D1598115

FDR's Quiet Confidant

Frank C. Walker in 1943.
Photograph courtesy University of Notre Dame Archives.

FDR's Quiet Confidant

The Autobiography of Frank C. Walker

Robert H. Ferrell, Editor

UNIVERSITY PRESS OF COLORADO

© 1997 by the University Press of Colorado
Published by the University Press of Colorado
P. O. Box 849
Niwot, Colorado 80544
Tel. (303) 530-5337

The University Press of Colorado is a cooperative publishing enterprise supported, in part, by Adams State College, Colorado State University, Fort Lewis College, Mesa State College, Metropolitan State College of Denver, University of Colorado, University of Northern Colorado, University of Southern Colorado, and Western State College of Colorado.

Library of Congress Cataloging-in-Publication Data

Walker, Frank C., 1886–1959
    FDR's quiet confidant : the autobiography of Frank C. Walker /
Robert H. Ferrell, editor.
       p.   cm.
    Includes bibliographical references and index.
    ISBN 0-87081-394-3 (alk. paper)
    1. Walker, Frank C., 1886–1959.   2. Politicians—United States—
Biography.   3. United States—Politics and government—1933–1945.
4. Roosevelt, Franklin D. (Franklin Delano), 1882–1945—Friends and
associates.   I. Ferrell, Robert H.   II. Title.
E748.W225A3   1997
973.917'092—dc20   96-54006
                                            CIP

This book was set in Adobe Caslon, Caslon Openface, and Omni.

The paper used in this publication meets the minimum requirements of the American National Standard for Information Sciences—Permanence of Paper for Printed Library Materials. ANSI Z39.48-1948

∞

10 9 8 7 6 5 4 3 2 1

CONTENTS

✱   ✱   ✱   ✱

FOREWORD

"There goes the best friend I ever had." These words, spoken by former U.S. president Harry S. Truman as the hearse was about to pull away from St. Ignatius Loyola Church on Park Avenue, reflect in so many ways the true nature of Frank C. Walker. They also could have been spoken by Franklin D. Roosevelt. For he, too, held no one man in his administration in higher esteem.

And what were the qualities that commended Frank Walker to such presidents as Truman and Roosevelt? He was hardworking, even-tempered, intuitive, gregarious, modest, loyal, ethical, and—to his family but also to others—loving. To be sure, such a catalog might seem impossible in a single human being; these qualities might seem more like those of a saint. But Walker possessed them in full measure.

He was, to begin with, hardworking. This quality might seem obvious, and yet it is not. It is the cardinal attribute, the necessary quality, of any man or woman who achieves high public office—or who gains recognition in any other walk of life. No one can accomplish great things without it. Yet the origin of the quality is not always discernible. In Walker's case it doubtless derived from his parents, who were hardworking—they had migrated west to Butte, Montana, when the city was a frontier town full of newcomers trying to make their ways. Labor was the necessary ingredient for achievement in Butte, and the Walkers knew it. The belief in the value of hard work passed easily from parents to son, and thereafter into anything Walker put his energies into.

Another Walker quality was the possession of an even temper. Achievement is not something that comes from emotionalism, an aspect of behavior that may have publicity value and perhaps qualifies a person for the theater. But for achievement there is no room or time for wasted motion. Each challenge of the day requires thoughtful analysis. Walker could look at his daily quota of difficulties and reduce his emotional response, thereby seeing more clearly what he was looking at.

And then there was his employment of intuition, which was marvelous to observe. Because his mind was constantly working, he could see many sides of an issue without being overwhelmed by them. And having seen many sides, he could sense the factors that might force a change in plan without being deflected from his purpose; he could then change his operating procedure to accommodate the likely intrusions and thus allow everything to go forward. Only his acute sensitivity allowed him to take the measure of whatever he confronted. Intuition it surely was.

All these aspects of his personality would have passed for nothing if this subtle "assistant president" (as people described him) had not been gregarious. Walker had come up the hard way, even if one might describe it as the almost sure way. In Butte he met all kinds of people, and there the fist dominated arguments more than did logic. At Notre Dame he learned about the latter. Then in law practice with his brother in the Butte firm of Walker and Walker, he applied the logic of the law to the problems of a great variety of people with an interest in mines or railroads but many times in concerns that were acutely personal. When he moved to New York to ally with his uncle in Comerford Theaters, Inc., a theatrical circuit with dozens of theaters, he again saw a great variety of people. By the time Walker went into politics he recognized the personality types, for he had encountered them all before.

Modesty was another of Frank Walker's principal qualities almost to a fault. He simply did not like to take credit. Although he was a principal assistant under Roosevelt, perhaps even the leading assistant, this is seldom recognized. Consider the large reputation of his predecessor as postmaster general. Everyone across the length and breadth of the United States knew who James A. Farley was. But Farley's successor, who probably was more influential with the president, did not seek or receive the credit Farley took. Walker retained FDR's confidence to the very end, whereas Farley lost it in 1938 or 1939.

Loyalty was a Walker hallmark. This loyalty he freely gave, and it demands some explanation in regard to his relations with Roosevelt. There were many qualities in Roosevelt that Walker did not admire, for instance a waywardness with the truth, the ability to say different things to different people that went beyond any well-intentioned effort to please. He disliked the president's family life—or perhaps the lack of a conventional family life. At the same time he understood the single essential of political life, which is loyalty. He was loyal to President Roosevelt, whatever he might have disliked about him personally. He understood that if he was to assist the president, to be his confidant and help the Roosevelt administration, he could not act in a double-dealing manner.

Frank Walker was an ethical man yet more, he was a religious man. He did not wear his religion on his sleeve or parade it, but he never missed mass on Sunday, never ate meat on Friday. Each night he said his prayers on his knees; friends who traveled with him and stayed in hotel rooms with him noticed this. The truths by which he had been brought up by the nuns, his teachers at St. Patrick's School in Butte, stayed with him for the whole of his life. He was no prude and could laugh at jokes and did not display a holier-than-thou attitude. At the core of his being, however, were the teachings of the Church, and if he did not measure other individuals by those teachings he assuredly measured himself.

All of Walker's traits—they were more than traits, they were qualities—could be categorized under the rubric of love: he liked people very much, even as he observed their misbehavior, and this was especially evident to members of his family, who saw him so much more than did casual visitors. Children not merely liked but loved him. One of my daughters was going to bed one night when she heard her grandfather moving around downstairs. Coming down in her pajamas and slippers, she spied grandfather at the bottom of the stairs and literally leaped into his arms, almost knocking him over. It was a scene I have never forgotten, for it was unforgettable. And it so well summed up, and sums up, his memory as I write about him thirty-eight years, more than a third of a century, after his death.

Thomas J. Walker

※   ※   ※   ※

ACKNOWLEDGMENTS

Thanks must go at the outset to Wendy Schlereth and Charles Lamb, director and assistant director of the Archives of the University of Notre Dame, and to archivists William Kevin Cawley and Jennifer A. Webber, for assistance with the papers of Frank C. Walker. Jay P. Dolan, director of the Cushwa Center for the Study of American Catholicism, kindly made funds for photocopying available.

Vincent P. DeSantis of Notre Dame's Department of History showed much interest in the Walker autobiography, as did Sister Helen Forge, community secretary of the Sisters of Charity of Leavenworth, Kansas. Elliot A. Rosen, the well-known scholar of the early Roosevelt period, read and commented on the manuscript. To these friends I extend appreciation for their help.

Publication would have been impossible without the support of Thomas J. Walker and Laura Hallie Jenkins, son and daughter of Frank Walker.

Lastly, a thank you to Luther Wilson, Jody Berman, Amy Sorrells, and Laura Furney, director, former managing editor, editorial and production manager, and acquisitions editor of the University Press of Colorado, for their interest in the project from beginning to end, and to Dianne Russell for her meticulous editing. They were a joy to work with.

R.H.F.

�֎ ✖ ✖ ✖

INTRODUCTION

rank C. Walker was a major figure in the administration of President Franklin D. Roosevelt. As such he deserves attention, for after all, the administration of FDR was pivotal, epochal, formative, and at the very center of U.S. history in our century. In Walker's later years (he died in 1959) he undertook an autobiography, this book, which shows what he did to support the man who held the presidency through peace and war, through the Great Depression and the greatest war in world history.

Walker's early years would seem to make him an unlikely figure to assist a president such as Roosevelt. He was born in Plymouth, Pennsylvania, near Wilkes-Barre, in 1886, four years after the child of Hyde Park. Not long afterward, his father went out to the American West, to faraway Montana, where in Butte the elder Walker prepared a place for himself and his growing family— Frank Walker was the eleventh of fourteen children. In this way he introduced to his sons and daughters an aspect of American life they never forgot; Butte was a rough and tough town that was growing into a city, and by all measurements it was one of the least-attractive towns in the entire United States.

It was, then, a translation from industrial Pennsylvania—if not the most pleasant state in the Union then still in possession of impressive mountains and, in places, lakes and expanses of forest that tended to cover its industrial ugliness—to a part of the West that few residents or visitors could forget. This was an expanse of mineral-rich country best symbolized by the word "raw." And at the center of the rawness was the town with the nondescript name of Butte.

Once in Butte, the Walker family rediscovered what its members, young and old, had known in Pennsylvania: that life was a scramble and not always an interesting one. But like so many families descended from Erin, they all knew that America remained the land of promise. The head of the family became a mine superintendent, and if he did not do well in his first post of responsibility he went on to another one. A moral man as well as an individual of authority, he did his best to combine honesty with his work, and in the way of much American experience was able to care for his family and give enough guidance, including formal education, to his children that they themselves could go out into the larger world beyond Butte and experience success.

Young Frank Walker engaged in his share of shenanigans as he came to manhood, but they were the typical behaviors of youth, and in addition to the parental guidance he received from his father and mother, he found his actions surrounded by the advice and occasional disciplines of the Catholic Church. The Walker family was devoutly Catholic, and the children naturally attended parochial schools as well as Sunday Mass and other church services. This upbringing was well known to the Irish Americans who became political leaders in the early twentieth century. Its importance is difficult to overstate. The backgrounds of most figures in the veritable galaxy of politicians who helped Franklin Roosevelt into power and kept him there were rigidly Catholic. To name those politicos of what is now long ago is to name men nationally known in the 1920s, 1930s, and 1940s. James A. Farley was best known, the national chairman of the Democratic Party; and then there was Frank Hague, who ran Jersey City as a satrap might; Edward J. Flynn, who ruled the Bronx and much of New York City; Edward J. Kelly, who governed Chicago; and other Irishmen too numerous to mention. All of them attended parochial school, where priests and nuns instructed them not merely in theology but in behavior, including the then signal necessity of politics, honesty. A Missouri politician rising to prominence at this time (rising far more slowly than did Franklin Roosevelt), Harry S. Truman, was well acquainted with the boss of Kansas City, Thomas J. Pendergast, and often remarked on Boss Tom's leading principle in politics: that if he, the boss, gave his word, it was his bond. Pendergast, Truman remembered, did not often give his word and hence often had no bonds, but if he gave it man to man (women received the vote in national elections in 1920 but were then mostly ornaments to politics), one needed nothing else to make a political equation—his word sufficed.

Walker went from parochial school to Catholic institutions of higher learning, which in the first years of the twentieth century were like all U.S. colleges and universities, with the exception of a few eastern institutions; that is, they were fairly primitive places of instruction and scholarship. He began at Gonzaga College in Spokane, later Gonzaga University, and after three years of what was virtually prep school instruction, a delayed experience with a good high school, he went to the University of Notre Dame, even at that time the leading Catholic collegiate institution in the United States. There he found memorable teachers in the shadow of the great golden dome that still shines above the trees and buildings in the northeast section of South Bend, Indiana. He met students from all across the United States, made lifelong friendships, and took on the sensibilities and understandings that would make him feel at ease when he entered the much larger world of business during the 1920s and of politics in the 1930s.

The translation of Walker to these larger worlds was not immediate, for after Notre Dame, where he studied law, he went back to Butte and, after a few preliminaries, including election to the Montana legislature, opened a law office with his brother Tom: the firm of Walker and Walker. As a practicing lawyer he handled the usual humdrum of cases. He also observed from his theoretical college and university background what politics meant in a city where among the laboring men and their hardworking wives the principal rivalries lay between the Irish Americans, on whose side Walker of course found himself, and the Cornishmen, the men and women born of or descended from inhabitants of Cornwall in England. The two sides, Catholics and Protestants, were separated by the wall of religion, and their politics were often defined—in subtle, not always clear ways—by the purposes of the industrial rulers of Butte and environs. These were the men who had profited hugely from the copper mines and who had removed themselves mentally if not physically from Butte after taking advantage of their miners, paying them far too little for suffering the atrocious working conditions in the mines.

If being a lawyer in raw Butte, with all its political and religious antagonisms, was good training for a politician, as Walker was to become under Roosevelt, then the continuation of his political education came in 1924, when he left Butte for New York City, where he went into the theater business. There he entered an arena as adventuresome, and also as political, as practicing law in Butte, Montana.

Walker's uncle, Michael E. Comerford, had gotten into theater management when the business was young, and he established what in the days of vaudeville was known as a "circuit," the Comerford circuit. For Comerford Theaters, Inc., he operated theaters that combined showings of silent movies with vaudeville acts. He needed someone to help him with the management of his theaters in New York, Pennsylvania, and environs, theaters that, financially, were almost too complicated to hold in mind, for his holdings varied wildly, from tenths to fifths to halves to full ownership. "M. E.," who was no naif in the ways of New York City, needed an assistant, ideally a partner, whom he could trust, and with a cunning sense of where he could find such a person he appealed to his sister in Butte, who identified the junior partner of the firm of Walker and Walker.

The result was a quick trial run in New York and then a decision to remove there, and for the rest of the 1920s Frank Walker was working as hard as he could in circuit headquarters in New York at 1600 Broadway; in Scranton, working with M. E. and his uncle's assistants; making deals with other circuit owners and operators and with vaudeville impresarios and their beaters and bearers; and with men in the theatrical business elsewhere in the country, including the moguls in Hollywood. It was a heady time for the theatrical business. The moguls themselves had achieved Mogul proportions, with their mansions and swimming pools and yachts, only a few years earlier. Everything—the circuits, Hollywood—was unformed. The talkies came in around the year 1927. M. E. and Walker backed the wrong horse, Warner Brothers Vitaphone, and then went over to the talking pictures of the Warners' competitors, Fox Movietone, which revolutionized movies and (something no one among the circuit operators foresaw) marked the end of vaudeville as the new movie palaces dropped their live acts in favor of screen performance.

After Frank Walker's training at Notre Dame and law practice in Butte and experiences in making deals in New York City, he naturally found himself, during FDR's governorship of New York, which began in 1929, being appealed to by the governor's liege man in the city and in Albany. This was the strangely enigmatic and yet effective Louis Howe, a gnomelike man who had been advancing the political cause of his mentor ever since the Wilson administration, when FDR had been assistant secretary of the navy. Howe had summoned up one of the principal Democratic money men of the city, Henry Morgenthau Sr., erstwhile ambassador to Turkey and father of one of Roosevelt's Hyde Park neighbors, Henry Morgenthau Jr. Howe and "Uncle Henry," as Walker described the elder Morgenthau, brought a group together after the 1930 reelection of Governor Roosevelt and began scheming to make Roosevelt president of the United States. The sitting president, Herbert Hoover, the "great engineer," as people said, was finding himself in the midst of the worst economic downturn in American history. Hoover, it turned out, was no politician and possessed a genius for alienating his supporters. A year or two before, in 1927–1928, when Hoover, then secretary of commerce, had begun moving toward the presidential nomination of the Republican Party, President Calvin Coolidge described him privately as "the wonder boy." By 1930–1931 Hoover was a sitting duck, as Howe and Roosevelt and Uncle Henry and Walker knew.

As one would have expected, Roosevelt and his New York City coterie worked with great care, for the vulnerability of Hoover made the Democratic nomination a great prize, and all the party hopefuls—and they were innumerable, for the party had been out of national power since the administration of Woodrow Wilson—sought to take it. Each one the governor of New York carefully finessed or foreclosed. The front-runner requiring the most delicacy and skill was Roosevelt's predecessor as governor, Alfred E. "Al" Smith. To finesse Smith was something of an operation, the more so because Roosevelt in 1924 had described him as "the happy warrior," a sobriquet that stuck. It became necessary to unstick it. Ever so carefully, Roosevelt moved away from the man he had praised and mounted his own campaign with such care that when it came time for the convention in 1932 there was no question but that he had separated Smith, still in his political prime, from the great hope of all U.S. political leaders. Walker took part in these maneuvers in the belief that Roosevelt, with his presidential personality, his own happy warrior stance, would do a much better job combating the Depression than could Smith, who carried the burden of defeat in the 1928 presidential election. Smith also, and Walker would have grimaced at the thought of it even as he understood it very well, was a member of Walker's church. But this was in the days before John F. Kennedy, when being Catholic was a handicap for anyone aspiring to the White House.

It is unnecessary and would be impossible here to set out Walker's subsequent service in the Roosevelt administration in Washington, first as executive secretary of the Executive Council, a coordinating committee of heads of cabinet departments and executive agencies involved with the New Deal, then as executive director of that group's successor, the National Emergency Council. He managed these tasks for Roosevelt in 1933–1935. Then, in 1940, when Postmaster General Farley took literally President Roosevelt's protestations about not running for a third term and envisioned a ticket consisting of Secretary of State Cordell Hull or Vice President John N. Garner for president and himself for vice president (perhaps even with himself heading the ticket) and the president encouraged him and then took the prize, Farley quit the cabinet and chairmanship of the Democratic National Committee. When this happened, the president asked Walker to become postmaster general. Walker was not anxious to displace Farley, whom he liked. But he saw that Farley had lost his head, had taken his own authority and personal attraction too far, and had thereby separated himself from the undoubted power center of the administration. Walker sided with the president, was appointed, and in 1943 became chairman of the Democratic Party for a year when Roosevelt's friend from the Bronx, Ed Flynn, gave it up.

As a White House insider, Walker witnessed the interior political moves of the 1930s and of the war years, the early 1940s. Men and ideas, or ideas that attached themselves to public figures, rose and fell. During the New Deal years he watched the impressive pyrotechnics of the man who for a brief time led the crusade known as the National Recovery Administration, wherein every store and factory in the United States seemed about to pass under national control with a series of industrial codes administered by the talented but ill-starred Hugh Johnson. Johnson lost to the Supreme Court, which ruled against the NRA, in 1935, and to such administrators as Harold L. Ickes and Harry L. Hopkins. The latter two men had the interesting habit of hating each other. In their hatreds Walker, as secretary of the Executive Council, naturally had to take part, and he quietly sided with the self-styled curmudgeon, Ickes, against Hopkins, whom he privately considered an untrustworthy adventurer. All the while, in the outer vestibules of power worked such New Dealers as Thomas G. "Tommy" Corcoran, who, because of his ancestry, one might assume would have attracted Walker but who instead repelled him because of what the Butte man saw as disdain for morality. Behind Corcoran, or at least beside him, he saw such youngsters (Walker once had counseled him to study law) as James H. Rowe Jr., who Walker believed had taken his ideas from Felix Frankfurter and Oliver Wendell Holmes Jr., the latter by the 1930s a New Deal icon, the former trying to become one.

In the midst of what Corcoran described (perhaps in sly criticism of Walker) as a center of power that did not possess any transmission lines, was the president, who fascinated the man who served him for twelve years. Walker knew that politics raised up clever people, for cleverness was necessary for any politician, as Hoover and Smith discovered. But there had to be something more than cleverness, Walker believed, and he was not sure Roosevelt possessed it. He greatly admired Roosevelt's leadership during the Depression and the war and watched closely as this great presidential figure displayed truly remarkable political instincts. Even if those instincts were interrupted by failures, such as the unsuccessful effort to "pack" (as opponents correctly charged) the Supreme Court, Walker knew he was looking at a real pro, a man with first-class instincts. No one could address the people quite like FDR, who, with a wave of his hand, a nod of his patrician head, could sway anyone watching him. Walker saw people go into the presidential office determined to tell the president off—sophisticated people—and saw them come out charmed by the man who sat behind the big desk and quipped and smiled and laughed and did not always listen but gave the impression that he did and seemed to approve what his visitors desired. But beyond all the talk and the movement of people and ideas through the Roosevelt administration, the discerning Walker (who smiled and listened, two qualities Roosevelt admired in assistants) was not altogether sure of the foundational ideas, the necessary (he thought) strong anchor. He was charmed and yet in an almost undefinable way not charmed.

The years passed, and the president, although weary in 1943, told Walker that he was going to take another term. Shortly thereafter Roosevelt became unmistakably a sick man. His White House intimates suspected that he had contracted cancer. They did not know that as early as 1941 his systolic blood pressure had risen to 160, the diastolic to 110. By 1944 the systolic was going over 200; in March of that year a cardiologist at Bethesda Naval Hospital found him in heart failure. Drawing the right conclusion (that the president could not possibly survive a fourth term) from the wrong evidence (weight loss and stomach upsets) the men around the president moved to ensure a trustworthy replacement when Roosevelt passed on. The Democratic Party's treasurer, the California oilman Edwin W. Pauley, joined with the president's appointments secretary, Major General Edwin M. "Pa" Watson, and the leaders of the party—Walker; Walker's sucessor as chairman of the Democratic National Committee, Robert E. Hannegan; Flynn; and Kelly—to arrange the departure of Vice President Henry A. Wallace from office and to replace him with a man they could trust—Senator Harry S. Truman—by nominating Truman in Wallace's place at the Democratic National Convention in Chicago that summer.

Some word is necessary about the provenance of the pages that follow. Walker dictated or wrote the autobiography between 1949 and 1956 with the help of an assistant, Paul K. Hennessy, who began the task of putting the material into chapters. Neither Walker nor Hennessy, nor another assistant, William Cronin, completed the work. Sometimes several drafts of a single chapter were prepared, yet everything remained unfinished. Walker occasionally dictated small portions of the manuscript, and fragments accumulated. Hennessy went on to other things, and Walker perhaps found his time taken by the increasing problems of the Comerford theaters, which were in disarray because of the inroads of television on theater attendance. When after Walker's death the draft chapters and fragments went to the University of Notre Dame Archives as part of the Walker papers, archivists filed them in four large storage boxes, where they remained for many years. In 1990, Thomas J. Walker and Laura Hallie Walker Jenkins added their father's wartime diary to the collection.

The task was to put this disparate material together. The rule of editing became that the autobiography would comprise, save for a very few changes for the sake of clarity, only its author's words, with the addition of the final chapter, which draws Walker's life from 1945 until his death. Occasionally material from different drafts is integrated into the text, and remnants are also brought in. Sentences or paragraphs have been dropped if they are repetitive or irrelevant. On rare occasions this means the omission of parts of sentences. The word "however" appears in the middle of sentences, so it stresses what precedes it, rather than being placed at the beginning, as Walker usually placed it. Contractions mostly appear as two words, on the theory that when Walker was dictating he spoke in shortened fashion but would have written out such words. The word "which," if a comma does not precede it, has become "that." For the rest, changes are in placement of commas, lowercasing of capitals, occasional eliminations of exclamation marks, insertion of question marks, and other minor adjustments in punctuation. These changes appear without ellipsis points or square brackets.

In such a way, after many years it has become possible for Frank Walker to tell his story, to speak for himself about an extraordinarily interesting life in which he passed slowly but surely from growing up in Butte to attending Gonzaga and Notre Dame to the practice of law to the business of booking moving pictures and vaudeville acts to, at last, the grand work of politics during the grandest presidential administration of our time.

R.H.F.

❋   ❋   ❋   ❋

FDR's Quiet Confidant

1

GROWING UP IN BUTTE

rior to our arrival in Butte my father had acquired a boardinghouse in
the town of Centerville, a suburb. It was located on the main street of
the town, which is right in the heart of the mining district and the shadows of
the Mountain Con and Green Mountain Mines. For years this hill was
referred to as "the richest hill on earth," and from here many millions of dollars worth of copper were taken. My mother conducted this boardinghouse for
approximately a year, and the family made its home there. From there we
moved to the city, to the McNamara house on West Copper Street.

During the early years of our stay in Butte my father was engaged in leas-
ing various mining properties and operating them. In the late 1880s he
acquired a lease and bond on the Ramsdell Parrot, which later became a great
producer, but lacking financial backing he lost his interest to others. He was
associated with different men. One I remember was quite an unusual
character—Joseph Laveaux; another was Dussalt. At first his operations were
conducted in and about the city of Butte, and apparently he did not meet with
any great measure of success because about that time F. A. Heinze of New
York, a stripling of twenty-four and graduate geologist of Columbia, took over
the famous Rarus Mine, and my father became his first superintendent. I
remember as a youngster of eight years going down the shaft of the Rarus
with my father to the 450 level. Seven years later, at the age of fifteen, I
worked in the Rarus for Heinze as a nipper, or tool packer. The Rarus in many

1

ways was one of Butte's most famous mines, but Father and Heinze disagreed on the policy to be pursued in its operation, and Father left. My good father always had a correct conception of the rights of labor. He was always loyal to his employer, but in handling relationships between employer and the working men he always favored shorter hours, improved working conditions, and better wages. Heinze, who would publicly support labor, was a ruthless, unconscionable fellow who would stoop to anything to attain his purpose.[1]

Father then moved his activities to the little town of Basin, twenty-five miles east of Butte, where he acquired a lease. He made a considerable amount of money in this operation, but the ore was found in pockets and the veins were not easy to trace, and most of his newly acquired fortune was spent in development. Vast fortunes in gold and silver were taken from this property later.

During the time my father was operating the lease at Basin, the family lived on East Quartz Street, between Main and Wyoming, in Butte. It was from this house that my sister Katherine was married to John W. Cotter in 1894. It was here, too, that my sister Pet was born. Nell, who later married John Gaul, was born in Centerville, and my brother Leo was born at the McNamara house on West Copper Street. Leo died as an infant. My sisters Katherine and Moll and my brother Tom, who were older than I, had of course been born back in Pennsylvania. It was from the East Quartz Street house that I started attending school at St. Patrick's, under the guidance of the Sisters of Charity, many of whom I came to know very favorably over the years.

In those days Butte was considered the greatest mining camp in the world, and even we youngsters used to boast of the $3.50 a day received by the miners—the highest pay ever known to have been received by labor up to that time anyplace in the world. I can remember the comparisons that were made around our household about the conditions in the mining district of Pennsylvania in the eighties and early nineties. I can remember my father speaking of so many men who worked for ninety-nine cents for ten hours' work under very unfavorable conditions, and how difficult it was for so many of the miners in and about the coal area at that time to eke out an existence. The hours were long, the working conditions were hazardous, and very little was done to improve the lot of the coal miner. This made an impression on me that I have retained throughout my entire life, and I remember it was very vivid to me even as a youngster.

Butte was a rough, tough mining camp in those days, but it was likewise an interesting, colorful, cosmopolitan town. In the early days of mining in Butte, the Cornish and Irish were the dominant nationalities, with a small scattering of Welsh and others.[2] The population of the city was in the neighborhood of ten thousand and, as I remember it, the population of the entire state, the third largest state in the Union in area, was less than two hundred thousand.

Frank Walker's siblings in 1930. *From left:* Kit, Tom, Nell, Moll, and Pet. Photograph courtesy the Walker family.

I have visited Butte many, many times in the years since I first left it, and now when I think of this little mining city with thirty thousand people, nestled in the heart of the Rockies on the western side of the Great Divide, I am satisfied that I shall always feel it means more to me than any one place in all America. It's as rugged as the mountains that surround it, just as rough and sharp as the crags above it, and just as strong and solid as the huge quartz rock that forms its foundation. It's an ugly sort of duckling at first appearance, yet it's as beautiful and grand and majestic to those who know it well as the great range of mountains that look down upon it. Its courthouse in the center of the city is more than a mile high. The workings of its mines beneath its surface are more than a mile deep.

> She's ugly, you say, Old Butte is
> And grimy and bleak and drear?
> Why, partner, I never could see it,
> And I've lived here many a year.
> There's nothing pretty about her,
> But somehow she's strong and free,
> And big and rugged and well, comrade,
> She looks pretty good to me.[3]

It is spread out over a series of hills on the slopes of the great mountain-side. Vast dumps of gray waste ore from the mines, and dark blue-black slag from its mills and smelters, strike the eye on all sides, and for many years but few blades of grass or green of any kind have broken the monotony of its dreary-looking surface. Yet during its short life, within an area of a few square miles more than three billions of wealth in copper, gold, silver, lead, and zinc has been unearthed from beneath its surface. Like Topsy, it just grew up.

I have no recollection at all of Pennsylvania in those days, but, strangely, I do remember my first day in Butte. I remember quite well looking out the front window of the hotel—I'm not sure whether it was the Southern or the Cottage Hotel—watching the streetcars go by. The streetcars, cable cars they were in those days, passed on Main Street to Centerville, and in the next year or two after we had moved to Centerville I came to know old Pete McDermott, the motorman, and Mike Pryor, the conductor, quite well, and took many trips with them in the old cable car from Centerville to the foot of Main Street and back.

On one occasion I had a very exciting experience. I was just a tad, but I managed to get seated on the high seat of a delivery wagon right in front of our home. The driver had gone in to make a delivery, and I was alone on the seat. The horses ran away and took me all the way down Main Street to where the post office is now located. Finally somebody grabbed the horses, and, fortunately, I was not seriously injured.

A neighbor of ours in those days was Kitty Williams, who later became a motion picture star. I remember when she played Cherry Malotte in *The Spoilers*. Her mother later married Joseph Laveaux, who was a partner of my father in some mining leases. We were accustomed to calling Kathleen Williams by her mother's new name—Kitty Laveaux. I can remember Kitty and I going sleigh-riding downhill on the main streets of Centerville.

We had many fine characters in and around Butte at that time. Dennis Driscoll ran a grocery store north of us. He had several daughters, one of whom became Mrs. John Corette. She was among the early graduates of St. Patrick's School. Another daughter, Margaret Driscoll, was a classmate of mine as we went through St. Patrick's. An unusually fine family lived across the street from us, the Ryans. A sister of Mrs. Ryan was Mother Irene, who was one of the pioneer nuns of the Order of Sisters of Charity. She was superior at the hospital in Anaconda at one time and later became superior at St. James Hospital in Butte. For a time she was also superior of the order.

It was at St. Patrick's School in Butte that I received my early education under the guidance of the good Sisters of Charity, who, next to my mother perhaps, made the finest impression upon me of my entire life. It was St. Patrick's Church that I first attended, just two blocks below the school. It was there that I came to know one of the finest and most ideal little pastors it has ever been my good fortune to have met, a little Belgian priest named Father Desière. He had a world of energy, a sweet face, and a fine character, and a habit of addressing you, no matter what the time of day, with "good morning." He would never say good evening or good afternoon. We all called him "Daddy" Desière. He always called me "Walker." I have read of many parish priests over the years, have met many, and have listened to others depict the fine qualities and virtues of many others, but Daddy Desière, as I knew him, and I knew him well, was my idea of the typical pastor. He was a part of my life, a part of me and a part of my family. He was our parish priest from the time I started to school until his death in about 1920.

I remember one incident in his latter years, which I always think of in connection with Prohibition.[4] Bishop Carroll, the bishop of Montana, had been made a trustee of the university in Helena. His excellency was a very distinguished man and had been an educator in Iowa, but he was a bit narrow in his views, particularly as regards Prohibition.[5] Monsignor Desière's views were broader. He, with resignation, accepted Prohibition as law but had grave doubts as to the wisdom of it in principle. Although he never indulged too freely, he did enjoy a nip once in a while, and when he came to our home, as he frequently did, my good mother always prepared a little drink for him. He had a strange combination—milk, whiskey, and salt, and Mother always would put in a little extra spirits, claiming it would be a very good thing for the little man.

On this occasion Bishop Carroll had written a three- or four-column article for the *Anaconda Standard* that was published in the Sunday edition in Butte, in which he ardently advocated Prohibition. The day after the article was published I met Daddy Desière on the street at about the corner of Park and Main Streets in the middle of the afternoon. He swung his gold-headed cane, stopped, and said, "Good morning, Walker! I'm so glad to see you. Did you read the disquisition by the Bishop in the paper yesterday? It was superb! Superb! Fine article!" Then he added: "But Walker, you know the Bishop does not speak ex cathedra."

This, to me, was typical of Monsignor Desière. He was perfectly respect-ful toward his bishop, but at the same time he knew his own rights. He knew the bishop had no authority in such matters because the question of Prohibi-tion was not a question of faith and morals.

The good Sisters of Charity were a splendid influence in the early days of the mining camp of Butte. They did much to develop the character of some of Butte's outstanding men and women. The early nuns whom I knew were all women of culture and intelligence, and well-educated. They were a fine band of self-sacrificing women who contributed a great deal, both intellectually and spiritually, to the pioneering group who later came to guide the destinies of the old mining town.

One I remember distinctly, and devotedly, was Sister Florence, because she was such a fine inspiration not only to me, but to all who knew her. She was quite young when she first came to Butte, and taught me in the third grade at St. Patrick's School. She had simplicity and charm, and wit and wis-dom. She had a superb influence on my life, not only as a youth but for all the years since. I shall always hold Sister Florence in fond remembrance because she was fine and sweet and gay of heart, and yet she was the most strict disci-plinarian. Sister Florence favored all the sports for the boys—baseball, box-ing, football—and threw in a bit of the dramatic. She was responsible for my first appearance in a school play, and she encouraged all of us in debate and public speaking. She was gracious and kind and competent, and came to be almost a member of my family.

Sister Emilda, too, I will always remember. It was she who instilled in me the spirit to challenge the conduct of some of our troops in the Spanish-American War. She later became superior of St. James Hospital. As a cub reporter on the *Butte News* some years later I was assigned to and did write the story of her death.

Sister Mary Xavier was in herself an institution—a stern, rigorous disci-plinarian. We came to be friends later in life, but my association with her in school was always one of quiet rebellion. I had respect for her competence but little affection for her. She and I were always at sixes and sevens. Sister Xavier had much to do with the training of the boys. She was a splendid mathemati-cian and was always considered one of the finest minds in the Order of the Sisters of Charity. She organized, developed, and trained St. Patrick's Cadets, a band of a hundred or more students ranging in ages from ten to sixteen or seventeen, and I do not think any of the generals of the last war could have been more rigorous in their discipline or more meticulous than Sister Mary Xavier was with her cadets—she was a real Spartan. We drilled for many, many hours if we wished to take part in a school play or any other production under Sister Mary Xavier's supervision. The outstanding event was the St. Patrick's Day parade. St. Patrick's Day was always a great day in the history of Butte celebrations. Several bands, fife and drum corps, many Irish societies, and, always, St. Patrick's Parochial Cadets took part in this great parade. On the seventeenth of March, 1897, I was the smallest of the cadets, the lowest of the privates in the rear ranks. I remember Bill McMahon, who is now head of the labor division of the Anaconda Copper Company, was our captain. The streets of Butte were not paved in those days, and we marched down the main street from Centerville to the B. A. & P. up to our knees in mud.[6] After boarding the train, we went to Anaconda, where a celebration was had in front of the St. Anne's Hospital. I remember John Curtis of the Curtis family, pioneers of Butte, gave a declamation on that occasion. Michael Gavigan recited—Mike always recited at such affairs. This was the day that the Cornishman, Bob Fitzsimmons, knocked out the Irishman, Jim Corbett. I received the news on the way home on the train and I was heartbroken to learn that my idol, James J. Corbett, had been defeated. My loyalties were decidedly with Corbett.[7]

Incidentally, I played hooky from school on at least two occasions, and Jim Corbett was the inspiration each time. The first time was the day of the Corbett versus Mitchell prizefight, and it developed into one of the outstanding events of my early business career. On the way to school at the luncheon period I met a friend of mine we called "Pig Fence" Harrington. The *Inter-Mountain*, which is now the *Butte Daily Post*, had issued an extra just about the time the afternoon classes were to begin. Most of the boys had already reached school, and Pig Fence saw a great opportunity to make a killing. I happened to have twenty-five cents to put us in business, so neither of us went to school. We played hooky and sold papers all afternoon.

This first venture was a successful business affair but a sad affair domestically and socially. That evening, proudly displaying my profits of $2.35 to my mother, I had hoped and expected real commendation, but instead of that I received a severe reprimand together with a good tanning. The nuns on the following day seemed to adopt the same attitude. It was made very evident to me that my parents and the good sisters were much more anxious to teach me how to live than how to make a living. At that time I could see neither common sense nor justice in their attitude. I am happy to say, however, that my thoughts have changed considerably over the years.

The second was an occasion later on, when Corbett came to Butte playing the hero in a melodrama. I joined a small group of classmates and attended the matinee at old John Maguire's Opera House. Corbett gave us a real thrill as he hurled the villain down the cellar stairs. Jack Dugan and I received a well-deserved and never-to-be-forgotten reprimand from our teacher the following day for our absence.

There were very few sissies among the kids in Butte in those days. They were a rough-and-ready crowd of vital, vigorous young fellows. Our delinquent youth seem to be one of the most serious matters that confronts us in this generation. I must confess it has disturbed me no little. I think it is a problem of serious moment and one that merits our most serious thought. Yet when my mind turns back to my own youth in Butte, I sometimes wonder whether in terms of proportionate population juvenile delinquency is more prevalent now than it was in my generation. The kids of Butte were no holy innocents. The ruggedness of a mining camp does not by any means lend itself to the standards of Lord Fauntleroy. That type of youth would not receive a high Hooper rating as the average boy of the town.[8] If I were pressed for my honest judgment, I fear I would be compelled to admit that there was a youthful delinquency problem in my time. I would also have to admit frankly that Mrs. Walker's son seldom rated an A for good conduct.

The St. Patrick's School kids had rock fights with the boys from the Colorado public school. We rolled boulders down the hills onto the roofs of Chinese laundries, and many Chinese laundrymen found their clean white linens dumped into Butte's muddy streets. We tossed each other's caps on the open fruit and vegetable stands on Park Street and grabbed fruit and coconuts and cantaloupe as we recovered them.

A great pal of mine, in the 1950s one of New York's leading physicians, and I had a little racket of selling empty beer bottles to old Mario Medin, the Italian merchant of the town. We knew that when Mario purchased his wares in the front of his establishment, he then stored them in the rear yard quite open to view, in addition to the dangerous exposure of his inventory. When Mario returned to look for new customers he would be resold the same bottles—a performance that was repeated as often as three times in the same day. I know that I passed through a stage of my life when as a kid I was a real thorn in my good mother's side.

There were several gangs in Butte in those days, but I think the hardiest of them came from up around what was known as Dublin Gulch and Hungry Hill. They were a venturesome lot and engaged in many escapades. Our house was not far from the entrance to the Gulch. Centerville and Walkerville also had formidable gangs of young fellows who could hold their own in any sort of contest. I got to know a good many of these youngsters because they were schoolmates and many of them classmates of mine.[9]

I know it was a happy day for my mother when we moved from East Quartz Street to another part of town where the boys were not quite so rugged. In those formative years a youngster could easily have embarked upon some hazardous venture that might have blighted his career. Fortunately, the guidance of my good mother and the kindness of the Good Lord saved me. I didn't pursue the course that brought me too far astray, but I still think it could have happened to me because it did happen to many of the unfortunate young fellows who were my boyhood friends. Several of them went on to acquire criminal records. Regretfully, later on as deputy county attorney I prosecuted and sent some of them, no few of them, to the state penitentiary.

We didn't feel any sense of being delinquents in those days, but as I see it now, if we lacked the proper supervision in the home and at school we could easily have gone to other and more serious offenses. The average citizen of Butte was engaged in hazardous occupations, which lends itself to a sort of daring and carefree spirit, and which undoubtedly left its mark on some of the young boys growing up. Men engaged in hard, hazardous occupations do not seem to acquire the caution and the prudence and foresight common to other men, yet with their spirit of abandon it seems to me they acquire a virile wholesomeness—a finer, more generous spirit and basically a nobler attitude toward their fellows than most men in other fields of endeavor.

The persistent discipline of the good mothers of Butte, of which my mother, God bless her, was the finest, was in my opinion the principal ingredient that changed the course of the lives of many of the youth of Butte and brought out the better things in them so that in the main a high percentage came to be outstanding citizens. I feel that the progeny of these men and women acquired many of these good qualities in great measure. The very ruggedness of life in Butte gave them something basic and fundamental that they could never have acquired otherwise. As they went on into new fields and accepted new opportunities for development and education they became much finer men for it all.

We had a football team at St. Patrick's that was called the Parochials. We had two or three very successful years in which we won most of our contests. I can remember very well playing against Centerville on the main street of the town of Walkerville, right in front of St. Lawrence's Church, which is north of Centerville. Still vivid is my recollection of having won the game and of being "rocked" home. Gus Dorais, who as a famous star played with Knute Rockne at Notre Dame later on, was a substitute on our team. Gus was younger than I, but our material was rather limited and we had to use the

At school in Butte in the 1890s. Frank Walker is in the center. Photograph courtesy the Walker family.

younger fellows to fill in. I remember, however, he did very well. His brother George was one of the real stars of the team.

About this time Butte had one of the best professional football teams in the entire country. It was composed largely of former college football players: giant, redheaded Jim Hooper, formerly of Michigan; Dygert, who was also a Michigan halfback; tiny Percy Benson, who played quarterback on the team; and Francis Brooks, later a lawyer and judge in Honolulu; and Donald Gillies, now vice president of the Republic Steel Corporation, and who was the real outstanding player of the team—on one occasion he made a ninety-four-yard run against, I think, the Reliance Athletic Club of San Francisco, a record in those days.

Cap Stivers, later a colonel in the Second Division in the United States Army (World War I), and a member of the legal staff of the Anaconda Copper Mining Company, was manager of the pro team and also played end. The team had the financial backing of young Charles Clark, son of former Senator W. A. Clark. Though I was but nine or ten years of age at the time this team was in its ascendancy, I think I still can remember most, if not all, of the lineup. I remember they used to run their plays in practice on the streets of town, many times under the arc lights, and as a youngster I used to follow them about. On one occasion old Bob Perham let me carry his nose guard so I could gain access to a game without paying.

One of the games that stands out in my memory was the game in which we played the University of Iowa, then coached by the famous Pop Warner.[10] John Cotter, my brother-in-law, was from Iowa. We went to the game in an old-fashioned hack, one side draped with Iowa colors and the other side draped with Butte colors, crimson and cream. The game ended in a brawl. Little Percy Benson, the light little quarterback who weighed only about 130 pounds, was roughly and unnecessarily pummeled by one of the Iowa stalwarts. Big Jim Hooper took it upon himself to care for the Iowan, and as a result the Iowa team finally walked off the field. The game ended before the first half had been completed. Despite argument, discussion, and protestation, Warner refused to let his team return to the field, and the game was awarded to Butte. I have a letter from Pop in my files giving his version of the affair. It is not unbiased. Pop had charged the spectators with firing off revolvers and intimidating his men.

The people of Butte were as enthusiastic about their old pro team as most of the young people are today about their college teams. Business came to a standstill the day of a game. They had a cheerleader and team songs; they wore gay colors and large bright chrysanthemums. The atmosphere of the present-day college football game was always prevalent when the Butte professional team got into action. The Perham boys, Billy Laswell, Trilby Davis, Patsy Sullivan the former insurance man, Mickey Harrington, "Snake" King, Bill Slater, Russell Matlock, the Boyce boys, Jack Mahoney and Jack Bahm, and Doc Blackburn are among the names I remember who were outstanding on the teams in 1894–1898.

Montana had many interesting pioneers. Three of the most outstanding in my mind were Marcus Daly, an Irish immigrant, who I think was about the first to recognize the vast stores of treasure that lay in the earth in and around Butte; W. A. Clark, who afterward participated with Daly in what proved to be Montana's greatest political fight; and Jim Murray, the uncle of a later Montana senator, whom I came to know quite well as a boy.[11]

Daly had been sent to Montana some years earlier by the Hearst interests of California and Nevada, and in the first few years after our arrival in Butte he was in charge of operations of the mines. He was a very strong, positive character, whom I came greatly to admire.

W. A. Clark acquired more than $100 million. He built a railroad from Salt Lake City to Los Angeles and financed it himself, mile by mile. He took a course in the treatment of ore at Columbia University after attaining the age of thirty and learned to speak two or three languages while attaining his fortune. I came to know Clark when I served as counsel for him in the years preceding World War I. As a boy I had carried a route on his paper, the *Butte Miner.* He was a man of great capabilities and had from my own observation one of the most amazing memories of any man I have ever known. He built a home on Fifth Avenue in New York, later styled by some Clark's Folly. He had difficulty in getting stone and bronze to erect this building, and I am told he bought a stone quarry and a bronze factory to get the necessary materials to complete this structure. He was a hard, cold, practical man as I knew him and studied him later on in my life.

Jim Murray was a smart, keen, alert Irishman who, too, acquired a very considerable fortune—not comparable, however, with Clark's. My only dealings with him in business were on one occasion when I was a young practicing lawyer. He had acquired a mortgage on one of Butte's better office buildings, the State Savings Bank building. He had loaned Creighton Largey $300,000 on the bank building at seven percent interest, which was pretty fair interest even in those days. Murray had always hoped to be able to take over the building on foreclosure, but when Charley Leonard refinanced it for the Metropolitan Life of New York at five percent interest, Murray's hopes were shattered. I took the certified check out to his bank on North Main Street, together with the satisfaction-of-mortgage papers. He sat in his office in plain sight of me deliberately keeping me waiting two hours before he reluctantly accepted the check and signed the release.

I have often heard stories of how Clark and Murray in the early days spent much of their time in Deer Lodge. In the evenings they would sit out on the porch and occasionally lay a wager as to the number of logs upon a passing sled. Some intimated that Clark on one occasion rode down the road a half a mile or so and counted the logs before they came by the hotel. Murray seemed to feel there was some merit in the suggestion. In any case it could be safely said that neither had much faith in the other.

As the stories go, on one occasion Murray from the window saw Clark measuring the height of a hitching post in front of the hotel one morning. Late that night, with the assistance of a wooden mallet, Murray drove the hitching post down several inches. When they sat on the porch in front of the hotel the next day, Clark expressed some doubt as to Murray's ability to guess the height of the post. They started wagering, first $100, until they got it up to a cool $1,000. Murray's mallet brought him victory. Clark's guess was six or eight inches off.

The coming of F. A. Heinze brought with it the beginning of the great battle between Heinze and the Anaconda Copper Mining Company at first, and Heinze and Clark against the company as the years went on. The litigation and quarrel that took place between them and Daly formed one of the most interesting parts of the history of western Montana and the cities of Butte and Anaconda. One of the fundamental issues was the question of developing the apex theory, which may be briefly stated as follows: The owner of a mining claim held title to a certain surface area in which an ore vein "apexed." On the surface his claim is limited by law to a parallelogram fifteen hundred feet in length by six hundred feet in width. But if his vein, *under the surface*, dips or slants to one side or the other, he may follow it and take out its ore—*it is his vein.*

I have during my mature life always had an opinion of myself as being rather quiet, retiring, and not at all assertive. But as I look back at some of the incidents in my lifetime I have come to think that, although in later life I have regarded myself as a sort of middle-of-the-roader, I was decidedly partisan in all matters in which I became involved during my boyhood and youth, and particularly so in some of the issues that involved the pioneers to whom I have just referred.

At the age of eight I was a strong supporter of Daly against Clark in the fight between Anaconda and Helena for the capital. I carried a flambeau in a torchlight parade boosting Anaconda. Money was spent freely and feeling ran high. It was a real battle, and I was a real zealot for Daly and Anaconda, but Clark won out and Helena became the capital.

As a youngster of ten or eleven I can remember taking an active and enthusiastic part in parades in favor of the eight-hour law. The companies insisted that they could not survive in competition with other companies working the ten-hour day. They did everything in their power to defeat a bill introduced by Jack Quinn in the Montana legislature. Jack was one of the real characters of Montana. He later became sheriff and afterwards ran for mayor and was badly defeated. Through the efforts of Quinn the Montana legislature passed an eight-hour bill, which was very helpful, and I was one of its most ardent and active supporters.

At nine I was in the midst of the memorable fight of the APAs against the Catholics.[12] Butte's miners in the early days were evenly divided between the Irish and the Cornish. At times, real bitterness and hatred split the two factions, finally eventuating in a real riot on July 4, 1894. The two factions were arrayed against each other in the heart of the city. Many eyes were blackened, many heads were broken, and at least one man was killed, a policeman named Daly.

The quarrel broke out in front of Simon Hauswirth's saloon, headquarters for the Cornish. Some of the Celts began an argument with the Cornish on the merits of the Irish and the British. The mayor, the police, the sheriff's force, and the fire department were all in action, seeking to bring order. Clubs, stones, brickbats, all were used on offense and defense. The fire hose was used in an attempt at suppression of the fighting, and the fire hatchets were used by the mob to destroy the hose. As Mayor Dugan entreated with the crowd from the balcony of the city hall I had a place in the center of it all—perched on a telegraph pole in the rear of the First National Bank. This was the real center or vortex. I remember Jack Collins, the stock inspector and a friend of the family, grabbing me by the leg, taking me by the ear, and marching me up Main Street in the direction of my home.

My father took a modest part in this affair, much to the disgust and consternation of my mother, and I think he came home with some evidence of having been part of the fray. It is needless for me to say which side my father and I were on.

On the occasion of my graduation from St. Patrick's grammar school I was vehemently critical of the Spanish-American War. I was critical of our military and their arrogance in the Philippines. My valedictory from grammar school was my first public address, and though I was but thirteen years of age at the time, my disquisition became the subject of editorial comment. The local paper editorial said of it: "The young man who gave the valedictory at St. Patrick's parochial school yesterday would feign believe that the moon was made of green cheese if the Sisters had told him so."

Even many years later, in college, in a debate between the University of Notre Dame and Georgetown, I argued with great conviction and enthusiasm, if not persuasion, for the guaranty of bank deposits. I remember how amused old Senator Carter of Montana was at what he styled a "most radical proposal." The debate was held in Washington. The senator, who was a real conservative, came to the debate, I think, in deference to the distant relationship that existed between us. He and my brother married sisters. Too, I was a constituent of his in Montana.[13]

When I think of some of these incidents I sometimes wonder just how much a middle-of-the-roader I am. After I graduated from St. Patrick's, I worked in the mines as a nipper. My father had become ill and it became necessary for me to contribute my mite for the support of the family. I worked in the Rarus Mine for Heinze, the bitter opponent of the Anaconda group, and the same mine where my father had served as Heinze's superintendent. Heinze was a smart, alert, and in my judgment a rather characterless tycoon, who was playing with the labor group. I always thought he did it selfishly, to win political favor, and not because he was at all interested in the welfare of the miners. Although my father had worked for him and my brother had joined forces with him in his fight against Daly and the Anaconda Copper Mining Company, I was never at heart for him, but I was for the support he gave labor. Even my brother-in-law, John Cotter, who married my eldest sister, was one of Heinze's leading counsel when the battle between Heinze and the company became so very bitter. Heinze had the very happy faculty of winning over the miners. He was much more popular with the hoi polloi than were the group at the head of the company, and the battle continued for a number of years with Heinze winning most of the fights in the courts and more or less dominating the political situation.

When I turned sixteen, a neighbor of ours, Mr. Campbell, offered me a position as his office boy. The job paid me more than my work as a nipper and was much safer and much more pleasant work, so I left Heinze. I worked faithfully in a most difficult position for Campbell, who was himself an important political leader, the real political leader of the Anaconda Copper Mining Company. Important conferences involving politics, labor politics and such, were discussed in his office. There I met Mr. Scallon, president of the Anaconda Copper Mining Company; John D. Ryan, who later succeeded Scallon and went on to become chairman of the board; C. F. Kelley, now chairman of the board; and Daniel J. Hennessy, the merchant who operated the company store. Hennessy became a close personal friend of our family. He was a very unusual man—a fine character—and I came to have great affection and respect for him, as did my mother and father. I will always feel that he was the finest citizen that the city of Butte ever had.[14]

This group discussed their most vital, confidential, and important political, labor, and business problems in my presence, while at that very time my brother-in-law, John Cotter, was Heinze's chief counsel, and my brother, just out of college, a great Heinze supporter. I will always hold Campbell and his associates in the highest esteem for permitting me to carry on in this humble yet quite confidential post under such circumstances. All of these leaders knew me and my family background, they knew the relationship of some of my family with the Heinze forces, yet they gave me no indication that they questioned my loyalty to my boss or to them.

To me, immature as I was, it was a fine demonstration of faith. I carried on there for more than a year, and in that short time—I think!—learned more about the fundamental issues disturbing capital and labor than in any other one year of my lifetime. It was an important year for that group politically, and I am happy to say that neither my brother-in-law nor my brother nor any of Heinze's associates ever at any time asked me a question as to the doings at the A.C.M. headquarters.

I felt kindly toward all of these men. I had great respect for all of them, and real affection for some. Yet through it all I did not lose my sympathy for or interest in the man who toiled.

In these early days the issue was not so much the question of pay as it was the relationship generally that existed between the company and the miners. The men worked ten hours a day, seven days a week, so that a man had little time for rest and recreation, little time to spend with his family. He had no sense of security and there was very little to look forward to in life. The working conditions in the mines were not good, and little was done by the operating companies in the way of timbering and ventilation to give the men protection. Many spots in the mines were dry, and the miners, running drills into the copper bodies, filled their lungs with dust. Mining was a very hazardous occupation in those days. Many were seriously injured and many killed. Many of the men who lost arms and legs or who were otherwise seriously injured were paid a mere pittance in settlement by claim agents. There was not even a reasonable attempt at social justice. At one time it was said that, proportionately, there were more widows in St. Lawrence's parish in Walkerville than there were in any other parish in the entire United States.

I do not wish to condemn any of these men. I shall always feel that at heart they were individually real humanitarians. They and their associates had aligned themselves on one side of a battle, and they seemed to feel deeply that they were in the right and that their opposition was bent on destroying the system that made for successful enterprise. They seemed to feel that there was no middle course.

I do not think that they knowingly, deliberately, and designedly ignored the rights of labor. They did not seem to understand, possibly because many of them had acquired fortunes easily in mining, industry, law, and finance, and some of them in the stock market. There were some who, I fear, did come to feel that the Good Lord had endowed them with such unusual talents that they were destined to serve as trustees for the masses—that they were of the anointed. They just did not seem to realize that labor too was making a very sizable contribution to the success of their varied interests.

2

EDUCATION

My father died in 1902 just after I went into Mr. Campbell's office. A year later I made plans to enter Gonzaga College in Spokane to renew my educational work. My mother's financial aid was rather limited; with the assistance of my elder sister, Mrs. John Cotter, however, I managed to get in a year of preparatory work and two years of college with the Jesuits at Spokane. Spokane was a mere overnight trip by train from Butte. The reasonableness of the board and tuition at Gonzaga and the proximity of it to my home fitted into my financial problem, and I spent three years with the Jesuits.

I had a smattering of Greek and Latin, some mathematics, and took part in some of the extracurricular activities. I took part in the elocution contests, with no great measure of success. I became quite a thespian—played Shylock in *The Merchant of Venice,* and played the lead in Richard Brinsley Sheridan's *Pizarro.* These were rather pleasant years at Gonzaga, and I made some very fine fast friends and acquaintances—some of the best in my lifetime. Father Goller, a delightful, scholarly man who was considered among the best of philosophers and theologians in the Jesuit order, was rector. He left a fine impress on all his students. I revered and respected him. I came to have great respect for the Jesuits, for their courses of instruction, and for the fine spiritual atmosphere that hovered over the place. I had been out in the world for two years and should have taken my work more seriously. I must confess that I really didn't do any serious work during my three years with the Jesuits.

In the fall of 1906 several of my classmates changed from Gonzaga to Georgetown. Among them were some of my closest personal friends, and for a time I gave serious consideration to joining them. My mother was adamant and held out against my decision. My elder brother's experience at Georgetown in the late nineties did not seem to have worked out so well. He did not seem to take his work as seriously as he might have done, according to my mother's ideas. He did not finish Georgetown cum laude; as a matter of fact, Tom didn't finish at all. He didn't return for his senior year. He was not expelled from Georgetown, but I think they made it clear to him and to my parents that his failure to return would not make them at all unhappy. My brother Tom was a type who did not seem at all disturbed by this. He was the most venturesome one in the family, and I think he was anxious to get out in the world rather than become a profound scholar.

After some discussion I decided to go to Notre Dame. The picture of the dome on the university advertisement on the back page of the *Ave Maria* came vividly to my mind and I think helped in some measure in this decision. In addition to this, an old friend of mine, Ed O'Flynn, who won the Breen Medal for oratory and also the state oratorical contest, had been at Notre Dame for at least two years. He was a real advocate of Notre Dame and a most enthusiastic booster. I think his description of the place helped convince me.

At that time Notre Dame was quite well known in the Far West, and I think it was held in high repute throughout the country. I placed it in the category of one of America's finest Catholic boarding schools. It just started its real development at about this period. It had but a few more than eight hundred students—this included minims, high school students, and seminarians.[1] The college consisted of approximately two hundred to two hundred and fifty men, with a faculty of less than forty, sixteen of whom were priests. Sorin and Corby were the only halls that had private rooms for students. Both halls were comparatively new, and for a Catholic boarding school to provide private rooms at that time was considered a very daring venture. High school students were at Brownson, the main building, and St. Edward Hall, and those of the student body who worked their way through college at St. Joe Hall. The church, the main building, the presbytery, infirmary, the kitchen and convent, the gymnasium and old science building made up the entire physical plant. General tuition at that time was $400.00. Fifty dollars extra was charged for a room at Sorin.

Of course, I came into a new and different world when I came to Notre Dame. I was a callow youth, raised in the rough, tough surroundings of a mining town situated in the heart of the Rocky Mountains. Save for three years at Gonzaga College, I had done no traveling of any kind and had had touch with only the residents of my own narrow sphere. I had come to know

The University of Notre Dame as Frank Walker knew it when a student there. Courtesy University of Notre Dame Archives.

only the natural beauty of the great mountains that surrounded me, and the lakes and streams that formed a part of it all. Notre Dame, its faculty, its men, and its campus unfolded an entirely new world for a provincial young mountaineer.

It was a busy spot when I first saw it. The student body was just returning for the new scholastic year. The first few weeks were a bit trying to a newcomer, and I suffered a real touch of homesickness. A month had not passed, however, until I seemed to fit in and become a part of it, and in my first thoughtful moments I came to realize that I was deeply impressed with Notre Dame. I was deeply impressed, above all things, by the tranquility of its atmosphere and by the fineness and wholesomeness of its men, its faculty, and the student body. These impressions have remained with me over the years, and to me it is a place cut out—a place apart. There is not any spot I know quite like it.

I spent the first two weeks at Notre Dame in what to me was very serious controversy with one whom I then considered an arrogant, petulant, irritable, condescending padre who was director of studies—Father William A. Moloney. We clashed head-on at our first meeting on the respective merits of the Jesuits and the Holy Cross men as educators. Father Moloney insisted that I have but one year of college credit for my two college years at Gonzaga, and I insisted that the excellence of Jesuitical training warranted two years' credit. I don't think he ever did care much for the Jesuits. It may have been due to his wholehearted devotion to Notre Dame and the Holy Cross order. He insisted that I take two conditions—one in Latin and one in Greek. He argued that I had not sufficient quantity. He and I argued the point of quantity and quality; I contended that I had had sufficient quality—he contended that I had not sufficient quantity. I volunteered to take an examination. He finally consented to this, and "Daddy" Scheier, who taught Latin and Greek, gave me the test. I remember I got a ninety in Latin and, by the grace of God and the help of Daddy Scheier, got an eighty-two in Greek. It so happened that he picked the only bit of Greek of which I had any understanding. It was Saint John Chrysostom. I did at one time know my Greek irregular verbs. I had learned them at Gonzaga one night from ten o'clock until eight o'clock the following morning. My knowledge of the Greek irregular verbs left me as I passed in my examination paper, which, fortunately for me, I passed.

I lost the battle with Father Moloney and finally got permission from my family to stay on at Notre Dame and take law. I didn't speak to Father Moloney during my first year at college. I went out for the debating team, which was then under Professor Reno. In the midst of the tryout for debating, Reno was superseded by Father Moloney. I was inclined to withdraw from the forums when he held them, but he told my friend O'Flynn the reason I was quitting was because of fear that I could not make the team. This infuriated me and spurred me on so that I did make the team for two years in succession. Incidentally, I had a unique distinction. Notre Dame had won thirteen straight debates. I was on the team that lost debate number fourteen, but I led the team the following year and was vindicated. Under Father Moloney's guidance I went to Georgetown and argued "guaranty of bank deposits" and successfully defended Notre Dame's honor. Father Moloney and I were fast friends ever afterward. I had real affection for him and held him in high esteem. He was an unusual person.

I took several elective courses in addition to law, logic, and psychology under Father Tom Crumley. He had a fine, good mind. He was a refined, gracious, kindly person and always most popular with the students. He was unusually slow and deliberate. I can still remember watching for him before class. As he turned the corner near the presbytery to teach his class, which was in the rear of the old Science Hall, I, seated on the grass in front of Sorin, would roll a cigarette, smoke it, then start and beat Father Tom to the class.

I say he was always fine and gracious. Yet on one occasion he flunked the entire psychology class. I thought I had done quite well. He told us later that he flunked us to see what our psychological reaction would be—he had used us for guinea pigs.

He had unusual wit and fine humor. I remember Father Charlie O'Donnell telling me he was seated with him in church during the stations of the cross, which were being said by Father Steiner. Father Steiner of course had a rather booming voice. As he would come to each station he would call it out in loud, stentorian tones. As he proceeded on his way, Father Crumley turned to Father O'Donnell and said, "Apparently Father Steiner has no faith in the acoustics of our church."

During my three years at Notre Dame I was really a student. I was far from brilliant, but I did work hard, not only in my study of law but also during the other courses I had chosen to take.

In addition to that, I indulged in a few extracurricular activities. I was living in Sorin Hall, and Red Miller and Rosy Dolan lived in the same place. I weighed less than one hundred and forty pounds with padding and cleats. They both told me they would help me out in trying to make the football team, so I tried for quarterback. The line in those days was two hundred pounds from end to end. They had such huskies as

Frank Walker when a law student, on the Notre Dame campus in 1908. Photograph courtesy the Walker family.

Ralph Dimmick, Sam Dolan, George Philbrook, Fay Wood, and Al Mertes, and in the backfield they had Red Miller and Dominic Callicrate, both of whom were powerful fellows and ran with their knees high. In those days they did little open field running. Mass formation was then popular. Backing up the line, which is now done by a fellow around two hundred pounds, then fell to the lot of the quarterback. I can still hear the coach shouting, "Under the play, Walker," then a stiff arm, a knee under the chin, and Callicrate and Miller coming *crash—bang!* This would happen after Dolan and Dimmick had done their share of pushing me around. After three weeks of this I turned in my suit. I was black and blue from the top of my head to the soles of my feet. The hopeful protégé of Miller and Dolan was scarred and disillusioned. I quit football. Miller and Dolan were names to be conjured with in my time. They were both great football players and fine men.

I also took part in debating during my last two years of college. I made the varsity debating team in 1908 and 1909, and made the law team in 1909.

I was editor of the *Scholastic* but made no great contribution to it. I was also editor of the *Dome*. During my last two years I reported for Indianapolis, South Bend, and Chicago newspapers. In my time the newspapers had no reporters on the campus. Ambrose O'Connell had what were called "reportorial rights," which to obtain from him one had to have the approval of the head of the English department and $125 in cash. I got the consent of the English department and paid Ambrose $125, which rights I sold later for $150. Strange to say, Ambrose later became my assistant in the post office department, and I purchased from him the first stamp that was sold in the new post office on the Notre Dame campus. I earned my way through college the last two years by writing for the various papers, and I occasionally sent a short story to a Montana syndicate and would pick up twenty-five or thirty dollars in this fashion, which made life much easier at Notre Dame, but with my extra work it kept me very, very busy.

In my days we had three class orators. I remember I was selected as one of the class orators and finished my paper on juvenile delinquency. I spent my days immediately before graduation in the hospital with appendicitis, and John Kanaley, who had been on the debating team with me, took my place as one of the class orators.

The good and fine and wholesome things that came to me at Notre Dame did not come from instruction that I received in the law school; they came from the general atmosphere and environment of the place, close association with some very fine wonderful men, some of them unusual spiritually and some intellectually striking. The Notre Dame law school of today is far from the Notre Dame law school of my time. It had some fine, intelligent, serious students, and perhaps enough good professors to guide us in our work, but I must say that as a whole it was not an outstanding law school. My three years spent there did give me what I consider a good solid worthwhile foundation in law.

A delightful old gentleman, Colonel Hoynes, a Civil War veteran, was dean of the law school. I remember we had large brass cuspidors in the lecture room. Old Dean Hoynes had his lectures marked at various points for little anecdotes that he told over the years. The seniors would tell us in advance what to expect. During the lecture the class would chew tobacco and punctuate the sentences of the old dean expectorating juice on the cuspidors that sounded to the high heavens. The dean used a magnifying glass for the finer print when he discussed Blackstone and the Code of Hammurabi, and would cite occasional cases that for those days were considered a bit on the risqué side. These were followed by the forced guffaws of the entire class. Old Dean Hoynes was a quaint, queer old character with many idiosyncrasies, quite pompous in his own fashion yet quite democratic with the boys and liked to be considered one of them. His story of the Civil War and his early career would not always adhere to the facts, I am afraid. Each freshman class would be told of the dean's early legal career. Pulling down his vest and nervously coughing two or three times, he always suggested that he had had a very active, thriving practice in his time and in one year made as much as five thousand dollars. He was not a great lawyer nor a profound scholar. He was a polished old gentleman and we all liked him, bore with him, and were many times bored by him.

At this time the law school had a fairly good faculty—old Judge Anderson and Judge Howard were very good teachers, and Sherman Steele, a former graduate of the university, was one of the finest teachers I ever had. Particularly his course in constitutional law was thorough and worthwhile. Later, Ed Schwab, brother of the steel man, taught us one or two courses.[2] He lived in Mishawaka and frequently came late to class. Old Judge Howard and Judge Anderson were many years his senior, and, rain or snow, hail or sleet, they were always on time. We became quite put out with Schwab coming late, so I headed a strike on one occasion. We waited until five minutes after ten, and when Schwab did not show up we all went to our rooms. Out of this resulted a hearing before the president on the right of students to strike. We did not win an outright decision, but neither did Schwab. Father Cavanaugh's reprimand was far from serious. Schwab became more punctual. I wonder if it was Notre Dame's first strike—it was mine.

Gallitzin A. Farabaugh, who is now an attorney for the university, also had a class in my time, as did Virus Jones, a South Bend lawyer. We also had other outside lecturers.

Being associated with the law school is not by any means the outstanding part of Notre Dame to me. I just cannot single out any one thing that won me over to the place. It was a combination of many.

Of course, of all, the one who left the greatest impression on me was Father John W. Cavanaugh, the president. I have always thought that we were especially fortunate in my time at Notre Dame in that we had so many preachers of different character and style—the saintly, esthetic Father Hudson, the cultured Father French, and the logician Father Crumley, and best of

all Father Cavanaugh. He was a tall, handsome young man. When I entered
Notre Dame he was but thirty-six and had taken over the presidency the year
previously, succeeding Father Morrissey, who had become provincial.

Father Cavanaugh was famed for his oratory. He indulged in elaborate
and somewhat far-fetched figures of speech. He used many refined distinc-
tions of the language and rather gloried in their usage. He commented on this
himself quite frequently, as he would discuss his own speeches and sermons.
He never hesitated to gild the lily. In his time that was the popular type and
form of speech. Bryan, Bourke Cochran, and many others who were famed
for their oratory indulged in florid style lavishly and received popular approba-
tion and acclaim for their efforts.[3] His sentences were of the long, involved,
periodic type, but he also injected sparkling wit, sarcasm, and irony. He could
express scorn and contempt; he could also vilify in striking fashion. He could
be high and mighty and lofty, and he was a master of fulsome praise.

It was his custom to introduce lecturers at Notre Dame. Oftentimes he
would present some diminutive speaker—one almost a nonentity, unknown
not only to the student body but also little, if at all, known to the president
himself. I can still see the little fellow with his feet dangling as he sat on the
high-back chair, swelling up, throwing back his shoulders and raising high his
head as Father Cavanaugh would laud him to the skies.

In later years at a public gathering I once introduced Father Cavanaugh. I
turned and referred to his introductions at Washington Hall and said, "You
could make a Robin Hood out of the much caricatured 'timid soul.'" It was true.

He always carried himself with poise and great dignity. It was his custom
to wear a frock coat and carry a gold-headed walking stick. They were a very
part of him. I can still picture him—head held high, shoulders thrown back,
promenading down the center lane of the campus bound for the city. At times
a gracious smile lighted his sort of cherub face, and other times a serious mien
gave definite indication of his mood.

I did not come to know him, save as a student comes to know the president of his college. I did, however, have direct contact with him on two or
three occasions, each one of which revealed to me a good quality in the man.

One incident stands out quite clearly—that I survived it whole-skinned
was no mean accomplishment. I was a member of a committee of three of the
student body who visited the president's office on behalf of the captain of the
football team. The captain, contrary to orders from his professor, had left for
home to attend an Easter party, as he had a date with his girl to attend an Easter dance. The professor advised the president of the absence of the student
and Father Cavanaugh wired him collect, telling him to return forthwith to
the campus. The recalcitrant student wired the president, collect, advising him
that he would return the Tuesday following Easter. It fell to my lot to plead

the case for the recalcitrant. As we all knew, Father Cavanaugh was a man who stood upon his dignity. I found myself with a task on my hands. After a summation of the case by the president, in which he stressed with great emphasis the fact that the student was captain of the football team and the best-known man on the campus, that he had practically thumbed his nose at the president, sending him an insulting wire collect, he said the student body knew all of the facts and knew of our presence before the president. He suddenly turned to me and said, "Frank Walker, I am going to let you decide this case, but I insist that you as a Catholic gentleman decide it on its merits." Then he turned and asked for my reply. I in rather subdued voice said, "The student returns," and the committee silently withdrew. I did not see Father Cavanaugh for about two weeks and was really fearful of what might happen at our next meeting. I met him coming down the steps of the main building. As he reached the bottom step he grabbed me by the arm and said, "Frank, where have you been? You are a sight for sore eyes." We had a short talk but no mention was made of the case. I think he wisely thrust the decision that he did not want to make on my shoulders, for he knew that I was not going to vote for expulsion. I think he handled the case beautifully. He demonstrated once more some of the fine qualities that were his.

An incident that showed how effectively he could indulge in scorn and irony I learned from one of the old-timers. One of the priests still at Notre Dame was more or less a protégé of Father Cavanaugh. He had a good mind, much literary talent, and was and still is a very personable man. On one occasion Father Cavanaugh was taking a distinguished visitor on a sightseeing tour of the campus, and he had his young priest protégé accompany him. In his own inimitable fashion he pointed out the various places of interest and at times let his imagination carry him off line a bit. The young man interrupted several bits of Father John's description in an attempt to set him closer to the facts. This irritated the president of the university no little. He accepted several interruptions with seeming calm, no comment, but finally his patience was tested too sorely (he did have a low boiling point at times). He stopped dead in his tracks just as a large jackass in one of the nearby fields gave a loud bray. Father said, "Young man, you just heard the beast roar, did you not? You know he is an aristocrat among jackasses. May I suggest to you that you are a jackass among aristocrats?" Then he went on with his description of the next scene.

On another occasion he was called upon to give the principal address at a Knights of Columbus affair. The meeting dragged on until after twelve o'clock. The toastmaster took it upon himself to make a speech before introducing each speaker. He finally introduced Father Cavanaugh. Father Cavanaugh, whose patience had been sorely tested, is said to have spoken as follows: "Mr. Toastmaster, you have introduced the Grand Knight elaborately, the Deputy Grand Knight, the Assistant Deputy Grand Knight, the Knights of the Garter, and several other Knights. May I in closing this function suggest to those present that we officially, here and now, declare you to be the Knight of the Big Wind. Good night."

Perhaps he was not profound nor a scholar, not a great teacher. I am told he was not even a good administrator. But he had wit and charm and poise and grace. His public speeches, after-dinner talks, and sermons from the pulpit left real impressions on all those who ever heard him. He was a master in the art of conversation and could hold his own in meeting with the outstanding men of his time. He had force and courage and he did things. He made a real contribution to the education of many Notre Dame men. The attendance at the university doubled in his fourteen years; considering all the circumstances, this was quite remarkable. Notre Dame came to be known in his time. We in the Far West knew much of Notre Dame long before the time of Rockne.

I feel that the idea of the foundation, which came into being because of Father Cavanaugh, was in great measure responsible for the comparatively large sums that have come to the university in the past decade. The foundation not only created an awareness of the financial problem but also it excited the interests and enthusiasm of Notre Dame men and Notre Dame friends throughout the country. Then, too, giving is a contagious sort of thing. The Sally Fisher donation gave it a start; the Science Building, the Morris Inn, and the O'Shaughnessy arts and letters gifts gave it real impetus. The distinguished professors program paved the way for the Ford grant and other corporate grants.

When first I talked with Father Cavanaugh in 1948, we agreed that $25 million in ten years was to be the foundation objective.[4] I think we both felt that we were perhaps a bit overambitious. In my present frame of mind I shall be sadly disappointed if we do not surpass this goal. The work of the foundation itself should be credited with practically all of these gifts and grants. I think Notre Dame has every reason to be proud and grateful for the foundation. There was a real need for all the things set out in the program, and they could not have been carried on to this stage if the plan were not conceived.[5] In this grand work one man stands out as clearly as the lighthouse in the sea— Father Cavanaugh. Beyond question he was Notre Dame's greatest president.

3

THE LAW

W hen I left college I took and passed the bar examination the following month, July 1909. In September I was appointed assistant attorney for Silver Bow County, which included the city of Butte, under my brother Tom, who was the county attorney. I carried on in this post until December 1912. During these years I gained some of the most valuable experiences of my lifetime. I tried a dozen murder cases and a number of important civil cases and had the opportunity to argue several cases before our state supreme court.

One little case that occurs to me is a good example of the bulk of the work I handled as a young prosecutor, and it is worth recording, I think, because it reflects some of the inclinations that moved me in those days. An Irishman had charged a Cornishman with third-degree assault. The Irish and the Cornish were about evenly divided in manning the mines, and though they differed quite often, most Irish and Cornish had the notion that their controversies were sort of private affairs, to be settled privately with fists or brickbats. I was one of the Irish who subscribed to this school of thought, and I had little zest for the prosecution, or for protecting in court the interests of an Irishman who had had his nose bloodied by a "Cousin Jack," as we called the Cornish. I did not show much enthusiasm arguing the case, and the Cornishman was acquitted, which was all right with me. Immediately after the trial the Irishman breezed through my office, with his nose in the air, into the office of my brother the county attorney, and asked him for the immediate arrest of his adversary. My brother Tom, quite surprised, said, "Why? That man was just tried and acquitted!"

"Yes," said the complaining son of Erin.

"You had an attorney looking after you for the prosecution, didn't you?" asked Tom.

"That I did not," he said. "I had your brother!"

I was out of college less than a year when I received my first political baptism, an experience that to me was an amazing study in human nature. Butte politically was a sort of little Boston, controlled in the main by the Irish Democrats, with the English always aligned with the Republicans. On this occasion, shortly before noon on the day the Democrats were to convene to nominate their candidate for mayor, I received a call from the chief of police, Jack Quinn, asking me to stop by at his office and walk over to the convention hall with him. I joined Jack and walked with him from the city hall to the convention auditorium, about two blocks distant. The convention was to be called to order at noon. As we were about to enter the building, Quinn, who was a very brusque, factual, and forthright fellow, suddenly turned to me and said, "Frank, when they ask for nominations, tell them Jack Quinn is running for mayor." He then turned on his heel and left me cold. His request took the very wind out of me, because if I was to do what he suggested I had but a few

The house on Granite Street, 1923. This was Frank Walker's house upon his return to Butte after graduating from law school. Photograph courtesy the Walker family.

minutes to collect my thoughts. I recalled that Jack Quinn had been our chief of police, that he had made more loans of a dollar or more to indigent miners in Butte than any other man, that I had been a disciple of his as a kid when he fathered the eight-hour bill in the legislature, and when they asked for nominations I made some sort of a rambling nominating speech telling everything good about him that I could remember. Jack was overwhelmingly nominated, and as a result he chose me as chairman of the Democratic committee to organize and conduct his campaign.

Quinn, of course, was an Irishman, living in an Irish community. His opponent, Duncan, was a Unitarian minister who wore pince-nez glasses, a bow tie, and spats. He spoke Oxford English and was rather a freethinker insofar as social and fundamental economic matters were concerned. He ran on the Republican and Socialist tickets.

I remember closing the campaign for Quinn from the balcony of the Butte Hotel, which was the historic rostrum for public speaking in Butte. Partisanship had grown to white heat, and there was a veritable riot. I could not be heard for the shouts of the opposition. Shrill voices jeered and derided me as I heard in a broad Irish brogue: "Hoorah for Dooncan! Hoorah for the minister."

Quinn under Walker's leadership took a terrible licking the next day. It was my first lesson in politics and a real example of democracy at work. The Irish were tired of the Democrats and turned them out, even for a Republican-Socialist minister.

Two years later the Democrats came back into power. I can still hear one of Duncan's former Irish supporters, who was disappointed with the Republican-Socialist regime, saying to Johnny Reilly, the new police commissioner, "Johnny, what are you going to do with these damned Socialist policemen that Dooncan forced on us?" Johnny responded, "I'm going to give the so-and-so's a fair and impartial trial and fire them!"

Jack Quinn was really one of Butte's most colorful characters. He died of Bright's disease sometime after his defeat for mayor. My brother Tom and I went to his home to draw his will a day or two before he died. We went into the room and were shocked to see this big, broad-shouldered, fine husky chap reduced to skin and bones by prolonged illness. The ravages of his disease had brought him not only weakness but blindness.

When we went in he was chuckling. He said, "Who do you think just left me? California Jack." California Jack had been jailer for Quinn when Quinn was chief of police.

Quinn, chuckling, said, "California Jack said, 'Quinn, you look terrible! You look very bad! But you'll have the biggest funeral any man ever had in Silver Bow County.'"

To California Jack that was a real accolade. He thought he could not have made a more comforting remark to his good friend Quinn.

In 1912 I ran for and was elected to the Montana legislature. I really was averse to running, but in a weak moment I succumbed to pressure and threw my hat into the ring. It was for the term following the very bitter session of two years before, when Tom Walsh had been defeated by the Anaconda group. I had been an ardent admirer and supporter of Walsh in 1911, and my efforts on his behalf were another one of my first election activities after leaving college.[1]

Shortly before I decided to run for the legislature, intimation had come to me from one of the heads of the legal department of the Anaconda Copper Mining Company that they were considering retaining me as a member of their legal department. Nothing came of it at the time, but since my term as assistant prosecutor did not end until the following January, I had the notion that the offer would definitely come as soon as my term expired. Meantime, however, I decided to run for the legislature, and it was after my election and arrival in Helena that some of the active heads of Anaconda, the men who did their lobbying for them, came to me and suggested that they would be very happy to have me look after some of their legislation.

I was not impressed with this offer, or the approach, and I made it very clear to them that I was going to represent the people of Silver Bow County and not any one company. I think this created in them an air of hostility toward me from the very beginning of my term in the legislative assembly. I cast my ballots from the beginning to the end of the session, however, according to my convictions.

A very considerable amount of legislation that affected the company came up during that session. I supported and voted for a bill to eliminate the defense of contributory negligence cases and advocated, supported, voted, and worked for the Workmen's Compensation Act. Montana was among the first states in the Union to pass this progressive legislation. A number of the fellows injured in the mines in those days had their actions to recover defeated by the defense of contributory negligence legislation. We amended the act so that it practically amounted to a striking out of that defense, thus placing the proper responsibility upon the company, and of course any employer.

Some of the measures were of a log-rolling character. And I think it was the fact that Anaconda attempted to dominate the legislature in some particulars that caused the men from the northern and eastern parts of the state to have a real antipathy for Butte and Silver Bow County. Of course, such an antipathy is true in most legislative assemblies for one reason or another. The fellows from the sticks usually are suspicious of the big-town fellows.

One important issue involved the creation of new counties within the state. The assemblymen from the eastern part of the state were very much opposed, while the company favored dividing some of the counties so it would have better representation for itself. At that time D. M. Kelly, who later became vice president of the Anaconda Company in charge of western operations, was attorney general. At his suggestion, I worked with an assistant attorney general with whom I had been previously associated, Louis P. Donovan, in drafting an opinion as to the constitutionality of the new county measure. Louis and I both agreed that the measure was unconstitutional, and a copy of that opinion was placed on the desk of each of the legislators. The company did its best to have the bill passed. I was opposed to it, and I refused to attend a caucus that would have bound me to support the bill. This added no little to the hostility that I sensed the company felt toward me, and by the time the session was adjourned they really felt unkindly toward me, which I learned quite definitely a short time later.

When the session was over, Charles R. Leonard, who had a very extensive law practice, and who himself was not a trial lawyer and did not appear in the supreme court, asked me if I would enter his office—on a very fine basis so far as I was concerned. It was an arrangement whereby I could handle my own litigation, and if there was any conflict between his and mine, mine would have precedence. He was to pay me $250 per month, pay my office expenses, and permit me the use of his extensive library, which, to me, a young fellow out of college just a few years, was a very fine offer. Before accepting Leonard's offer, however, I told him that the Anaconda people had sometime since indicated to me that they might desire my services. So I went to see the vice president and general counsel of the company who is now chairman of the board, C. F. Kelley.

Kelley and I had quite a discussion, winding up in a very unfriendly fashion. Kelley intimated that I catered to the hoi polloi, that my ideas were not at all in harmony or in sympathy with the Anaconda Copper Mining Company policies or its type of corporate entity. I lost my temper with him, in any case, and pointed out that I had gone to the legislature to represent the people and not the company. I told him that I remembered quite well that when he himself had been in the legislature earlier, at the time of the Clark and Daly battles, nobody could tell him how to vote, and I told him that nobody was going to tell me how to vote when I attended the legislature.

We have remained quite friendly socially over the years, but that ended our business relationship. For some time I felt that Kelley had been very unfair in the matter, and I felt rather unkindly toward him. I got over my personal experience with him many, many years ago.

My days in the legislature were most interesting. The Woman's Suffrage Bill, for example, came to the committee of which I was chairman. Jeannette Rankin, who afterward went to Congress and voted against both world wars, was very active in the suffrage cause. She and Mary O'Neill and many others bombarded me from day to day in an endeavor to get the Woman's Suffrage

Bill out of the committee. I was not at all enthusiastic for woman's suffrage at that time, and I am not sure I am in entire sympathy with it now. I undertook to see to it that the bill did not leave the committee, and it did not come up for passage in the thirteenth session of the Montana legislature.

There was a lot of rancor and bitterness between the A. D. MacDonald crowd and the group headed by E. C. Day. MacDonald was from Kalispell, and he had defeated Day for speaker, which caused the hostility. The Day crowd would not accept MacDonald's nominee as chairman of the steering committee because, according to the rules, the chairman of the steering committee had control of the order of the house for the last twenty days of a session and could pigeonhole any bills that he did not wish to see come to the floor. At one stage the proceedings got to a point where MacDonald's friends feared his opponents might try to oust him by force, and several husky pro-MacDonald representatives lined up in the corners of the room, near the speaker's rostrum, to protect him. MacDonald had his troubles during that session, and if I am not mistaken he established a record for the Montana legislature on one occasion when, during a filibuster, he did not leave the chair for thirteen hours. As a result, the chairman of the steering committee was elected from the floor, and I was chosen.

I would not want to say that I am not superstitious. Incidentally, I have always considered the number thirteen lucky for me because of the series of times it popped up during these first days of my life spent in the legislature. I was elected in 1912, which numbers, when added, total thirteen; it was for the thirteenth session of the legislature, which convened in the year 1913; there were thirteen members of the delegation that went from Silver Bow County to Helena; the room to which I was assigned in the hotel was marked thirty-one, but it was plainly legible upon the door that these numbers had been transposed and that the room had previously been number thirteen; I was appointed chairman of the judiciary committee on January 13 and elected chairman of the steering committee on February 13. This is one for Ripley.[2]

When I returned to Butte from the legislature in March 1913, I accepted Leonard's proposition and really settled down to the practice of law. I only stayed with Leonard for about a year, however, because I began to feel that I was not there to take the brunt of the blame for any mistakes that were made in briefs and court but could pass thereon. I felt I would do better on my own. It was at that time that my brother Tom and I agreed to engage in the practice of law together under the firm name of Walker and Walker.

The practice of law, at first, was at times rather trying for me because of my early background. I had come of those who had been in travail over the years. I lived among and was closely associated with the working classes from childhood and was a part of them all of my life. I knew their problems well—

and I always hoped that the time would come when they would find surcease from their sorrow.

In my new profession, accepting the run-of-the-mill business that comes to the average law firm engaged in general practice in a small city, I found that many of my clients, in fact most of them, were of the wealthier class. I served, in association with my brother, as local counsel for the Northern Pacific, and the Chicago, Milwaukee, and St. Paul railroads. We represented the telephone company and outstanding contractors who were building railroad extensions through the Northwest, and we had a bank or two among our clientele. And I think I veered away from my social and economic principles for a short time because, earning a livelihood practicing law in a small city, I was obliged to take the cases that came my way to eke out an existence. My horizon was not too broad.

Our clients' problems sometimes met with opposition from labor, and I contended for my clients' rights vigorously and forcefully, as a righteous advocate should. I even occasionally appeared on behalf of the Anaconda Copper Mining Company or one of its subsidiaries. I think it is interesting to note, however, that neither I nor my firm ever received a check for services performed for Anaconda. The check never came to me or to Walker and Walker but to my brother, T. J. Walker, despite the fact that I did my share of the work and, I do not say this boastfully, often a bit more than some other members of the firm. The reason for the retainer not coming to the firm but to my brother Tom, I have always felt, dated back to my term in the legislative assembly. Tom always got on much better with the company group than I. But despite the fact that there were times I was not in sympathy with the general objectives of some of our clients, my sense of propriety did not prevent me from accepting fees when I had given my best effort and felt I was entitled to share in the reward.

Billy Gemmel, who was one of Montana's real characters, had come to Butte in the early days as an employee of one of the railroads. He, by the way, was the first curve pitcher ever to play on Butte baseball diamonds. Bill had acquired a good coal business, an interest in the local racetrack, and some considerable real estate holdings. He was one of my first clients. On the occasion of one of the local dinners, Bill referred to me as "one of the young lawyers who had been graduated from Notre Dame but really educated by Bill Gemmel." He said I had tried seven or eight lawsuits for him, all of which I had lost, but for which he paid me several thousand dollars in fees. I think my average in the cases I handled for Bill was better than he publicly declared, but I am sure I had my share of defeats.

One of the really exciting experiences in the history of Butte occurred only a short time after Tom and I opened our new office, in the late summer of 1914, and lent an additional touch of color to what always was a colorful mining city. It happened as an aftermath of the Moyer, Haywood, Pettibone incident, which occurred in the adjoining state of Idaho and resulted in the blowing up of the miners union hall in Butte by a group of union members in broad daylight.[3] Few places in America saw more violent controversy between capital and labor, and battles between one labor union and another, than Butte, and I think this was about the worst Butte experienced.

It was in the heyday of the IWW, and a band of IWW supporters moved in on the miners union hall, which was under the control of the American Federation of Labor, and took out an immense safe containing the union funds.[4] They placed the safe on a truck and marched down the main streets of the town in parade formation to the flat below, where they dynamited the safe. Later the miners union hall itself was blasted, and during the hubbub attendant upon the dynamiting of the hall, Moyer of the AFL and several union officials escaped by a rear exit and left town. Acting Mayor Curran, while speaking from a windowsill on the second floor of the hall, was hurled to the ground and suffered a broken leg. The chief of police then, an old and respected friend of mine, Jere Murphy, was hit over the head and knocked unconscious. He had been chief of police for years but was serving at that time under George Ambrose, the Socialist.

The police force in Butte was small, and the sheriff's force even smaller. The sheriff was Tim Driscoll, a modest, retiring man, mild in character. His force was composed of courageous men, but he could not bring himself to order them to shoot on the mob, and thus the affair got entirely beyond his control.

Mucky McDonald, president of the local IWW and head of the Wobblies, as they were called, actively took over the control of the city, and for several days the city was under the complete control and domination of his group under his leadership.

The headquarters of the union was in the basement of the office building in which my brother and I engaged in the practice of law. It was in the very heart of the city that McDonald, in high-handed fashion and with no interference of any kind, set up his seat of government, issued edicts and pronunciamentos, and in generous fashion assured the natives that if they would follow his edicts they would not be molested.

As a preliminary step toward recovering jurisdiction from the new dictator, Governor Stewart called upon Frank Conley, warden of the penitentiary, to take over as provost marshal. Conley, a big, heavyset, rugged man who had been a deputy sheriff in the eastern part of the state at nineteen, came up from Deer Lodge to assume his new duties.

He stopped by my brother's house and picked up Jim Galen. Jim was of the courageous rugged type too, and did not fear man nor beast. He came of an old pioneer family, had been a superintendent of Glacier Park, and ran a transportation company in and around Mount McKinley Park in Alaska. Incidentally, Jim was the brother of my good sister-in-law, Mrs. Tom Walker.

With forty-fours in their pockets, the two hied forth to the IWW headquarters, where a meeting was being held. The place was jammed. Conley, followed by Galen, brushed his way up the center aisle and mounted the rostrum, where McDonald was presiding. In calm tones and cool manner, Conley said: "McDonald, I just want to tell you, and this group here, that at the instance of Governor Stewart, I, as provost marshal, have taken command of this city. I intend to maintain law and order and will brook no interference from you or anyone else."

McDonald, in patronizing fashion, said: "I'll render every assistance to you and be glad to appoint a committee to aid you in restoring law and order, Mr. Conley."

Conley replied: "I don't want assistance from you or any of your ilk. I just want to let you know I'm in charge here and that the first fellow who creates trouble in this town goes out in a black box."

Conley said it and Conley meant it.

The state militia came in that night and took over. We lived under martial law for about ten weeks, from September 1 to November 5, to be accurate. It was an unusual experience for us to be governed by the military. Colonel Dan Donohue, related by marriage, incidentally, to Admiral Leahy, later aide to Presidents Franklin D. Roosevelt and Harry S. Truman, did a very fine job.[5] There was little disturbance or trouble from the time he took over until the troops departed in November. Jesse B. Root, one of the outstanding lawyers of the town, a swashbuckling man at heart, gloried in presiding over the military court. It chafed a bit to live under such conditions.

Afterwards the sheriff, Tim Driscoll, was charged with misfeasance in office for failure to act in an emergency. Our law firm was retained in his defense. A judge from the eastern part of Montana, who later served in Congress and was governor, Roy Ayres, was called in to preside.[6] The night before the trial, my brother Tom and I, who had been working on the case, dropped in the Silver Bow Club for a nightcap. Seated on a couch in a corner of the club we found, much to our discomfiture and surprise, the three men who had started the ouster proceedings in close consultation with the judge. It seemed obvious that this meeting would be of no great help to our cause, and as the case proceeded from day to day it became very evident that Driscoll would not long be sheriff. The trial was held shortly before the fall election, and Tim was a candidate to succeed himself. I became so incensed at the unfairness of the judge's rulings that I turned my back when it came time to argue the case and directed my remarks to the crowd in the room rather than to the judge. My efforts, including my rather contemptuous attitude toward the judge, availed

Frank Walker, identified by the penciled arrow at right, marching in the Veterans' parade in Butte, 1916. Photograph courtesy the Walker family.

poor Tim not at all. The judge ousted him, though he did not fine me for contempt. Charley Henderson defeated Tim for sheriff, and that ended one chapter in Butte's many labor difficulties.

A few other incidents that occurred during these years were the blasting of the time-card office that very same summer, on August 20, 1914, and the shooting on Anaconda Hill where several strikers were shot, which was one of the most terrifying things that happened in my time. The hanging of Little, an IWW, on the trestle south of the city one Sunday morning by anti-IWWs was a gruesome affair.[7] I do want to emphasize that almost every such incident was inspired by the struggle between capital and labor that was taking place through the years. These were grave and serious times in the history of our little city and were evidence of the tension and bitterness that existed.

My brother Tom and I carried on, actively practicing law together in Butte, for the next ten years, until I left Butte in 1924 to accept the position of general counsel of Comerford Theaters, Inc. under my good uncle, Michael E. Comerford. Those last ten years, of course, included some of the busiest days of my lifetime while Tom and I tried to and did develop our law practice into a thriving business.

4

THE COMERFORD THEATERS

During my lifetime my mother spoke to me often of her brother and my uncle, M. E. Comerford, but I really did not come to know him well until 1913 when I came east on a business trip that took me to New York City and up into Montreal. I spent some very pleasant hours with him on that occasion, and I believe it was the mutual friendship developed at that time that resulted ultimately in my coming to New York.

My mother always seemed to me to look upon M. E. as a son, and while she always spoke well and hopefully of him, it seemed to me that she spoke a bit fearfully. She felt that M. E. was a good and fine character but a bit too worldly wise for his own good. She had a maternal interest in him. It was her idea that he had not had the affection and care and training of a mother and that he was somewhat handicapped because of that. His mother died when M. E. was very young, and for a time my mother assumed charge of his early training. Mother had a fine, keen mind. She had great vision, understanding, and prudence. In the latter years of her life, in kindly and respectful fashion, I nicknamed her Prudence. The family adopted that name for her. Though mother had little formal education, she did teach grade school as a young woman. She had unusual powers of observation and kept herself well informed on current events. She was keen and in my judgment an unusual judge of human nature. Her mind and heart centered in her family. She had ambition, but it was only for them, their good and their welfare.

Save in respect of being a real home person, my mother and M. E. were much alike. I had a full and complete feeling that I really understood M. E. when I first came to see and observe him. This I think was due to the fact that he had so many of my mother's qualities and quaint ways. In so many ways they seemed to think and act alike. Each had acquired the habit of speaking in parables. Each had the habit in the family circle of casually discussing the qualities of some particular character or characters in such fashion as to make it obvious that the point or moral of their remarks was directed straight at one of those who were present.

I can recall so well my mother telling me about certain young men who had ninety-five percent averages at college, and commenting on the fact that the boys' mothers must have been very happy. She was not always too adroit. On one occasion she happened to choose for her example a friend of mine whose college rating I well knew. She styled him a cum laude, when to my own knowledge he had gone through Yale with a gentleman's C average.[1]

This similarity in their minds was strikingly brought home to me later. I can remember shortly after I had come to New York to work with M. E., he very casually told my cousin M. B. and me about meeting Adolph Zukor and his son hurrying down Fifth Avenue the previous morning at 7:00 A.M., bound, so he said, for a secondhand

M. E. Comerford, the uncle of Frank C. Walker. Photograph courtesy the Walker family.

store where at very low cost they were to acquire beautiful furnishings and draperies for one of Zukor's new theaters.[2] I was quite certain that Adolph was comfortably ensconced in his Fifth Avenue apartment at that time any morning. He made his point, however, and I was struck forcibly with the realization that M. B. and I had an immediate problem with our newly completed theater in West Scranton and that we had better have it beautifully furnished at reasonable cost.

Knowing my mother so well, I came to acquire a correct appreciation of Mike Comerford. Inspired by the respect and affection I had for my dear mother, I came to respect and love him, too.

M. E. had his start in the amusement business with a minority interest in a partnership. Partnerships were the very foundation of the Comerford organization. His first undertaking was in a combination with two or three others. With but a minority interest he could carry on an enterprise with a conviction, determination, and enthusiasm that brought the respect of his associates and made for his and their success as well. Over the years, as he continued to expand in theater and real estate business, his business was conducted in most instances in the form of partnerships in which he held either minority or majority interests. It is most unbelievable, but when I first joined him he had no less than one hundred associates or partners. He was a real pioneer, starting in the motion picture business in 1906.

It struck me that Mike Comerford was very constructive in all his plans and action. He had none of the defeatist in him, and he seemed to have unusual vision. When he came into the motion picture industry, rules and standards were just in the making. Many of the newcomers had been in various lines of endeavor and acquired the beginnings of sizable fortunes with little previous experience and little effort. Many in production, distribution, and exhibition were working out their lot by trial and error. Few had an idea of the great possibilities that were ahead. Beginning with small one-reel pictures shown in abandoned storerooms at a price of five cents admission, it grew and expanded amazingly. Fortunes came and went in very short periods of time. New rules and regulations came into vogue, and standards of practices and ethics developed gradually.

Mike Comerford had little formal education, very little comparatively. Yet he became a well-read man with a goodly knowledge of history, particularly American history. He had innate refinement and culture and a wholesome philosophy. Nothing of the rude or coarse or vulgar ever became part of him. During a good part of his lifetime his associates and friends were of quite a worldly type. He had friends among the high and the lowly. He had the common touch that never became common. He tried to conceal his emotions but concealed them less than he knew. He had a high temper and at times could be as cold as steel.

I have known few, if any, men who had greater simplicity of soul. He did many charitable acts that by his own arrangement and design will never come to be known. He did more for the early friends of his life than any man I have ever met, but he did it quietly, unostentatiously, withal intelligently. He had none of the show-off in him. He measured men well and capably, giving in correct measure to those who were deserving and needy as they merited it, and in keeping with their needs and responsibilities.

He was neither extravagant in his giving nor in his living. I doubt that I have ever known any man who lived more modestly or had less desire for the luxuries of life. He dressed well but not fastidiously. He was temperate in all his habits. He drank but little and smoked sensibly, always cigars—he had an old-fashioned contempt for cigar-eets, as he styled them.

He was not given to praise, particularly in the presence of those he would praise. His form of rebuke was a model of self-control yet could be forcefully expressive. It would never be done in a violent or angry mood and seldom if ever in the presence or hearing of others.

My first business association with him and the Comerford organization came in the summer of 1924. I was east on legal business and had agreed to confer with M. E. during my trip. He had suggested to me prior to this meeting that I become associated with him in business. He had also mentioned it to my sister, Mrs. Katherine Cotter.

On this particular occasion he requested me to attend the closing of a deal he had with Ed Fay in Providence. We had discussed the question of whether or not I was coming east, as I had given some thought to locating in New York. In closing the deal with Fay, he suggested that he was going to give me a third of his newly acquired interest. This he did. He also gave a third to M. B. and retained a third himself. He acquired a half-interest in the Fay circuit from the Samuels brothers, merchants in Providence, and from an associate of theirs named Herzberg, for $250,000. Attorney Higgins, former Rhode Island governor, served as legal representative for M. E. and for Fay.[3] Fay, who was a stockholder in the circuit, acquired a further interest for himself and his brothers, so that under the new arrangement the Fays owned half of the outstanding stock and the balance was divided between M. E., M. B., and myself. M. E. aided Fay in financing his part of the deal.

At that time Fay's circuit consisted of Fay's Theater, Providence; Fay's Theater, Philadelphia; and Capitol Theater, Rochester.

After closing the Fay deal we returned from Providence to New York. It was at the time of the famous 1924 convention, when the Smith-McAdoo ballot went on for 103 ballots.[4] I knew the Montana delegation very well, so M. E. and I spent a few days as their guests, watching the proceedings. M. E. renewed his suggestion that I come east and join him. I told him I knew nothing about the theater or motion picture business and had no ambition in that direction; I had practiced law for fifteen years and wished to carry on. I felt I had reached the top of my possibilities in Montana, as possibilities there were limited. My brother and I were associated in a partnership that was making about $50,000 a year. I could see no possibility of increasing our income in that territory. I told him I was thinking about a broader field in the law and had not given consideration to any other business.

He said he contemplated enlarging his field of activities. He desired to extend his vaudeville circuit and acquire more theaters, not only in Pennsylvania but in other areas as well. He felt that I could aid him in his work and still look after my practice of law. After considerable thought we finally agreed that I would come on for two or three years and try it out. He offered me a contract with one of his companies. I was to work as counsel and adviser. The term was three years and the compensation $24,000 a year and expenses.

I got in touch with Mrs. Walker, who was in Montana. She came on to New York and looked over the field with me. She had been raised in Montana and was not enthusiastic about coming east. I told her that I had practically agreed to go along for a time with M. E. After a month's visit, during which we looked over the field and gave the matter more thought, we both agreed that we would go into the new venture. We returned west after we reached this decision so that we could talk with my brother Tom and make our plans for the future.

I returned east in the fall to size things up and went west during the holidays to bring the family back. We arrived in New York City in January 1925. I was then thirty-eight years of age. Mrs. Walker and I had been married ten years and had two children: Tom, four years of age, and our daughter, Laura Hallie, who was but ten months old when we came east. For Mrs. Walker it was quite an ordeal. She was born in Butte and had lived there all of her life, save for a few short visits. She spent two years with her mother in Europe, where she studied in Paris and Switzerland. Montana meant much to her, and to me as well. Though I was born in Pennsylvania, the family went west when I was but four years of age. Save when at college and law school and one year in the army in World War I (a safe war for me: I was ordered up the line at 8:00 A.M. and the armistice was effective at 11:00.), I had spent my childhood and adult years in Butte. I had practiced law there for fifteen years with some measure of success. I loved Montana, and Mrs. Walker and I were attached to our friends. It was a daring move to make, but I was anxious to try a bigger and broader field. Whether our choice was correct, only time will tell

Soon after coming east, in keeping with M. E.'s plans to widen his vaudeville activities and theaters, we moved the company offices from a small space at Forty-first Street and Broadway to our present site, 1600 Broadway. This was in June 1925. We enlarged our organization, acquired more spacious quarters, and started booking additional theaters. We spent more than $25,000 renovating. At that time we employed Miss Dooley, who served with us well and faithfully. Not long afterwards we negotiated with Alex Pantages, the western vaudeville magnate, for a joint venture in booking vaudeville.[5] According to a proposed plan, we were to book theaters east of the Mississippi and Pantages to book theaters west and bring his acts into Chicago. We had practically closed a deal with Mike Shea in Buffalo to take over a half-interest in his circuit and run it. He had vaudeville theaters in Buffalo, Niagara Falls, and Toronto. But just about the time the deal was to be consummated, Sidney Kent, representing Paramount, stepped into the situation, made a deal with

Frank Walker with his son, Tom, and daughter, Laura, in 1928. Photograph courtesy the Walker family.

Shea for Shea's manager Franklin to operate the Paramount houses in New York City, and Paramount took an interest in Shea's circuit. Shea's action disappointed us. M. E. was particularly put out, so we looked around for an alternative plan that would fit into our plans.

We eventually formed an alliance with William Fox and built the Great Lakes Theater.[6] I personally took charge of negotiations. M. E. purposely, I'm sure, avoided taking part in the deal. I am quite certain he was trying the newcomer out. He was gambling a half-million to find out if I would do. I negotiated the entire deal—agreed on the terms of the lease, passed on construction contracts, and handled all negotiations with Fox and his lawyer, Saul Rogers.

The alliance with Fox was made largely because of Winnie Sheehan, Fox general manager, who was a native of Buffalo and desired theater representation in his hometown. About that time, M. E. hired Walter Keefe, an old Pantages associate, for the purpose of acquiring additional vaudeville houses to book. He was sent out into the territory to line up theaters. E. F. Albee was then in charge of the National Vaudeville Managers Association, a very strong vaudeville combination, and was very anxious to have the Comerford interest join with his vaudeville booking combine.[7] Comerford had different ideas—he wanted to carry on his own.

He and I, at the solicitation of John Harris of the well-known family of Pittsburgh, had several conferences with Albee. I always felt M. E. treated these rather lightly. I do not think he ever intended to close with Albee. He never did. Albee was then head of the Keith organization, the outstanding vaudeville combine of all time. He impressed me, a newcomer in the amusement world, as a rather dictatorial and demanding person. At that time he was completing the erection of splendid but really extravagantly conceived vaudeville theaters around the country and had not the least awareness of the real importance of the motion picture in the entertainment world. The motion picture was really coming into its own.

After one of the conferences that M. E. and I had with him, we left his office, which was in the Palace Theater building, and stopped in an adjoining restaurant for lunch. During our discussion of the Albee conference, M. E. asked me my opinion of Albee. Quite spontaneously and without lowering my voice I indicated that I thought he was an arrogant, self-opinionated old so-and-so. Here I, a lawyer from a small western town, learned my first lesson in New York business tactics: the walls have ears. Our conference with Albee was to carry on the next day. As it opened, Albee turned directly to me and ventured that, despite my opinion, he was not an arrogant old so-and-so and said he hoped to change my opinion of him. Though we made no deal with him, he and I personally became quite good friends. Later, when some of his associates voted to take him off the National Vaudeville Managers Association board, I, who was one of five or six directors, was one of two to support his position. I did learn to follow my mother's advice and be more prudent and cautious in New York dealings.

M. E. and I spent much of our time during this period surveying various cities and conferring with theater owners. Jerry Cadoret, who had been associated with M. E. for a number of years, served as sort of bird dog for M. E. in flushing up prospective deals. He and I covered a good part of the East; I think Jerry and I visited every city in New York State of a population of five thousand or more. Mike Kallet traveled with us frequently. His advice and suggestions were always helpful, and he was a great assistance to me particularly.

M. E. at this period had an unusual group of men in his employ. Most of them he had taken on from time to time as his circuit was enlarging and expanding. Sam Friedman, who as a boy sold M. E. newspapers, was manager of the Strand, which was the ace house. George Morris, who was originally a painter, had come to be in charge of maintenance and construction. Bill Cadoret, a brother of Jerry, had run a theater in Kankakee, Illinois, and had just come on to take over the purchase of film. Joe Duffy, Martin Caffrey, Art Luce, Mike Gallagher, Professor Sharer, and many other old cronies of M. E. who had been in various fields of endeavor became ticket takers or house managers. Harry Spiegel and Arthur Cohen, Hank Stezar, were all busy—Harry at the Family Theater, and Cohen and Stezar running fights and other forms of entertainment at Town Hall. Jack Jones, an old-time showman, ran the Capitol.

Kate Luxemburger had been M. E.'s secretary and sort of guardian angel. For a number of years she ran the switchboard, acted as secretary, guarded the door, and kept many favor seekers away from M. E.'s doorstep. Johnny

Roberts then was booking theaters. Luke Farrell, our old partner, was running Carbondale.

The Breig brothers were engaged as contractors for most jobs and were doing a certain amount of building each year. Lempert, architect from Rochester, designed most of the theaters that were constructed in the period from 1923 to 1930.

The Ryan brothers were not very active during my time with M. E. but had been most active earlier. Bill served on and off in our accounting department but seemed to spend very little time around headquarters. Joe had moved to the Comerford building across from the cathedral, where he was situated for about a year after my arrival. He then severed his relations with the company. I never did get to know Joe Ryan well. My knowledge of him was based in the main on hearsay.

As I gleaned it from those around in my time, Joe for some years was a sort of righthand man to M. E. But for many reasons, I was told, he became persona non grata. M. E. mentioned him but seldom to me and others. I did get the notion that he was most bitter toward Joe Ryan but had no real ill feeling toward Bill, who seemed to him and others to have no great sense of responsibility. He was a man, I think, of some capacity and I am told had much to do with setting up the system of accounting followed by the organization for many years.

From what I gleaned from general conversations with M. E., M. B., and different men in the organization, the early days of operation were interesting, colorful, and extremely hectic.

M. E.'s early associates were Mike Blewitt, Frank Treon, L. A. DeGraff, and Fred Herman. They engaged in a number of different ventures. Blewitt and Treon were the first to drop out of the picture. Herman became an employee and manager of different houses in Wilkes-Barre. DeGraff and his family were quite close to M. E. and his family and remained so for years, until DeGraff pulled up stakes and moved with his wife and daughter to Canada. The DeGraffs have passed on, as have M. E. and his wife, Margaret. Norma DeGraff, who still lives in Canada, and Mariel Comerford Friday are still most congenial and have carried on a very close and friendly relationship. DeGraff, when I joined M. E., was interested in the Poli houses in Scranton and Wilkes-Barre. They were owned by the Union Theater Company. He also had a minority interest in the Binghamton houses. In 1932–1933, M. E., M. B., and I acquired DeGraff's theater interests and his Binghamton stock and also took over Kornblite's and Cohen's interests.

We had some interesting and colorful experiences booking vaudeville in my first days with the organization. Most of the stellar attractions in vaudeville played our circuit, and the grosses of our vaudeville reached the high mark of all time in the days from 1924 to 1929. Though the Keith circuit was more or less in control of vaudeville on the East Coast and used every sort of tactic to make our path difficult, we managed to do very well.

No little amount of my time when I first became associated with M. E. was in supervising his vaudeville enterprise, then operated under Amalgamated Vaudeville Agency, Inc. Of course, vaudeville began to decline in the late twenties, but I did take an interesting and active part in it in its declining days. It really started on its way down in the middle twenties. It was a thrilling and unusual experience for me, a small-town lawyer, to match wits with Broadway vaudeville managers and bookers of acts and attractions. They were a smart, shrewd, clever lot, worldly-wise and with a code of ethics and rules of conduct all their own. It was really an education for me, and I found it to be a most interesting period of my life. I came to know many charming, delightful, and interesting people in this part of the amusement world. Most of them had a fine sense of honor, some a strange philosophy. I remember one of the outstanding men in the vaudeville field who was credited with saying, "Don't make gentlemen's agreements, you have to keep them." Also, "Get a good lawyer to draw up your contracts so that later he can break them for you, if and when necessary."

It became my privilege, too, to meet and know some wonderful stage and vaudeville stars: George M. Cohan, Al Jolson, George Jessel, Eddie Dowling, Ray Dooley, Frank Fay, Fred Waring, Will Rogers, Sophie Tucker, Ed Wynn, and James Barton. Eddie Dowling and Ray Dooley became close friends, not only of mine but of M. E. and of my family.

The men who were active in operations of the booking office were a sort of dedicated lot, with different hopes, ambitions, and standards. Our chief booker was Harry Padden. He had an unusual combination of qualities. He devoted all his working hours to booking the acts, fighting and then making up with his agents, spending his all for the show. He seemed to have the certain necessary faculty of blending a show properly, the ability to get the show on the road, and his bookings in regular order, on time. He burned himself out, giving so much to see that the show would go on.

Bud Irwin, his assistant, who later took over the management of the booking office, was a capable, efficient booker, and an extremely reliable and dependable man. He spent many years booking vaudeville and later managed the Riviera Theater in Binghamton.

We had a number of characters among our employees and agents. They all seemed to add an unusual and a different bit to several very interesting years. One of the best was Harry Shea, who was a fine character. He was a real New Yorker. He and his wife, May, came to be close friends for whom I had respect and regard.

Ed Fay, an associate of ours, was part owner of and operated the Fay circuit. This circuit originally consisted of theaters in Providence, Philadelphia, and Rochester. He devoted much of his time and effort to the booking of our vaudeville attractions. Ed had some very definite ideas of his own about the theater. He was an outstanding pioneer in the musical world, vaudeville, and motion pictures. Ed Fay in my opinion was one of the finest of M. E.'s partners and associates. He and M. E. had been friends for some time before I came on the scene. Theirs was an unusually close and fine friendship. Ed had great respect and affection for M. E., and M. E. had real affection for Ed Fay and had a fine appreciation of Ed's capabilities, loyalty, and his fine, wholesome philosophy. I, too, came to know and respect Ed Fay. He made a fine contribution to our organization and was always a friend and adviser to me. He had the Feinberg brothers, Abe and Joe, working under him. Both were smart, shrewd bookers. Ed kept them busy and on their toes at all times.

Ed was in some measure helpful to the men who organized National Screen Service Corporation, the outstanding producer and distributor of advertising trailers for motion picture theaters.[8] This association brings to my mind a little incident that revealed in unusual fashion some of the finer qualities of some of the men in the amusement world.

In the early thirties Ed became financially involved in a little venture in an industrial enterprise foreign to his field of activities. He placed confidence in an associate who betrayed his trust and found himself involved to the point where he needed $40,000 instantly. Herman Robbins loaned him the cash immediately with no security and told him he could pay it back when he got around to it.

At the inception of my association I had a number of conferences with M. E. and M. B. Comerford with reference to the status of the Comerford theaters generally. I learned largely through M. B. that ninety-eight percent of obligations was short-term paper due in ninety days or less. I felt this was a serious financial position for M. E. After some deliberation I took it upon myself to have a frank, candid talk with them about the matter. During this period M. E. and I had several discussions about the future operations. He had great imagination and was exceedingly ambitious. He felt that he could build up a great theater circuit and was desirous of keeping the interest intact in the family. He seemed desirous of building up his organization so that it could and would be capable of developing and expanding efficiently. He was laying his plans for the long-term future and made it very clear to me that he was most anxious to have me a real part of the organization. M. E. and I succeeded in making arrangements with Brooks and Company in Scranton and Bankers Trust in New York for an issue of Meco Realty for $1.8 million in twenty-year bonds bearing interest at the rate of six and one-half percent.[9]

Shortly afterwards another issue was negotiated for $1.25 million in North Penn bonds, twenty years, at the same rate of interest. I think at this time another was issued for the West Side Amusement for approximately $250,000. This improved our financial position decidedly.

The Meco and North Penn issues formed my first real experience in so-called big financing. I was a small-town lawyer who knew nothing of Wall Street and million-dollar issues. Confronted with the need of money for M. E. and our circuit, I called on some of our big financial houses. Going from one to the other I soon learned on my own that it was not all Greek. I also learned that the fellows who had what is now styled the know-how were the younger men from the back office, who were called in after the front-office fellows put on their act. They were the ones who knew how and who really did the work. It did not take me long to learn the fundamentals, to get the corporate setup, the appraisals of the property, the required picture of earnings, the term of issue, the amount of it, the favorable and unfavorable stipulations as to paying off in full when desired; sale of properties under the mortgage requirements on approval, the percentage required for payment on early retirement, etc. I got to know enough in any event to work out a deal that later proved to be the saving of our fate.

During the period from January 1925, to September 1930, M. E. Comerford and I made a number of deals that enlarged the holdings of the Comerford organization very considerably. We negotiated a lease of land and erected the Great Lakes Theater in Buffalo. It was centrally located and seated three thousand people. As I earlier suggested, M. E. took practically no part in arranging or closing this deal. He left practically all the negotiations and all the details with me. I think he was in Europe with his family when the deal was closed, and it was several months after his return before he would even listen to a report from me on the deal. We also acquired an interest in the Bill Dillon theaters in Ithaca, which later developed into a merger with the Bernsteins, who had laid plans for the erection of a theater in Ithaca almost simultaneously with our Dillon deal. It further came to pass that we merged the Dillon theaters with the Bernsteins' newly built theater, bought Dillon out, and became fifty-percent holders with the Bernsteins. We acquired with Fay the Majestic, Carlton, Capitol, and Modern theaters in Providence. We took over the Weber and Feeley interest in Hazleton, Pennsylvania. They each retained an interest as we erected the new Capitol Theater in Hazleton.

M. E. was always a great believer in keeping his properties in good condition. We did business during the years with Lipman-Spanger, who built box offices and remodeled theater fronts. M. E. decided to take an interest in this business, which we did. He felt we would do better this way with our own theaters and could branch out into the field generally. This was, of course, like the vaudeville booking, and the main thought guiding us in operating this business was service to all our theater holdings. Finally we took over the Lipman-Spanger Corporation. We also invested in Eddie Dowling's show, *Thumbs Up*, and in Harry Crandall's *Pantheon*, a huge panoramic picture of gigantic proportions. This was done by corporations owned by all three of us, suggested first by M. E. but carried on with our approval. Crandall was an old friend of M. E. and an old-line showman. He was a pioneer in movie exhibition and had suffered severely when a heavy snowfall brought about the collapse of the roof of one of his theaters in Washington, causing many deaths and great loss. M. E. felt the panorama that was shown at the World's Fair had good possibilities as a moneymaker.[10] We tried it out in several spots but met with no success. Dowling's show and the Libman-Spanjer affair also failed to be profitable. They were joint enterprises, however, that looked good to M. E. and at the time appealed as well to M. B. and myself.

During the latter part of 1926 and 1927 many in the motion picture industry began to feel a bit disturbed about the trend in the business. Grosses were dropping quite decidedly and it was manifest that interest in the business was beginning to wane. For these reasons the motion picture industry generally and the Comerford interests particularly were highly gratified when Warner Brothers came to the fore with talking pictures. Some experimenting had been done in the early days with so-called sound pictures, but the coming of Warners' Vitaphone marked a new era in the entertainment world. It was truly a savior for those interested in motion pictures.

Mike Comerford, Ed Fay, and I accepted an invitation from Albert Warner and Sam Morris to attend one of the first presentations of a Vitaphone program. The program consisted of a speech by Will Hays introducing the new medium; the Philharmonic Orchestra of 107 men, conducted by Henry Hadley, played the *Tannhäuser* overture; Roy Smeck, a then popular vaudeville star, played a solo on his Hawaiian guitar and ukulele; and the great tenor of the Metropolitan Opera, Giovanni Martinelli, sang the aria from *Pagliacci*.[11] At that time I was a mere novice in the entertainment world. I was stunned by this amazing performance. M. E., old veteran and a showman for years, was really impressed, and Ed Fay, who was a musician in his own right and of some repute, was convinced that something worthwhile had come on the horizon. I had a number of my friends attend the showing of this program in the following days, among them Mrs. Walker and her father, who was visiting us from Montana. Everyone seemed greatly impressed and many seemed thrilled by this new form of amusement.

M. E., Ed Fay, and I conferred with Warners within the week following this demonstration. At their insistence I examined the proposed contract. When they asked my legal opinion, M. E., Ed Fay, and I were gazing out the window of Warners' office. The Warner offices were then on one of the upper floors at 1600 Broadway. I said in answer, "It seems to me it's like jumping out that window there, and expecting to land on your feet on Broadway. It's a great feat if you do it. However, I'd take a chance." That day, M. E., Fay, and I obligated our various companies for about a half-million dollars. Of course, Mike Comerford was the guiding genius, but we all took the chance. I followed his lead with some foreboding, but I confess I was really for it, as was Ed Fay. We signed up for about forty installations at this point ,and for some weeks afterwards the Comerford chain had more Vitaphones on order and being installed than any other chain in the United States. Neither Paramount nor Loew's followed the lead for some considerable time. Shortly afterwards Fox came out with his Movietone, and we followed on with Fox. This Fox system is practically the same form of sound motion picture now in general use; the Vitaphone has been abandoned. Majestic Theater in Providence, then owned by the Fay brothers, M. E., M. B., and myself, was the first real sound talking theater in the United States.[12]

In October 1928 we showed Fox Movietone at our Great Lakes Theater: Al Jolson in *The Singing Fool*. It was the first time in the history of show business that a picture ran three weeks in a town the size of Buffalo, which was then approximately 570,000 population.[13]

In 1928 and 1929 the larger theaters such as Paramount, Fox, and Warners started a campaign for the acquisition of theaters and began a real sellers' market. They were all trying to fortify their positions by acquiring more and larger theater chains. Paramount, Fox, Warners, RKO were reaching out to all parts of the country trying to acquire theaters. I kept in touch with the situation, and M. E. and I had many conferences with reference to the mad scramble for theaters. We both agreed that I should keep my ear to the ground and have discussions with heads of the various chains so that I could ascertain the possibilities for sale of the Comerford chain. Many propositions were made, with stock passing as consideration. We both agreed that if we made any kind of a deal we would not accept stock. We would insist on cash.

I had a number of conferences with Warners, Fox, RKO, and Paramount in the early part of 1929. Sidney Kent and I, among others, were representing the film industry in hearings that were being had with the Federal Trade Commission. During this period we began serious discussions of the sale to Paramount of the Comerford chain. One evening after a meeting of the Trade Commission in the bar association building, Kent and I rode as far as his home in a taxi—he was then living on Park Avenue. He and I sat in the taxi and talked for about an hour. We finally agreed upon a formula and shook hands on a deal whereby Paramount would take over the Comerford circuit. I told Kent at that time that they were to assume certain mortgages, pay a substantial amount in cash, and give us ample security for the balance, that we did not wish to take any Paramount stock, and that in all negotiations to be had, Kent would represent Paramount. I insisted that I would not deal with several individuals; full responsibility was to be Kent's. I wanted responsibility fixed in one man. I told Kent that Warners, Fox, and RKO had all approached us with a view of acquiring the Comerford chain. Sidney said that his association with M. E. Comerford had always been of the finest order, he had done business with him for a number of years, that Paramount and its men were perfectly familiar with the circuit, and that he was very anxious to make a deal with us.

I told Kent that M. E. and I both felt that it would place us in an unfavorable position if the word was bandied about that we were trying to dispose of our circuit. We both agreed that the understanding we had would be confidential in character and confined to the principals involved—Comerford (M. E., M. B., and myself) and such top officials in Paramount as were absolutely necessary to effectuate the closing of the deal. This, of course, would include Zukor; Austin Keough, the counsel; Ralph Kohn, the treasurer; George Schaefer, who was Kent's assistant; and the accountants who would have to check the figures. Again I told Kent that I did not wish to deal with a group of people, that the deal was to be made with him and with nobody else. I exacted a promise from him that if others interfered and the deal was not consummated, he would resign as vice president and general manager of the Paramount organization.

He told me that Zukor was leaving for Europe that night and that he would get in touch with him before he left, advise him of our understanding, obtain his approval, and advise me. Kent got in touch with Zukor that same evening and called me on the phone. He said, "Frank, it's a deal."

I advised Kent that some of our associates might not wish to sell but that M. E. and I both would do our best to prevail upon them to do so. If they were adamant, however, we would not insist. We would acquire as many partner interests as we possibly could. The deal further contemplated that Paramount would provide sufficient funds for us to acquire the interests of the partners so that the deal could be fully consummated.

As we were drafting agreements and making preparations to present our accounts, which took a very considerable time, the stock market took a bad turn, and in the midst of our negotiations the 1929 crash came. Kent had made all arrangements for his financing, and we were ready to close the deal. One day Kent called me to his office and told me that his bankers felt that they could not go through with the financing at this time. I got in touch with M. E. He and I had a further conference with Kent and both agreed with him that he should be relieved of his obligation. We both felt that a situation had arisen over which he had no control and under those conditions without further ado we released him from his gentleman's agreement. Kent suggested that if conditions improved he would then like to renew our understanding. We left him with that understanding.

Shortly after the first of the year the financial market improved considerably and we again began our negotiations, which ended in the closing of a deal in September 1930. When the time for the closing of the deal came, which was Labor Day, there were more than fifty questions, involving clouds on titles and other matters, that had not been settled. Austin Keough and I entered into a gentlemen's agreement that we would iron those matters out to the mutual satisfaction of both parties. We turned the theaters over to Paramount and they turned the money over to us.

In the fall of 1932 I was called into conference with Leo Spitz, who was counsel for Paramount. Spitz advised me that Paramount was on the brink of bankruptcy and it looked as though bankruptcy proceedings would be had, and that it might be necessary to make our circuit part of bankruptcy proceedings. I listened to him for some time. I had very little to say. After this conference I immediately went to see Keough, who was still general counsel for Paramount, and Y. Frank Freeman, now vice president of Paramount Pictures. I told them both that I would have no further discussions about the problem with Leo Spitz, that if they wanted any further discussions with me on the solution of our problem I would be very happy to discuss the matter with them, but I was not going to permit Spitz to hold the sword of Damocles over my head and have us appear as a claimant in bankruptcy proceedings. As a result of this conference I again had a conference with Spitz, which resulted in the 1932–1933 agreement. I thought then and still think that this was a very fair agreement from Paramount's standpoint and ours as well. It meant that we both would carry out the understanding we had originally made. Of course, we might have foreclosed on Paramount and taken over the whole circuit, or might have filed as claimants in a bankruptcy proceeding, in which event we might have had to settle for a small amount on the dollar. We would be taking quite a chance, as would they. I felt the agreement was wise and more prudent.

Word had come to me that certain individuals in the Paramount organization were quite anxious to acquire the Comerford circuit and felt the clever way to do it was to threaten us with bankruptcy proceedings and thus acquire the circuit for about twenty-five cents on the dollar. This was merely supposition. It came to me, however, from well-informed executives of the Paramount organization.

In conformity with our new contract, we again took over operations of the circuit in January 1933. At this time Paramount owed us. According to the new arrangement, we were to have management of the theaters until our obligation was paid in full. Fixed amounts were to be set aside and paid to us annually, and if additional earnings were made Paramount was to receive certain fixed payments that were intended as reimbursement to them of the purchase price paid to us. After we were paid in full, Paramount was to take over management and retain it until they were fully reimbursed, after which we were to be joint owners and operators.

The theaters were not in good physical condition when they were returned to us. The morale of the men was not at its best. Paramount's financial difficulties had to some extent dulled the enthusiasm and interest of its executives, and this feeling seemed to exist with many of the men down the line. The country generally was close to an all-time low. Unemployment was at its highest, and many felt that we were on the brink of disaster. It was less than six weeks after we took over that Franklin D. Roosevelt closed the banks.[14] Many of the banks in our area had closed. We did suffer some small losses; fortunately, none was serious in character. Anticipating that we might have difficulty in meeting our payrolls and taking care of our employees in the event of further bank failures, I took it upon myself to place $100,000 in cash in one of our safe-deposit boxes at the Guaranty Trust Company in New York. I did this mainly to care for our employees in case a real emergency might confront us. Fortunately, we came through the bank holiday with no great loss and survived the Depression.

5

THE ROOSEVELT BOOM

I remember well and favorably my first meeting with Franklin D. Roosevelt and the impression he made on me. It was during the presidential campaign of 1920, when Roosevelt, wartime assistant secretary of the navy under President Wilson, was vice presidential candidate on the Democratic ticket. That was when Governor Cox of Ohio was running against Harding for president.

Bruce Kremer was Democratic national committeeman for Montana and in charge of the arrangements for Roosevelt when he came to Butte, which at that time was my home. I was chairman of the local reception committee.

Roosevelt made a speech from the courthouse steps and I recall how impressed I was—I remember everybody was impressed—by this tall, vital, handsome man in the very prime of life. The picture is still clear to me. With his cap and pinchbacked suit with sloping shoulders—that was what we wore in those days—he really looked like a Hart, Schaffner and Marx model.[1]

Roosevelt's personality stood out, too. He liked people and mixed well with them. After the doings in Butte we motored down to Deer Lodge, about forty miles away. Deer Lodge is the site of the state penitentiary, and Frank Conley was still the warden. He was also a rock-ribbed Republican. Notwithstanding all this, he and Roosevelt got on splendidly together—Conley was our host at luncheon. From that time on, regardless of politics, Conley regarded himself as a personal friend and supporter of Roosevelt. In fact, when we passed through that section of the country during the 1932 campaign, Roosevelt remembered his earlier visit and was perfectly clear as to the details of his luncheon with Conley.

As just noted, Roosevelt made a good impression during that 1920 visit to Butte. Under adverse circumstances he did well. He was forced to buck a lot of hostile sentiment. The Democrats in Butte were in great part of Irish persuasion, with little enthusiasm for the League of Nations. It should be remembered that fear was widespread throughout this country that we'd be outvoted by the rest of the world. Then, too, Roosevelt made one statement that did not go over too well with the crowd and in fact did cause him some national embarrassment later. Referring to some country in South or Central America, he said, "I've got them right in my pocket." That particular remark achieved prominence as one of the real faux pas of his campaign.[2]

After the election and the Republican victory, I began to get letters from Roosevelt. He was maintaining touch with those he had met during his nationwide campaign, discussing policies, trying to keep alive some of the objectives he and Wilson had believed in. And kept vivid in my recollection, too, was Roosevelt as I had seen him in 1920—his youthful gaiety, his light-hearted gregariousness, his magnificent carriage and trim waistline—in every way he looked the ideal young American.

But my next glimpse of him was in shocking contrast to that earlier picture. It was in 1924 at the Democratic National Convention in the old Madison Square Garden in New York—the scene of the marathon battle between Smith and McAdoo, when John W. Davis was nominated as the compromise candidate only to lose to Coolidge the following November.

It was during this convention that Roosevelt made his celebrated "happy warrior" speech nominating Al Smith. I first saw Roosevelt near the platform, making his way from the New York delegation up to the rostrum to put Smith's name in nomination. I was in back of him and to me he seemed to make his way with extreme difficulty, walking with his crutches widespread. His legs seemed powerless and he was literally pulling himself along by his arms. He won everybody's sympathy.

Once up on the platform it was easier for him. He still seemed to walk with his arms but appeared to do it with less effort and bending over. It was three years then from the time he had first been stricken, and he had developed great strength in his arms and shoulders, neck and chest.

As I look back on that occasion, I remember how stunned I was. Roosevelt was still tall and impressive, but his gaunt, wasted figure supported by crutches was a shocking contrast to the smiling, vibrant American I had met in Butte a few years back.

I did not actually meet Roosevelt again until he was governor of New York State, after he had agreed to run for governor in 1928 at the suggestion of Al Smith, who was the Democratic candidate for president in that year. Smith lost his race for the presidency overwhelmingly, including his own state of New York, but Roosevelt was elected governor and thus succeeded Smith in Albany.

Roosevelt and Smith of course had been close friends over the years, and particularly so from the time Roosevelt made his happy warrior nominating speech in 1924 until Roosevelt was elected governor in 1928. But Smith had the impression that Roosevelt, while most amiable, was nevertheless the unsure and vacillating character that rumor had pictured. When Roosevelt moved into the executive mansion, Smith took an apartment in Albany and apparently expected to be consulted by the new governor on matters of patronage and policy. This to some extent is understandable, because Smith was quite bitter about his defeat for the presidency and attributed its proportions and the loss of the South entirely to the fact that he was a Roman Catholic. He had decided he would never be a candidate for president again and was undoubtedly happy to be able to go back to Albany, where he had been head man for eight years and had made a great record as governor. He may have felt that it was due him to be consulted.

Almost immediately, however, Smith was to discover that Roosevelt was neither weak nor vacillating, and that Roosevelt, and Roosevelt alone, was going to be governor of New York.

I did not realize it at the time, but later on Roosevelt indicated to me that the first breach came when Roosevelt failed to follow Smith's recommendation that Bob Moses be appointed secretary of state. Roosevelt decided he was going to appoint Edward J. Flynn of the Bronx. He had real admiration and great affection for Flynn, and they had been quite friendly for some time. The new governor was going to have some of his own people running the affairs of state for him in Albany, so he called Flynn in and immediately announced the appointment.[3]

This independent action greatly disturbed Smith. In addition, it widened an already-existing breach between Roosevelt and Moses that had existed for some years. The original cause of this disaffection arose, as I heard the story, when Moses, then Governor Smith's chairman of state parks, rather brusquely refused to put Louis Howe on the state payroll, figuring correctly, as Ray Moley has put it, that Howe's mending of Roosevelt's political fences could not be considered a parks project.[4]

As a matter of fact, when Smith recommended Moses, he asked Roosevelt to forget this earlier unpleasantness between himself and Moses. Smith believed, and in this I am in full agreement with him, that Moses was a competent public servant and would be very helpful to Roosevelt in his administration of New York State. But as Smith was fast learning, Roosevelt had a mind of his own, and he had decided he was going to have none of Bob Moses, who by the way was himself a very set fellow.

As often seems to be the case, particularly where former close friends are involved, there followed a succession of little strained incidents. Roosevelt functioned as the chief executive of the state of New York, and as various measures came up he would proceed to announce publicly his own policies and ideas without first consulting Smith.

I could not name the next most important breach. For all I know it may just have been a continuation of trifling incidents, but probably the case of Belle Moskowitz was more than a trifle.[5] She had been a close friend and adviser to Governor Smith for many years and had been active in all his campaigns. In 1928 when Smith was campaigning for the presidency she was very active. In fact I would say that she and Judge Proskauer were two of the closest and most important political advisers in Smith's entourage.[6] She was a brilliant woman, and Judge Proskauer also was a man of considerable ability. Smith wanted Roosevelt to keep Belle Moskowitz at his side and to follow her political judgment. I have no doubt he was sincere, but Roosevelt's instinct warned him—and he told me this himself—that Mrs. Moskowitz was a Smith adherent and could never become a Roosevelt follower. He felt that her loyalty to Smith was so deeply rooted she could never accept Roosevelt. And he wanted his people thinking of his cause first and not of Smith's.

A continuation of trifling occurrences rather than any important issue served to widen the breach between the new governor and his predecessor. I know that Roosevelt had great respect for Smith, and he definitely did not want to incur his hostility. Of course it must be remembered that at this time, during 1929 and 1930 and even during 1931, there was no indication that Smith might change his mind and become a candidate for the Democratic nomination in 1932.

I followed Roosevelt's career as governor with attention and interest, and when I found him advocating and supporting most of the things that the great American, Senator Thomas J. Walsh of Montana, stood for—the man who inspired and solidified my economic and political thinking in my earlier years—I became his supporter.

The governor's sensational victory in the 1930 New York State gubernatorial election was the cue for action for all Roosevelt supporters. Considering the results and what the future held, Roosevelt's success in winning reelection not only made political history in the state but also materially affected the course of the twentieth century.

It was not so much that Roosevelt won; that was more or less expected. But the margin of his plurality, an unprecedented 725,000 votes as compared to Al Smith's top plurality in 1922 of 386,000, and the fact that Roosevelt had swept upstate New York—something Smith had never even hoped for—by a plurality of 167,000 votes and forty-one of the fifty-seven upstate counties: all this signified in unmistakable terms that as a vote-getter Roosevelt could surpass Al Smith on his own ground.

Not only to me but to millions throughout the country "the name of Roosevelt was magic," and this victory definitely established Roosevelt as the leading contender for the Democratic nomination for president in 1932. I know I personally thought Roosevelt was by far the best choice of those within the realm of possibilities. His record as governor of our greatest state during his first term was outstanding, and the policies he had pursued were popular in the country at that particular time. Roosevelt was a liberal in every sense of the word, and his probable opponent, Herbert Hoover, the symbol of the Republican Party, was his direct opposite so far as policy was concerned. For Hoover was as much a conservative as any man we have ever had in public life, during the depression days from 1929 to 1932.

Hoover and the Republican Party generally appeared helpless to check the economic crisis that developed during these years. The prospects began to look so very good for a Democrat to be elected president in 1932 that Al Smith, believing that this time any Democrat could win, decided to become a candidate.

During the 1930 campaign for governor I became fairly well acquainted with Louis McHenry Howe, Roosevelt's devoted personal secretary, and Ed Flynn, and Henry Morgenthau Sr., President Wilson's ambassador to Turkey and known affectionately as "Uncle Henry."[7] It was through Eddie Dowling, Broadway actor and producer, that I first met Uncle Henry and began to take a more personal interest in Governor Roosevelt's hopes.

It was very soon after the 1930 election that Louis Howe set the wheels in motion. Quietly and unostentatiously the first steps were taken. It was really an education to observe the mental processes of Louis Howe during this early period, when the Roosevelt presidential boom began to jell. Quite obviously, the idea was no overnight improvisation. As the plans took shape I became the more convinced that Louis had hatched his scheme quite a while back. I would not go so far as to say that FDR was an archconspirator of this well-laid plan, but a search of the records discloses no violent disapproval. It was Arthur Mullen's opinion, as I recall it, that Roosevelt was already looking ahead to the White House before his first inauguration in Albany in 1929.[8] My personal belief is that when Roosevelt decided to run for governor in 1928 he also weighed in his mind the possibility of becoming president. Nor would I consider this a vainglorious speculation, since both his own Uncle Ted and before him Grover Cleveland had occupied the governor's mansion at Albany in the course of their respective journeys to the White House. It is quite possible, too, that Louis Howe was more ambitious for Roosevelt than even FDR was for himself. And as a team they proved practically unbeatable.

It was in January or early February 1931 that I realized something really definite was afoot when Uncle Henry rather casually invited me to join him for cocktails at his home on Fifth Avenue.

At Morgenthau's I found other guests: Louis Howe; Bill Woodin, head of American Car and Foundry; and Colonel House, the staunch supporter of Woodrow Wilson.[9] Morgenthau opened the session and then Louis took over. In his own circuitous and secretive fashion—Louis always had an air of mystery about him—he let us know that it had occurred to him and other Roosevelt adherents that there was a demand for FDR to run for the presidency. Louis went on to tell us how astonished he had been to discover in Franklin's mail an extraordinary number of letters demanding that FDR become a candidate. He clearly intended to convey to us that this influx of mail was in fact an avalanche. It was a matter of some concern to him as to what should be done about it. So he would like to have our considered opinion and advice so that he could then talk the matter over with Franklin and, if we in our mature judgment considered it wise, recommend to him that he permit us to formulate plans to inaugurate a campaign.

As a result of this meeting, and as a surprise to no one, Louis at our suggestion spoke to FDR and received authority to proceed. Without expressly saying so, Louis left me with the thought that he wanted each and all of us to pledge our undying fealty to the cause and with our fortunes and our sacred honor to carry out this pledge, so help us.

Soon after this we formed a finance committee with Uncle Henry as the treasurer. Uncle Henry, Colonel House, Bill Woodin, and I pledged ourselves to raise, get, or give, or in any event to have on call $10,000 apiece when needed. To all appearances FDR and Louis had decided sometime earlier that Jim Farley was to be the advance man for the big show. Ed Flynn was to be Roosevelt's chief political adviser.

A little later this group met with Roosevelt at his home in New York, and from then on until the eve of the convention in 1932 there were frequent huddles of this small group.

Early in 1931 at Louis's instance I assumed the responsibility of feeling out sentiment for FDR in the Northwest. I had had a unique and privileged relationship with Senator Walsh, and Uncle Henry invited the senator to attend a dinner for a small group of us that he was giving at his home. Senator Walsh was of course one of the outstanding figures in the Democratic Party.

I do not recall much about the dinner itself or the other guests, but I remember distinctly leaving with Senator Walsh. Morgenthau lived at 1100

Frank Walker, *right,* with, *from left,* Louis M. Howe, Governor Roosevelt, and James A. Farley. Photograph courtesy University of Notre Dame Archives.

Fifth Avenue, and we came down toward my own apartment at 1035 Fifth Avenue in a taxi. We sat in the taxi for some time and discussed the election and the candidacy of Roosevelt. Walsh made it very clear to me that he would be for Roosevelt. Sitting there I recalled to him what I had heard during the 1924 convention, that when the impasse between Smith and McAdoo had deadlocked the convention he, Walsh, had been offered the nomination and declined. Walsh informed me that the story was correct. He was chairman of the convention and he said he declined because in his opinion the situation was too delicate for any man in his position to accept the nomination. No one presiding over a convention should take advantage of such an impasse and allow his name to be offered in nomination.

Walsh continued that he didn't think the time was ripe in this country for a Catholic to be nominated or elected president. He doubted if that would come in our generation. The people, the senator thought, would have to be educated to the idea that a Catholic did not intend to have the Catholic Church take over the government of the United States. Many Protestants still had an erroneous conception of a Catholic's loyalty to his country. Many Protestants were quite intolerant and did not possess the true and correct understanding of the Catholic concept. It was going to take many years to educate them to the realization that a good Catholic could still be a good president.

With Senator Walsh's assurance of support for Roosevelt in the Northwest, I felt sure we were on solid ground. Senator Burton K. Wheeler, the junior senator from Montana, and I had known each other in Butte and tried many lawsuits against each other. Socially we were on good terms, but politically we seemed invariably to be aligned in opposition as frequently as we had been in the courtroom. But in this campaign for FDR we worked together. Wheeler was of great assistance to us in lining up delegates in the Midwest and Northwest.[10]

Bruce Kremer, who was dean in point of service on the Democratic National Committee, had a wide acquaintance throughout the country. And Bruce was of great help, too. My brother Tom, who had served several terms in the Montana state senate, contributed a great deal. Tom's hearty personality and wide range of respected and influential friends was most useful, especially in lining up the Montana delegation. And farther west than Montana we had valuable friends. Scott Bullitt, national committeeman from Washington, promised support and delivered results. In January of 1932, as a birthday present to Roosevelt, he guaranteed him the delegation from the state of Washington. Less than a week later, on February 7, under the unit rule Washington gave sixteen delegates to Roosevelt.

Since Washington was the first state to select its delegates and the game of follow-the-leader is always an important part of political psychology, the stimulus to the Roosevelt forces from this Washington triumph may well be imagined. Scott Bullitt, I am sorry to record, did not live long enough to participate in the victory he had helped to shape. He died, too young, soon after Roosevelt's election.

Early in the Roosevelt preconvention campaign I became associate treasurer, working with Uncle Henry. Treasurer of such a committee was no mere honorary assignment, not with Louis Howe in the picture. I can still hear Louis's piping voice on the phone: "Walker, we're very low on funds. Can't you and Morgenthau do something about it?" To record a prize understatement, business conditions were not very good in 1931 and 1932. Most of the "money boys" downtown were very hard hit, and those who still had money could hardly be sold on FDR.

It was amazing to me, therefore, that we did succeed in getting sufficient funds to carry on a fairly decent campaign. During the first year of the committee's existence we got approximately $78,550, the period from March 1931 to the same month in 1932. From March 1932 up until the opening of the convention in July, an additional $36,000 was contributed, including $10,000 from Joseph P. Kennedy.[11] All in all, this was really a respectable total, considering the unusually tight money market and Roosevelt's unpopularity in the business world. The real bulwark was Bill Woodin. He always came through at the right time. He told me to go ahead and not be fearful, that he would see to it personally that we would have no deficit. He was an extraordinary combination of a hardheaded executive with a flexible, alert mind more indicative of creative intelligence. In Ray Moley's language, Bill Woodin was "half businessman, half artist." Later, when he was appointed secretary of the treasury, he asked me to become his undersecretary. It pleased me to have him offer the position, but I told him I knew my own limitations and did not think I was qualified for the position. My university education had included courses in economics, banking, and currency, but I was obliged to confess that I knew very little about money. Incidentally, I am not sure there are many men who do have a real and complete understanding of money. This is my honest opinion, but in recording it I do not mean to reflect disparagingly upon our present-day bankers.

Others who, besides contributing themselves, took an active part in raising funds included Ed Flynn; James W. Gerard, who, like House and Uncle Henry, was an honored name in the Wilson tradition; Joseph Guffey; Eddie Dowling; William Julian, later appointed treasurer of the United States; and Larry Steinhardt, who later served efficiently in several of our embassies and who came to an untimely and tragic end in an air disaster just a few years ago.[12]

As for Joe Kennedy's substantial preconvention donation, Louis Howe definitely is not credited with an assist. This came about as the result of one of the most aggravating yet amusing incidents that I can recall in connection with either Louis or Joe.

I took Kennedy up to Albany on his first visit to see FDR. They had had some association, I subsequently discovered, in World War I, when Joe was active in some phase of shipbuilding. I appraised Joe as a fellow who had a few ideas of his own and did not classify him as one lacking in guile, but for very obvious reasons I was anxious to have Joe Kennedy on our team.

In lining up anyone to work with and for Roosevelt, however, there was always the inevitable problem—in this case "obstacle" might be the better word—of Louis McHenry Howe. Years later, in Hugh Johnson's second book on the New Deal, *Hell-bent for War*, when Howe was gone and Hugh himself was soon to follow, he described Louis as follows: "that strange, wise, little, gnomish, loyal, hero-worshipper, guide, philosopher and friend,—the patient, selfless architect of Mr. Roosevelt's political destiny over many years—many seemingly hopeless years—the late Louis Howe."[13]

Louis well deserved that tribute, but there were times when he could be outrageously obstinate and perverse. At best he was never exceedingly gracious in manner.

Realizing only too well Louis's unpredictability, yet realistically facing the fact that he and Kennedy would have to meet, I made the appointment. In advance I gave Louis a preliminary briefing: Joe could be helpful; the spark would be kindled and Joe would take fire if Louis would come out of his shell and for once, *just this once,* show some evidence of graciousness. Louis's reaction confirmed my deep-rooted conviction that miracles can happen. For Louis gave me his promise that he would be the very essence of cordiality. With Louis in that frame of mind, the rest was going to be easy.

So, completely at ease and warmed by the sense of a battle well won, I brought Joe in and presented him to my friend Louis. Louis had his head buried in his hands, resting on his usually cluttered and disorderly desk. With seeming effort he reached out his hand limply, sort of peeked out of the corner of an eye, and in an exhausted whisper, without rising, murmured, "How d'ya do?"

I plunged in, still afire with the miracle I thought I had achieved, told Louis who Joe was, outlined his earlier associations and career, and then, pulling out all stops, I predicted how this association of Roosevelt's two tried and trusted friends would do so much for the success of our campaign.

Somewhere along the line the miracle had evidently been cancelled. Louis froze up like the proverbial clam. We stayed on for ten or fifteen minutes, through one of the most tense sessions I have ever endured. Seconds seemed like minutes; as for the minutes—well, I began to have a faint conception of what was meant by "eternity."

My friend Howe, my very good friend Louis, despite all my wiliest strategy and efforts, would not say ten words. He managed with seemingly his last mortal effort to give Joe another limp handshake, and I have yet to find the word or phrase that could really describe how limp Louis's handshake could be.

We retired, and as we closed the door Joe not unreasonably looked at me quizzically and asked, "What kind of a so-and-so is that fellow?"

As soon as Kennedy left I went back in and told Louis off as best I could, but it was all wasted effort. He was always opposed to Joe Kennedy and raised a protest every time Joe's name came up for an appointment.

Despite Louis's ardent welcome we had our miracle, or the equivalent thereof, after all, for Joe came into the fold and did much to advance our cause financially and in other equally important ways. After this fiasco with Louis, I took Kennedy up to see Roosevelt myself. In contrast, FDR was most cooperative. He carried the ball, put on the charm as only he could do, and I think made a very good impression on our new supporter. From then on, always except for Louis, Joe was "in."

6

NOMINATION

The question was whether or not John J. Raskob and Alfred E. Smith were sincere in 1931 when they urged the Democratic National Committee to declare for repeal.[1] I firmly believe it was a sincere effort on the part of Raskob to bring Prohibition repeal to the fore. Raskob, in my judgment, was really the dominating factor in the management of the national committee at that time, much more so than Smith or Jouett Shouse.[2] Shouse worked under Raskob and took his directions from him. So did Charlie Michelson, and I'm sure Smith did, too.[3] Yes, Raskob was quite sincere in advocating Prohibition repeal. I think it almost became a mania with him. In his judgment it was one of the most important problems confronting the people at the time, and he wanted to bring it to the fore. So he felt it the wise thing to bring it up before the national committee.

Most of the men I knew, however, seemed to think it was inopportune and thought that instead of promoting harmony it would just bring a lot of disharmony to the front. All the southern senators and congressmen and the members of the national committee from the South, even though they felt in their heart that the repeal of Prohibition was a good thing, were not in a position politically to support repeal publicly. They were all very fearful about the question being raised, and some were quite furious about it. They thought all it would do would be to confuse the issue and put the Democratic congressmen and senators and national committeemen on the spot with their constituents.

The Roosevelt group also were opposed to bringing it before the national committee. I think all the wise heads were opposed to bringing it up at that time because they said it was not the prerogative of the national committee to determine the question; that was a matter of the convention. They did not even want to discuss or debate the question before the national committee. It was quite an interesting meeting, and quite tense at some times. One senator (Robinson of Arkansas) gave a very forceful talk, was very rapid, and he became very heated during his discussion.[4] He was rather hotheaded. He let loose a regular diatribe against Raskob, charged him with stupidity and with being dictatorial and trying to control the national committee by bringing up things that would damage the party greatly. In fact, he made an out-and-out talk for Prohibition and against repeal. Robinson did have quite a temper and could make a very strong and forceful talk. To show the temper he had, on one occasion he was playing golf with Senator Walsh, and he got in an argument with somebody who was going through. He struck the other man during the discussion.

Raskob was badly defeated in his motion to have repeal discussed and to declare that it was the sense of the national committee that they place a plank in the coming platform repealing Prohibition.

If this was the same committee meeting at which the nominations for the various cities were discussed and considered for the site for the coming convention, I remember quite well Bruce Kremer, who was quite eloquent, had quite a command of language, and had that old style of flamboyant oratory. Bruce, in his inimitable way, going from rock to rock and pinnacle to pinnacle, started to describe the beauties of San Francisco and the City of the Golden Gate, and he got so high up on the ethereal heights that he couldn't find a parachute to get him down. He had the devil of a time closing his speech, but finally, amid the laughter of the group, he did finally get down to earth and nominate San Francisco as the site for the convention.

The Roosevelt group was very anxious to have Chicago. Chicago had made the best offer—several cities were bidding—and the Roosevelt group supported Chicago.

At that time a good many of the southern senators and congressmen and the southern national committeemen had not made up their minds as to whom they were going to support in the convention. We all felt that Smith at that stage was not a candidate. There had been considerable discussion as to Newton Baker, Jack Garner, Ritchie of Maryland, and Roosevelt. I'd say they were the outstanding names discussed.[5]

It seemed to be quite generally agreed that Al Smith would not be a candidate. I remember having talked with Jim Farley and Ed Flynn later about this, and they indicated to me that they personally had gone to Al Smith sometime in 1931 and asked him if he was going to be a candidate. He made it very clear that he was not going to be. Now, both Farley and Flynn were admirers of Al Smith, but his statement relieved them of any obligation.

I think it was early in 1932 when Smith indicated that he might be a candidate. I remember his Jefferson Day speech in Washington when, without mentioning Roosevelt's name, he took a blast at Roosevelt. Roosevelt and Smith had been very close friends over the years, especially from 1924 until Roosevelt was elected governor in 1928.

All during the early part of the preconvention campaign much consideration was given to what Roosevelt's headquarters felt would be Smith's attitude. I know that various emissaries were sent to Smith to have talks with him. Roosevelt, I know, on a number of occasions asked Smith to come and have coffee with him. But at that time there was no indication that Smith would be a candidate himself; but there was no indication, either, that he would support Roosevelt. I think the indication was to the contrary. It was felt at headquarters—and I think there was some justification for it—that Smith was actually hostile to Roosevelt's candidacy.

News came, whether warranted or not, that Smith on many occasions had belittled Roosevelt and had indicated that Roosevelt was neither an able governor nor could be depended upon to stand fixed on any program or on any promise that he had made. Word came back, at least to Roosevelt and Howe and to many of Roosevelt's supporters, that Smith had said that Roosevelt was weak and vacillating and was not big enough timber for the presidency.

I've forgotten what time of the year it was, but it was some time before the convention that Smith started getting some of his friends out on his candidacy. These included Mrs. Moskowitz and Proskauer and more of his friends, who went to various delegates around the country. I remember at that time the then governor of Massachusetts, Ely, was a very strong supporter of Smith, and of course Raskob as well.[6]

I can't tell much about the various polls that were sent out by the Roosevelt group, such as the Strauss polls, showing Roosevelt's ability as a vote-getter. I didn't have any idea that Roosevelt had gone as far in preparation for the national campaign as he had. It was amazing to me that every plank he wanted in the platform he had given serious consideration to: he knew exactly what he wanted to say, where he wanted to say it, and when he wanted to say it. He was not thinking at all in terms of the Democratic convention; he was thinking in terms of the national election.

There never was any great doubt in my mind that Roosevelt would get the nomination; I felt that from the time he was elected governor for the second time in 1930. I felt that he was almost certain to be the nominee for the presidency. He was the only one on the horizon.

Ritchie had been pronouncedly a wet, against Prohibition, and he would get no enthusiasm from the South. Smith had been defeated in 1928, and besides, I didn't think it desirable for Smith to run again, although I had a great deal of respect for him. Baker, I thought, was a man of great ability, a great secretary of war, but I do not think he had the personal warmth, the charm; I do not think the people recognized his ability. I just did not think that Baker would be as good a candidate, as appealing a candidate, as Franklin D. Roosevelt. There was not anyone west of the Mississippi. There seemed to be just Baker and Ritchie and Smith, besides Roosevelt.

Garner, of course, was being considered by many. I got to know Garner later and got to like him very much personally, but most political-minded people regarded him as pretty much of a conservative. He came out openly for a sales tax, which I thought would not be a popular move as far as the election was concerned. It was a very unwise move politically for him to come out with that type of tax measure. But Garner had great courage and evidently thought he was right. I thought he was a pretty shrewd man, and he was an able man. But then I thought, situated as far south as he was, that would be a handicap to him in seeking the presidency.

As for his campaigning, Garner never did make speeches. I remember—I am talking about 1936 now, when he had been Roosevelt's vice president—Garner spent most of his time in Texas, and he was not at all active in the campaign. Not in the early part of the campaign, nor did he become very active afterwards. I was not active myself in campaign headquarters that year. Forbes Morgan became treasurer, and I had very little to do. My cousin had died, and my time was taken up with looking after the new details of my business—I had succeeded him—and I had had very little to do with the operation of the company, so I was busy acquainting myself with operating conditions.[7] But when they could not get Garner, I finally called him on the phone and asked him if he would not come up and talk at a dinner we were going to have at the Biltmore Hotel. We had asked people from downtown New York City; it was a dinner to raise funds.

Garner finally agreed to come, and arranged with me that I was to meet him for breakfast the morning of his arrival. I went to the Biltmore that morning and found Silliman Evans, an old friend of the vice president's, with him. Silliman left and Garner closed the door, letting Silliman out. Before he finished closing the door behind Silliman, Garner turned back to me and said, "Walker" (he always called Roosevelt "the captain," by the way), "I'm going along in this election with the captain. It's a good thing and the captain wants the election. But I'm against a third term. How do you stand on the third term, Walker?"

At that time no one was talking about the third term; there was little if any discussion at all about it. I don't remember having heard any. We were all opposed to it at that time. So I told him honestly and frankly that I agreed with him, that I was surely not for a third term.

"Well," he said, "I'm glad to hear that." Then we sat down and had breakfast and he made his speech that night.

I am not certain, but I think it was the only speech he made during the campaign. If I remember rightly, I think he went back to Texas. Garner never was much of a campaigner when it came to making speeches.

That discussion I had with Jack Garner came back to haunt me on another occasion. I went to see Garner after he had announced his candidacy in 1940 for the presidency. I don't know whether he had announced it, but it was quite evident to everybody that he was lining up with Jim Farley as a candidate. It was my custom to drop in and see the vice president whenever I went up on the Hill, and he and I, as he used to call it, would "strike a blow for liberty." On this occasion, knowing I was going up on the Hill, I thought that he might hear about it and that I'd have to see him, so I was wise and took George Allen with me.[8] This would avoid having a showdown on the very subject of the third term that I was quite sure that Jack would bring up. But wise old Garner saw right through my strategy. He said nothing about it until just when we were leaving. He let Allen go out the door first, and then he called me back. Then he said, "Walker, do you remember what you said about the captain back in 1936? I told you I was against the third term and asked you if you were against it, too? Well," he said, "I'm still against it!"

Now to get back to Chicago and the 1932 convention. With the Garner deal, Roosevelt was nominated on the fourth ballot with 945 votes out of a total cast of 1,148.5. Al Smith got 190.5 and took his defeat with poor grace. He refused to make the nomination unanimous and went right back to New York without waiting for Roosevelt's acceptance speech.

History records how Roosevelt broke all precedent the next day and for the first time, as the nominee, flew from Albany to Chicago to accept the nomination in person. I did not go with the others to the Chicago airport to greet him upon arrival. I remained at the Congress Hotel to see that everything was in order there. The governor was to come to the hotel immediately after his ovation and the delivery of his acceptance speech at the convention.

This, of course, was on Saturday, July 2, the day after Roosevelt had been nominated. After I had seen the others off for the airport I went back into the Congress Hotel, and there I witnessed a very poignant scene, which is still fresh in my memory. Al Smith was there in the lobby, a solitary figure, alone—at least for the moment—standing with four or five suitcases at his feet, evidently all set to take the train back to New York. I continued through the lobby and down the corridor to where the Roosevelt headquarters were located. But, and this is just as vivid to me as if it happened yesterday, I remember saying to myself: "Al, what a terrible mistake you're making, a mistake in every way, and, especially politically! Why, if you were out there at the airport, the first to greet Roosevelt, you'd be in the picture so completely nobody could ever get you out. Except that Roosevelt would be in the White House, it would really be your administration." That is what I thought then, and my opinion has not changed since. But history was not to be written that way, for Al Smith, his sportsmanship and sense of fair play, to say nothing of his political aptitude, deserting him for once, left Chicago without even waiting to congratulate his victorious rival.

I don't believe Smith ever even sent a wire to Roosevelt. It is true that they had some sort of a staged reconciliation later, but that was strictly for public consumption. The "Hello, you old potato" story was also synthetic. Fred Storm, I believe, was responsible for that.

In spite of this, I feel that I should record here that never at any time did I ever know Roosevelt, or Farley either, for that matter, to utter a single word against Al Smith. Which reminds me of a story about myself.

My uncle, M. E. Comerford, was a staunch supporter and a close personal friend of Al Smith. M. E. had had Smith down to Scranton more than once as his guest. So sometime during the campaign, or at least after I had become openly associated with Roosevelt, someone asked Governor Smith if he knew me. "Yes," grunted Al noncommittally, "I know him. He has a very fine uncle."

Except for Smith, it was an harmonious convention after Roosevelt was nominated. The rest of the candidates—Ritchie, James J. Reed, Baker, Harry Byrd, and the others—were all good sports about it.[9] And there was one erstwhile opponent of Roosevelt who went far beyond the "good loser" attitude and turned himself into a cringing hypocrite. I am referring specifically to Frank Hague.[10] He had been selected as the floor manager for the Smith forces, and before the convention opened he had gone on record that Roosevelt could not carry a single state east of the Mississippi River and even if nominated had "no chance of winning the November election." In addition he had made many nasty and unpardonable remarks about Roosevelt, the mildest and most printable being that "Roosevelt was crippled, both mentally and physically." When Roosevelt arrived at the Congress Hotel after delivering his acceptance speech, Mr. Hague was among the very first to call upon and pay his respects to the new nominee. He almost fell all over Roosevelt in his anxiety to make an impression. Roosevelt wasn't fooled a bit but, always the practiced politician, he greeted Hague pleasantly enough and took his fulsome compliments in stride.

Incidentally, Barney Baruch was not, by his own admission, a "Roosevelt before Chicago" man. He was a Ritchie supporter then. Ben Smith told me, however, that Baruch earlier had contributed $500, and that he contributed $1,500 at Chicago.[11]

In closing these remarks on the 1932 convention in Chicago, I think it is fitting and proper for me to record that the Shouse-Raskob-Smith faction, who were in control of the administration of the Democratic National Committee, was so uncooperative that we had to buy tickets for the members of the Roosevelt family to sit in the galleries of the convention hall.

The Democratic National Committee had authorized its committee on arrangements to hold a preliminary meeting in Chicago on April 4, 1932, to set the stage for the national convention. I was not present at this April 4 meeting, but I remember very distinctly Bob Jackson's version of what happened at that meeting, and to the best of my knowledge it stands unchallenged.[12] There had been considerable discussion as to who would be chosen as temporary chairman and who would be chosen as permanent chairman of the convention, and when the issue was taken up by the committee on arrangements, it was evident that there was considerable support behind Jouett Shouse for the temporary chairmanship or keynoter of the convention. The Roosevelt group naturally did not favor his candidacy because it had been evident for a long time that Shouse had been anti-Roosevelt, and he was suspected of working in league with Raskob and Smith, actually conducting an anti-Roosevelt campaign.

According to Jackson, after there was some discussion of the subject generally, Harry Byrd, then governor of Virginia, seeking to resolve the issue offered a compromise resolution recommending unanimously Senator Barkley as temporary chairman, and "commended" to the convention "for consideration as permanent chairman the name of Jouett Shouse, of Kansas."[13] It has always been my understanding that this arrangement was satisfactory to both factions, and Shouse said he would agree to it if it had Roosevelt's approval. Jackson and Farley then called Roosevelt in Albany, and Roosevelt promptly raised the question of the right of a subcommittee such as the committee on arrangements to dictate the selection of the permanent chairman. He felt that this was not one of their prerogatives, and he then made the suggestion that Barkley be chosen as keynoter and that Shouse be "recommended"—the committee used the word "commended"—for the post of permanent chairman.

However worded, the intent of the committee's resolution was very obvious, and Jackson himself admitted this. It was an agreement that Shouse should become permanent chairman. Jackson has always felt that he had made a definite promise to Shouse, a promise that later was not lived up to.

There were many reasons, however, for the subsequent abandonment of this agreement. And in my opinion, these reasons were justifiable.

The most important reason was the fact that at the convention Roosevelt was by far the leading individual candidate. All of the other candidates were lining up on a stop-Roosevelt basis. This accomplished, they figured they could trade, and individually, I presume, they each hoped they would be the selection when they combined upon one candidate. Under such conditions we feared that if Shouse, who was known to be anti-Roosevelt, was selected permanent chairman, Roosevelt might be subjected to so many hostile rulings detrimental to his cause that the convention might select a candidate other than Roosevelt.

The Roosevelt forces therefore rejected Shouse, but in doing so they engendered a very considerable amount of bitterness. We also furnished the anti-Roosevelt factions an additional incentive to gang up together, even if only temporarily.

When the convention formally convened on June 27, this matter was referred to the committee on permanent organization. The majority report of this committee recommended Senator Walsh of Montana as permanent chairman, and a dissenting minority report held out for Shouse. This was in accordance with a blueprint, so to speak, that had been drawn up at a meeting of the Roosevelt forces at Hyde Park held on Sunday, June 5. There were about twenty of us present at that meeting, and it was our unanimous decision that Senator Walsh would be our nominee for permanent chairman. Senator Walsh was present and agreed to have the Roosevelt forces put his name in nomination. While Walsh was known to be definitely pro-Roosevelt, we knew that he was of such stature that even his most bitter enemies would never question for a moment the impartial justice of his rulings.

On the floor of the convention Walsh was chosen by a vote of 626 to 528, and the prestige of this preliminary victory did much to enhance Roosevelt's prospects. The proceedings were going along smoothly, in accordance with our blueprint. Before the actual balloting for the permanent chairmanship we knew Shouse would get substantial support, but we never had any doubt as to the result. In the days before the convention actually got under way we had prepared an estimated poll on every important question that we thought might be put to a vote by the convention, and as I remember it on no occasion were we off more than five percent. Shouse did poll a much greater vote than we had originally anticipated, but we were so sure of our own strength that we deliberately refrained from using our Ohio votes. We felt safe with what we had, and this early in the proceedings we did not want to "tip our hand," as the saying goes, and reveal our unsuspected reserve in Ohio. It may be worth noting, to complete the record, that the Ohio delegation of 52 votes, wherein we had hidden support, voted 49.5 to 2.5 for Shouse.

At the June 5 meeting at Hyde Park to which I have referred, I had an opportunity to see a good deal of Senator Walsh. It was the first opportunity I had to talk with him since the night of Uncle Henry Morgenthau's dinner early in 1931, in the taxicab. During a recess in our meetings, immediately after lunch, he and I walked together around the grounds, and our conversation at that time is still fixed in my mind as one of the most pleasant I ever had with him. He told me of his situation in Washington. His wife had died some years before, and although his daughter lived with him, he struck me as being a very lonesome man. The senator had had money most of his life, and I think in the few preceding years he had lost most of it. He had now arrived at the time of life when he wanted to take things easy, but indicated that he found it very difficult to do so on the comparatively small income he received in the Senate. He discussed these and many other personal matters during our long walk around the grounds, but to me he did not seem to be a happy man.

At this same June 5 Hyde Park meeting it was decided to designate Jim Farley as Roosevelt's representative at the convention. Cordell Hull, senator from Tennessee at that time and a strong Roosevelt supporter, was our first choice for chairman of the committee on platform and resolutions, but Hull preferred to stand aside on this, and another senator, Gilbert Hitchcock of Nebraska, agreed to serve. Hull's reason for declining was the fact that he was an avowed dry, and he intended to defend Prohibition on the convention floor. With Senator Walsh also on the dry side and the Prohibition question itself likely to be an explosive issue, it would be wiser, so Hull thought, to balance the Roosevelt forces by naming Hitchcock, a wet in favor of repeal, as our choice for chairman of the committee on platform and resolutions.[14]

All during the week preceding the formal opening of the convention, the various candidates' organizations were setting up headquarters in the different Chicago hotels. Farley and Flynn had their official suites at the Congress Hotel, and Al Smith's headquarters were there, too.

It was during this preliminary period that I first heard Senator Huey Long in action.[15] I had met Huey once before, in his suite in the Waldorf-Astoria in New York one morning, when he was dressed characteristically in very loud green-striped pajamas. He and I had a discussion at that time as to whether or not he would support Governor Roosevelt. He said he had not made up his mind. The next time I saw him, and the first time I ever heard him speak in public, was on this occasion in Chicago, when he orated on the two-thirds resolution. It was at a get-together meeting of the Roosevelt organization on the Thursday previous to the opening of the convention, before about sixty-five leaders of the Roosevelt delegations assembled in a small room in the Congress Hotel. He put on a typical Huey Long act. When he managed to get the floor, Huey with no warning suddenly and unexpectedly offered a resolution to the effect that the supporters of Governor Roosevelt intended to abolish the two-thirds rule. He was allowed to second his own motion, and with arms waving he really went to town.[16]

I will never forget one phase of his speech, because it really sickened me. Very blatantly he boasted of having stuffed the ballot boxes in the state of Louisiana elections. He made capital of this, and bragged about it, stating that it was very helpful in carrying the elections down there. He said he always made sure that there were enough ballots to win the elections actually in the ballot boxes before the polls were officially open. All this he stated openly, in the presence of the entire group of approximately sixty-five delegates, and it didn't seem to bother Huey in the slightest. On the contrary, he seemed rather proud of his method of carrying elections.

I was very much opposed to bringing up this issue of the two-thirds rule, and so was Burt Wheeler. We felt it would furnish the opposition with a rallying cry on a most popular issue, especially in the South. And, speaking of opposition, I recall in particular the sentiments of Senator Bailey of North Carolina. He was a hotheaded personality anyway, and a very strong character. He was most outspoken in his objection to abrogating the two-thirds rule.[17]

When Huey had finished, and it must be admitted he carried the meeting with him, his resolution was adopted and I was sure we were in trouble. Burt Wheeler and I got into a huddle and agreed that I should talk to Roosevelt personally as quickly as possible. On the telephone I explained to the governor, who of course was still in Albany, that we were on the verge of a very serious mistake on this issue, that he was still the number-one target for all the opposition, and that we had worries enough without antagonizing many of our old friends. In Jim Farley's first book I believe he discusses this incident.[18] It is my recollection, too, which agrees with Jim's version, that Louis Howe did not arrive in Chicago until just after this meeting, although the two-thirds question had been previously discussed with him. In any case Roosevelt agreed with me that our forcing the issue was, to say the least, mistimed, and that it was much the lesser of two evils to retreat from this stand, retreat gracefully if we could but in any case abandon our position. I was for an immediate withdrawal, but Louie and Jim preferred to bide their time. They also talked with Roosevelt, and he expressed the opinion that it might not be advisable to disturb the current status quo. It was decided that when the furor had subsided we could quietly withdraw from our position. But Burt Wheeler supported me in preferring an immediate and frank abandonment of our untenable resolution. Otherwise we felt we could be—and we were—accused of unsportsmanlike conduct and of changing the rules of the game in the middle of the contest.

The issue was finally compromised. There would be no demand for a change of the two-thirds rule that would affect this convention. Instead, by unanimous vote the convention adopted a resolution specifically submitting the question to the 1936 convention and directing the national committee to include that question in its call for the convention. The 1936 convention abrogated the two-thirds rule.

At the last moment there was a serious hitch. Even Roosevelt's agreement to call off the fight was not sufficient, at least in the beginning. Huey Long was still feeling his oats, and he persuaded Bruce Kremer, chairman of the rules committee, to suggest a recommendation that if the first six ballots under the two-thirds rule did not produce a nominee, a simple majority would suffice on any succeeding ballot. This belated proposal gave new vigor to the charges of bad faith and trickery, but after considerable debate Bruce was persuaded to shelve the whole business.

This particular controversy was only one of several dramatic conflicts that engaged Huey Long's time during the 1932 convention. When the proceedings were formally opened he soon had another and more personal battle on his hands. It involved the seating of the Louisiana delegation.

The committee on credentials had to consider the claims of three factions from Louisiana. There was the delegation chosen by the Democratic state central committee, controlled by the Long machine, and there was an opposition group that declared that Huey had illegally selected his own delegates in a "rump convention."

Two contesting factions claiming the right to represent their state are not an uncommon feature of a national convention, whether it be Democratic or Republican, but this time there was a third protesting group. Officially and for the record it was led by a former lieutenant governor of Louisiana who claimed its authority from a state convention held in Baton Rouge. Whatever the official record might show, we all as a matter of practical fact regarded this last group as just a bunch of stooges set up by Huey himself. I think he did this with an eye to strategy, figuring that if there were three delegations he could pull off some support from the legitimate opposition. Moreover, the type of clowning act that this group put on tended to inject a note of burlesque into the seriousness of the situation, which of course Huey figured would redound to his advantage.

In whatever dialect they speak down there, sort of a French-English combination, Cajun or Creole perhaps, the leader, this lieutenant governor, really made a very humorous talk. An extract, taken from the record of the proceedings, is an example. This chap, Fernand Mouton his name was, said: "There are three contesting delegations here—there are three kinds of fishes here, the Kingfish on one side, the ex-fishes on the other, and I am the little fish."

It was all set up by Huey to draw the lightning away from his own delegation, and when it came time for the final summations Huey stopped all the clowning, addressed himself to the committee, and made a splendid defense for his own claimants. He did have a very good mind, there is no question about that, and he presented his case in a very lawyerlike fashion. He argued his case so well the committee seated his delegation. He might have lost otherwise, but his masterly presentation saved his delegation.

The Roosevelt forces also faced a battle in the Minnesota delegation. Bob Butler, later President Truman's ambassador to Cuba, was on the fence, or at least that is the impression he gave, stating he was undecided as to Roosevelt or Smith. Very vividly I recall how Bob came up to me just before the balloting and shook hands with me, volunteering the statement that he would vote for Roosevelt but favored Smith. He was a nephew of Pierce Butler, Mr. Justice Butler of the United States Supreme Court.

There was another episode of fence-straddling that gave me a great deal of enjoyment at the time. For some time back in New York we had been trying to line up Colonel Joseph Hartfield, a rather small but politically active chap who in certain quarters had a bit of influence. I talked to him personally and he finally assured me that he was "all for Roosevelt." Hartfield, incidentally, was an alternate delegate from New York. My brother Tom, who was a delegate from Montana, was a graduate of the University of Virginia law school, and he and Hartfield had known each other there. When they met at the convention in Chicago and the inevitable and meaningless remarks about "the good old days" were behind them, Hartfield immediately began to high-pressure Tom with a great sales talk on behalf of Smith. While Tom was quietly explaining to the colonel that he was a Roosevelt supporter, I happened along.

Tom casually introduced me to Hartfield as "my brother, Frank. Maybe you've met him. He's living in New York now and very close to Roosevelt."

Hartfield's crimson face would have made a Turner sunset seem pale by comparison. He knew us, all right, knew also that I had heard part of his sales talk for Smith, and realized all too clearly that his previous promises of support for Roosevelt were very vivid in my mind at that moment. All this, I say, he knew too well. What he had not known was that Tom Walker had a brother named Frank who had come east about eight years previous. That particular boom for Smith came to a most abrupt standstill.

While on the subject of individual delegates and the embarrassments that can result from their efforts to make their presence felt, I am reminded of another story.

As is well known, Roosevelt had an almost infallible and sometimes disconcertingly retentive memory. Among the delegates from the District of Columbia at the 1932 convention was an attorney named Arthur O'Brien, who later on married one of the Roebling daughters. In agreement with the unit rule, the District delegation voted solidly for Roosevelt. O'Brien, however, was a Smith man and something of an obstructionist besides. He was continually rising to his feet to make one objection after another. And just as in the 1924 convention the "Alabama casts 24 votes for Oscar W. Underwood" became a monotonous but very famous statement, the 1932 convention and radio audience became very well acquainted with the distinctive and increasingly familiar voice of Arthur O'Brien saying: "Mis-ss-s-ter chairman!"[19] And in disciplined but weary tones from the chair the reply: "For what purpose does the delegate from the District of Columbia arise?" And then O'Brien would continually launch into an irrelevancy.

Smith man or no, once the administration was in power in Washington, O'Brien qualified as a "deserving Democrat," and at various times his name was suggested to the president for some appointment. Roosevelt had unique gifts as a mimic, and each time O'Brien's name would come up for something Roosevelt would put his head back and intone "Mis-ss-s-ter chairman!"

O'Brien received no appointment while Roosevelt was president.

Another very, very vivid recollection I have of that convention—a problem that is still something of a nightmare on television twenty years later—concerns the number and volume of seconding speeches.[20] The proceedings were all broadcast, of course, which to the politicians apparently meant only one thing—a countrywide audience and an opportunity to reach the home folks.

Having had that experience I quite agree with what Jim Farley said in one of his books. A politician will give you his party loyalty and his life's blood and perhaps even his wife, but never, never will he relinquish his assigned radio time.

It was essential for our chances that we make a strong showing right at the start and if possible put Roosevelt over on the second or third ballot. Hence speed was of the essence, or if not speed at least uninterrupted and smooth-rolling action. But the course of events plus some of our best friends' reluctance to abandon their cherished radio time thwarted us temporarily and could well have upset us permanently.

The nominations for president began on Thursday afternoon, June 30. John Mack had been personally selected by Governor Roosevelt to place his name in nomination, and he made a succinct and good job of it. In addition to Roosevelt, eight other candidates for president had their names placed in nomination.

Imagine what happened to our time schedule and desire for speed then when Roosevelt alone had at least nineteen delegates seconding him.

The story of that long Thursday night and how Roosevelt was nominated on the fourth ballot the following evening has been told so often there is no need of my recording it. The break came of course when Garner switched, concerning which there are many versions. Curley and Arthur Mullen and Hearst have all either claimed or been given credit for the switch.[21] To the best of my knowledge, however, Sam Rayburn and Silliman Evans were the men who were really responsible, although the services of Pat Harrison, who held his Mississippi delegation together, should not be overlooked.[22] It is probably true that others may have had the same idea and were working on the business of persuading Garner to switch from some other direction at the same time we were, but Rayburn and Evans really engineered the deal.

Garner had a big conservative following, and he held the trump card, so to speak. Yet he, like McAdoo, saw that only the two-thirds rule could stop Roosevelt, and nobody really wanted another 1924.

On that Friday night, July 1, therefore, after Alabama, Arizona, and Arkansas had voted for Roosevelt, upon the call for California's vote Bill McAdoo asked unanimous consent to address the convention. The rest is now history. I think McAdoo was sincere when he said he did not want a repetition of Madison Square Garden in 1924, but he was not averse to giving Smith the coup de grace either.[23]

Cermak came along right afterwards to switch Illinois, but he had missed the driver's seat and could only be the first to jump on the bandwagon.[24] Garner and McAdoo had beaten him to it.

When, through Rayburn and Evans, Garner agreed to release his delegates, it was decided that it would be better to let California make the announcement, which gave McAdoo his great opportunity. And, as I have previously suggested, he did not find the assignment unpalatable.

One indirect result of this maneuver, which proved to be of great importance during Roosevelt's terms in office, was the disappointment it inflicted upon Burt Wheeler. He wanted the vice presidential nomination desperately. He had never quite recovered from the sting of his defeat when he was the vice presidential candidate with the elder La Follette on the Progressive ticket in 1924.[25] In my opinion, his being passed over in 1932 was what originally soured Wheeler on Roosevelt. He never was wholeheartedly for him after that, and he displayed his genuine animosity five years later in 1937 during the Supreme Court fight.[26] It seems that this vice presidential bug is not easily dislodged from the system. Even in 1940 when Roosevelt was up for the third term and Garner was not a candidate, Wheeler tried to come in again, through Mose

Cohen of California. He would have made peace with Roosevelt in a minute if he could have secured the vice presidential nomination.

In connection with the Garner switch, I have made reference to Hearst and Arthur Mullen. When Hearst died a few years ago, a good many newspapers, including his own, in paying tribute to him gave him the credit for engineering the Garner switch. The fact is he did not, but to give him his due I do not think that Hearst himself ever made that claim.

In 1940 Arthur Mullen published a book entitled *Western Democrat* in which he relates how Roosevelt selected him as floor leader in 1932, a story that I thoroughly enjoyed. Although there was considerable difference of opinion on the subject, Mullen had absolutely no doubt whatever about his own abilities in any way, on any subject, at any time.

Arthur wasn't exactly a shining success as a floor leader. He had difficulty making up his mind, was not crystal clear in getting his points across, and seemed confused a good part of the time. Senator Walsh as chairman was caused a great deal of difficulty because Arthur was not on the alert at the proper time to present the appropriate motions. Arthur was rather hotheaded, and occasionally at the psychological moment, when he should have been on his toes with his eye on the chairman, alert for his cues, Arthur would be off in some corner or involved in some controversy of relative unimportance.

Nevertheless, I had a real affection for Arthur Mullen. I thought he was a fine old fellow. Throughout his life, as I knew him, his outstanding characteristic seemed to me to be his faculty for more or less bulling his way through the issues and the problems of life.

Arthur had been active at Democratic National Conventions back through many years, and at that time he pulled considerable weight in Nebraska, and we needed support in the Middle West. In many respects Arthur was a pretty alert fellow politically. In previous years he had been opposed to Bryanism, and probably still was, but in a more subdued tone in 1932 because Charlie Bryan still had some strength after having been nominated for vice president in 1924.[27] Arthur advised Farley to keep on good terms with Bryan and not to incur his hostility. As a matter of fact, however, I personally did not feel that Bryan had much force. He certainly did not appear to me to be as strong a character as Arthur.

There was one personal encounter I had with Arthur later on that I have never forgotten, and that gives me a laugh every time I think of him because it seems to me to typify his many gruff, bulldoggish characteristics perfectly. Arthur was very anxious to become attorney general. Soon after the convention, and still very early in the campaign, he came into my office, closed the door, and sat down. Then, in his characteristic whisper that could be heard all over the place he asked me how I stood on a candidate for appointment to the office of attorney general. He said he would like to have my support.

I explained to Arthur that already I was in a very embarrassing position about this, even before he had come into my office. I told him there were three men from my own state who had their eyes fixed on the same post Arthur coveted. And one of these three I knew was being considered very seriously for the appointment and in my opinion had the inside track. That individual was of course Senator Walsh. But Bruce Kremer wanted the job and so did Burt Wheeler. So I endeavored to explain to Arthur that even without his entry I was in a most embarrassing position, indicating that it would be very difficult for me to back anybody for the appointment when three of my close personal friends were candidates.

Arthur left my room in high dudgeon, and I could hear him going down the hall talking to some fellow in that stentorian whisper of his. "Well," said Arthur, "I just talked to Walker and he won't go for me for attorney general. He wants Tom Walsh to have it so he can be United States senator."

Arthur's companion, and I have forgotten who it was, hesitated, and then said, "Why, Walker couldn't be senator from Montana. He's a resident of New York now." In addition to being a resident, I had also been an accredited delegate from New York State to the Democratic convention!

"Well," said Arthur, not yielding an inch, "then he wants it for his brother."

Arthur was magnanimous and forgave me personally afterwards. He was not a fellow to hold a grudge, being at heart a very kindly person, but I always felt that he nursed a grievance against the Roosevelt crowd generally after that because he felt that the Democratic victory had brought him nothing. He was not offered any worthwhile position, only something of minor importance that I cannot even recall now.

Arthur opened a law office in Washington and materially at least was probably reaping some reward, when quite unexpectedly a new development undoubtedly intensified his resentment. In December 1933 the president issued an edict stating that members of the Democratic National Committee then practicing law in Washington should either resign from the national committee or close their offices. Arthur resigned, but none too happily.

The first trip I ever took with Roosevelt was the trip to St. Paul, when he outlined for me in great detail, months before he was even nominated, his plans for the campaign, and the nature and location of the speeches he would make. In only two instances did he change the schedule he had originally planned, and every major project of his first recovery program, except the NRA, was touched upon in his campaign speeches.[28] The two changes in his original plans were minor indeed and consisted simply of switching the Salt

Lake City speech, where he originally planned to speak on power but actually did speak on a program for relief of the railroads. He delivered the power speech a few days later in Portland.

An addition but not a change in his plans was the Pittsburgh speech, where he spoke on economy. Roosevelt personally never wanted to make that speech and in fact never planned to make it. He yielded only after considerable pressure was brought to bear by Louis Howe, Barney Baruch, and some others, and he lived deeply to regret it. This of course was the famous "economy speech" wherein he announced he was going to cut government expenses twenty-five percent.

I remember vividly that during the 1936 campaign—and Rosenman has an amusing account of this in his book—he asked Sam if he could not get up some sort of a speech that would explain away his Pittsburgh address.[29] He felt he had to give some answer because the opposition was picking on him for having gone so definitely on record on the subject of economy in 1932 and not following through.

About two weeks after he had first asked Sam, the president wanted to know if he had thought up an answer. Sam said: "Yes, I think I have. I think I've got the answer. You should deny that you ever made that speech. That's the only answer you can give that will satisfy the public." The speech, incidentally, was made before one of the largest crowds of the campaign, about fifty or sixty thousand people.

Roosevelt made many other less important speeches during the 1932 campaign, one of which was in Baltimore, which we feared would, and which did, cause some repercussions. The *New York Times* referred to it as his most belligerent speech of the campaign, principally because he took a blast at the Supreme Court. The *New York Times* quoted Roosevelt as follows: "After March 4, 1929, the Republican party was in complete control of all branches of the government—*the legislature, with the Senate and Congress, and the executive department and, I may add, for full measure, to make it complete, the Supreme Court as well.*" The italicized part of this quotation from Roosevelt, to make matters worse in emphasizing its significance, was pure ad-lib, and the conservative Republicans promptly raised a justified outcry. We were very much concerned about it, but the *New York Times* dismissed the matter in an editorial two days later, as follows: "All he [FDR] probably intended to indicate was that a majority of the judges in that tribunal are, as they long have been, Republican in politics. . . . It was a needless and foolish remark by the governor." And, in effect, the editorial went on to say, "So what?"

In a final word on Roosevelt's campaign talks in 1932, I want to repeat that it is still amazing to me to look back and realize how far in advance and how well he laid out his plans for his campaign, election, and his administration's

With Raymond Moley, Henry Morgenthau Jr., and the candidate, 1932. Photograph courtesy University of Notre Dame Archives.

policy and program. These were the things that were on his mind at a time when many, many people gave him very little chance for the nomination, and many more were calling him vacillating and saying he did not have a plan, that he did not know what to do.

One incident of the 1932 campaign I would like to forget because it depicts me either as the goat or the villain, depending upon the way one looks at it. This also had its beginning on the St. Paul trip, when I became quite well acquainted with several of the newspaper reporters.

It seems that I had had an opportunity, on that occasion, to tell them in some detail about the wonders and charm of my old hometown of Butte, boasting perhaps a little about what a palatial spot it is, and modestly admitting that it is the tops in scenic beauty.

In any case, Jim Farley and I joined Roosevelt at Salt Lake City on his campaign trip west that fall, and naturally, because Roosevelt was the leading presidential prospect, a large group of star reporters, some of whom had been with us on the earlier trip to St. Paul, were aboard his train. Key Pittman and Senator Walsh were there, also Al Frank and some of my personal friends, and Roosevelt spoke at the Mormon Tabernacle in Salt Lake City.[30] Among the reporters present were Walter Brown, Jim Kieran, Ernest Lindley, and Louis Rupple, and the next stop on the itinerary was to be my hometown of Butte.

It was the morning of September 19, 1932, and I will never forget the curious expressions on the faces of some of my reporter friends as that train pulled into town. Roosevelt made his talk from the courthouse steps on West Granite Street, and as we made our way there and the meeting got underway I soon noticed my reporter friends, or at least the fellows I thought were my friends, whispering and looking at me, and holding their respective noses very significantly.

It did not take me very long to get the drift, because with a very guilty feeling I remembered my extravagant and magnificent description of Butte on that St. Paul trip. And Butte in all its history never looked worse than it did that September morning of the third Depression year. The mines were all but completely shut down, the stores were doing no business, and the town was thoroughly in the doldrums.

The reporters in the days to come did not allow me to forget all this in a hurry, and as may well be imagined I was very much on the defense.

Butte always offers something nice to look back upon, however, and Depression or no she could still manage to have a parade, even on this occasion. My wife, Hallie, and my two children were visiting in Butte at the time, and when Jim Farley, who was in the parade, spied my daughter, Laura Hallie, watching from the family porch, he called to her, took her in his lap, and she rode in style in the rest of the Roosevelt parade.

And my young son, Tom, did not allow his little shadow of a sister entirely to monopolize the spotlight that day. In the usual reception line to meet the governor, Tom went through, shook hands, and then went back to the end of the line and repeated the performance. This time the governor looked down at him very attentively and inquiringly and said: "Don't I know you, young man? Haven't you been through here before?"

7

THE EXECUTIVE COUNCIL

I n the early part of July 1933, Marvin McIntyre called me on the phone and asked me to come to Washington to meet with the president.[1] He said that the president wanted me to handle a matter of some importance for him that would require three or four weeks of my time. The president was then in Maine waters and was to return to the capital the following day. Mindful of the generally accepted rule that a request from the chief executive is a command, I left for Washington the next day. Despite the fact that I had told the president and Louis Howe very definitely that I had neither desire nor ambition to hold public office, I must confess that I was intrigued and somewhat flattered to learn that FDR wished to entrust me with an important mission. In my innocence I believed Mac when he said that a very few weeks of my time would be required.

I arrived in Washington and was invited to dine at the White House that evening. I really became "the man who came to dinner." On and off I stayed in Washington for more than half of the Roosevelt regime.

We had a cocktail in the Oval Room before dinner.[2] Roosevelt was his usual charming self. He indulged in pleasantries, told some interesting anecdotes, and we reminisced a bit. After dinner we got down to the business at hand. The president went into detail concerning his plans. Some fifteen measures, as part of his recovery program, had been passed by the Congress. This meant the creation of fifteen new governmental agencies, all of them with different functions. Some were designed immediately to relieve existing conditions and others in a more or less trial-and-error fashion to bring about a permanent and a somewhat altered and improved economy.

Many of us can still remember that at this period the banking situation was far from cleared, the agricultural problem was most serious, and home mortgages were being foreclosed by the thousands. Insurance companies were in a confused state; mortgage concerns and building and loan associations were becoming bankrupt. The heavy industries, particularly the construction branch, were at an all-time low. Big as well as small business was crying out to Washington for aid. Most serious of all, unemployment was reaching a tragic and dangerous state. The exact statistics are not known, but it is a safe venture to put the number of unemployed during the summer of 1933 at somewhere between thirteen and fifteen million. These are the stark figures, estimated by impersonal calculations and formulas of economists. What it meant in lost homes, broken families, and frustrated dreams no one will ever know.

It was obvious that such a condition of affairs necessitated drastic and immediate action. Hence the hurried creation of these new agencies and bureaus to combat the conditions confronting us and to bring relief to the nation. If not the most serious it was, perhaps, the most confusing period in the existence of our government.

It was the president's thought to create a sort of cabinet that would comprise the heads of all the new agencies as well as those of the regular departments of government that were directly involved in the new emergency legislation. It was his desire to start these new agencies off in orderly fashion, to set out and define their functions clearly so that they would fit into the regular pattern and not infringe upon or conflict with one another or with any of the regular, old-line government departments. He planned to meet with this group of departmental and agency heads at stated periods, to have them report on their efforts and keep him informed as to their accomplishments.

On that July night in 1933 the president and I sat together in the Oval Room and collaborated upon the draft of an order creating what was to be styled the Executive Council—a sort of emergency cabinet. Incidentally, this same draft, with FDR's handwritten revisions and corrections as well as his signature and date, hangs as a framed and treasured memento in my library.

So on July 11, 1933, by executive order "to provide for the orderly presentation of business and to coordinate interagency problems of organization and work on the new governmental agencies," the president appointed a temporary Executive Council.

As originally constituted, the Executive Council consisted of twenty-one members, with the power to appoint additional members being vested in the president. The executive order also provided that in the absence of the president, "the senior cabinet member present shall preside."

The president selected me to serve as the executive secretary. At first he had suggested that I serve as director. Mindful of the fact that some members of this new organization were cabinet members, and having realization of the temperaments of the heads of departments, I prevailed upon the president to permit me to assume the title of executive secretary.

Right from the start I knew it would not be easy to direct this group. I knew also FDR's weakness for dealing with men directly and personally. Over the many years I knew Roosevelt, he was never what I would style "organization-minded." Organizational charts, jurisdictional functions, protocol, and such things always meant little to him.

The heads of about ten newly created agencies together with the ten cabinet members (and one or two others) made up the Executive Council. I was not only to guide this group, serve as sort of mentor, keep them in alignment, and fit them into the planned pattern, but also I was to serve as the coordinator.

Now the word "coordinator" has broad significance and can be made to cover a multitude of sins. I remember quite well that I had just begun to function in my new position when Frank Kent of the *Baltimore Sun* (although he was a Democrat, Kent managed without great effort to suppress any enthusiasm he may have felt for the Roosevelt administration) wrote that I reminded him of the preacher who was trying "to coordinate the incoordinatable and unscrew the inscrutable." Many times during those years I came to feel that his were words of wisdom.

I set up our first office in a small suite in the Treasury Building and began selecting personnel to start on my new venture. Bill Cronin, then my secretary, was the first man I selected. He came to serve as a jack-of-all-trades. He was a tactful, prudent, and wise person with a very pleasing personality. Bill saved me many headaches and arduous tasks over the years, and I shall always appreciate his sense of fidelity. Bill had the happy faculty of saying no more pleasantly than many men say yes. He also had a sense for spotting the type who had an axe to grind and saved me from many an ardent enthusiast who insisted on giving me all the answers to the then current difficulties. About this time also I called in a close personal friend, Colvin Brown. Colvin was in my judgment a fine analyst, a good organizer, and a clear thinker. He had the Yankee type of mind both hardened and sharpened a bit by his early career as a journalist in Illinois. That combination in my opinion makes for a rare and shrewd and practical individual.

I brought in a few others in the early days of the council. Then I began a study of the recent legislation passed and an analysis of the functions of the newly created agencies. I learned quite soon that no organization charts had been set up and that no clear understanding existed as to the functions of any agency or the duties of its personnel.

It was a surprise and a shock to me to learn that none of the permanent departments of the government had changed or modified their organizational charts for years. In fact, with one exception, I found no evidence that any such charts had ever existed or that any provision had ever been made for a systematic compilation of functions or duties of all government departments, whether old-line or emergency. The single exception was, if memory serves me right, the Navy Department, where under the direction of the assistant secretary of the navy during World War I charts had been prepared.[3] These charts defined the duties and functions of all navy personnel from the secretary on down to the newly enlisted apprentice seaman.

I drew up an executive order for the president's signature requiring each regular and emergency department to prepare the necessary functional charts and entrusted to Arthur Mullen the task of seeing that the provisions of the president's order were duly carried out. I am quite certain that this was the first time a real effort was made to chart the activities of our vast government. In fact, we drew up our charts in looseleaf form so that changes could be easily made as new agencies came into being and existing departments kept expanding.

The tempo accelerated. Government activities increased. Almost overnight, or so it seemed, jurisdiction of functions would be transferred from one division or one department to another, new headquarters opened, old ones either moved or disappeared. It seemed to the average man coming to Washington that sheer confusion met him on all sides. To remedy this we established an information bureau. It was the first of its kind ever established in our government. It served its purpose well and was of much assistance and provided splendid service to the general public, especially those having business with various governmental departments. Through the facilities of this information service it was possible to obtain immediately the name and location of the individual in charge of any particular problem, and if desired, appointments could be made for those desiring conferences. This eliminated much confusion and lost time and motion, both for those doing business with the government and for the officials themselves. Later, this phase of the information service was extended, where practicable, to the activities of branch and regional offices in the field.

A system of individual reports was set up so that at weekly or biweekly intervals the president and members of the Executive Council received information as to the workings of each governmental department. Thus we were kept in touch with the progress—or lack of it—being made and were immediately apprised of any possibility of clashes or overlapping.

At this time I set out to select an economic adviser and statistician to the council whose duty it would be to analyze these reports as they were filed and then make such recommendations to the Executive Council as his judgment dictated. I felt, also, that it was essential that the council should have the services of an experienced economist who could observe current business trends and at all times keep the members of the council informed as to business conditions in the country.

In selecting the right man for this exacting post I sought the advice of the outstanding economists and statisticians in the country. After an exhaustive survey of the field it became quite evident to me that Winfield W. Riefler was the man I had been seeking. At that time in his middle thirties, Win had graduated from Amherst, been a foreign trade officer in South America for the Department of Commerce, and since 1923 had been rendering increasingly valuable service as a statistician with the Federal Reserve Board in Washington. His analytical reports served us in good stead. He expressed his views with clarity, pointed out the many weaknesses in our economy, and predicted the trends with real vision. The fact that he served as chairman of the Central Statistical Board afforded him the opportunity to obtain at firsthand the views of a very important group. This board had a staff of thirty. As soon as each governmental agency, pursuant to executive order, submitted its weekly report to the board, the economists there broke down and coordinated the findings. From these findings, Riefler in his capacity as interpreting economist to the Executive Council prepared his official report, which was first sent to me and then formally presented and made part of the records at the meetings of the Executive Council.

Our overall survey had revealed the startling and unmistakable fact that nowhere in the governmental structure was there a branch or an agency that served as an informed administrative control facility for the president. In my opinion the Bureau of the Budget was the logical agency to take over this assignment. But our more detailed study of the bureau revealed the fact that thus far it had exercised but little of the authority granted it by Congress when it was established in June 1921. In the twelve years of its existence the Bureau of the Budget had concerned itself mainly with the mechanics of preparing the formal budget. Little if any attention had been given by the bureau to the merits of any requests for appropriations that were submitted to the Congress for approval. Less thought had been devoted to the structural setup of the government. As a matter of fact, the Bureau of the Budget knew very little about the organization and functioning of the regular old-line departments, to say nothing of the mushrooming emergency agencies and their proposed programs with their continual shifting in emphasis and direction.[4]

So from 1933 on, the Bureau of the Budget developed and expanded to the point where it is one of the most important departments of the government. President Roosevelt and President Truman in turn leaned upon the bureau for advice, assistance, and information, and the budget's reviews of departmental requests for appropriations have been most helpful to department heads and to Congress.

The meetings of the Executive Council were held weekly, Tuesday being the appointed day, and the place the Cabinet Room of the executive offices in the White House. I prepared the agenda based upon the reports filed in the council office prior to the meetings—twenty-four hours previous to the meeting being the deadline—by the individual agencies concerned. We made a digest of these reports; this was discussed and brought to the attention of all members at the meetings of the council so that any existing conflicts or overlapping could be ironed out.

The president was in the chair at all sessions. If he were unable to attend, the senior cabinet officer present presided. I sat at his right and, having prepared the agenda, in effect directed the course of the meetings. As has already been stated, the report on current business trends and a forecast of future developments by the economic adviser, Win Riefler, was one of the most important items. The president, finally, would outline in general fashion the status of government affairs and report the progress or lack of progress that in his judgment was being made.

When one considers that the Executive Council was, by the original executive order creating it, empowered "to provide for the orderly presentation of business" and also "to coordinate . . . work on the new governmental agencies," the far-reaching and diverse items that appeared on the agenda should occasion no great surprise. All matters of top policy in emergency agencies were to be weighed and considered here with a view of determining their effect on the separate agencies involved. An examination of the minutes reveals that at one time or another the Executive Council had before it the question of investigating drought-stricken areas, whether government contracts entered into before the provisions of the National Industrial Recovery Act went into effect should be adjusted accordingly, proposals to provide work for city youths in rural areas, the financing and the general policy of the consumers division under the "blue eagle," the effect of the gold policy, and so on through a seemingly endless list.[5]

Although these and others—many, many others—were brought up for discussion, it is safe to say that most of the functions of the council could be classed in the coordination category. First, last, and always, it had to be a question of making the gears mesh, of making the wheels go round.

I can make another fair comment at this point. Many serious controversies had their beginnings at the council table, but very few of these came to the fore in open discussion. The heads of the agencies who constituted the Executive Council were in the main smart and alert fellows. Instead of voicing their dissents openly at the council table, they were eloquently silent. Once away from the formality of a council meeting they would lose no time in taking their individual problem up with me personally. When my ruling failed to conform completely with their views, invariably they sought out the president in private conference.

It is generally admitted that Roosevelt was never a strictly organization executive or administrator. For one thing, he wanted to know firsthand what was going on. He liked to break through the top-line executives in departments and get down into the lower echelons. I think there was some wisdom in this, but his problems were too many and varied, the details too numerous, to do this successfully. Such procedure created considerable animus and friction with department heads and resulted in much confusion. Fortunately for me, I sensed this characteristic early in my association with FDR. I can't say I completely agreed with his policy, but after all, he was boss. I was merely an aide who wanted to be helpful, so I accepted it all in stride and did the best I could under the circumstances.

The president had another unorthodox habit in this respect. He would assign matters to as many as two or three men in one agency and have them report directly to him and not to the head of their bureau. It gave him firsthand knowledge and insight into what was going on down the line but tended to create no end of confusion and some very bitter battles.

Of necessity my work brought me in very close touch with the president. I recall going over his list of appointments and finding that many times on the same day he would confer separately with Secretary Cordell Hull, Undersecretary Sumner Welles, and Counselor R. Walton Moore, all in the State Department. Later it would come to my attention that none of the three knew what matters the other two had up for consideration. This was also true as regards agriculture, with Henry A. Wallace, Rexford G. Tugwell, and George N. Peek each telling the "father confessor" his own particular tale. It also applied to the Forest Service, WPA, War, Navy, and Labor Departments. It did not apply to Interior or PWA, both under Harold Ickes.[6] Heads would have fallen in any department run by Ickes if matters were ever taken up with the president by any subordinate.

The Boss many times tried to get into the lower levels of the RFC, but with no great measure of success. Jesse Jones was smart, too. He had many and devious ways of blocking interference with his branch of the government. As a consequence, little or no information about or from the RFC came to

FDR that didn't reach him directly from Jesse. The latter made his own personal appointments, most of them—at least a high percentage of them—from big business. To each and all he gave definite instructions that, to use Frank Hague's famous expression in Jersey City, "I am the law here."

As 1933 wore on I came to have high regard for the shrewdness and keenness of mind and the trading ability of my old friend Jesse. He was made of tough fiber and got his own way in the majority of conflicts in which he was involved in Washington. One incident comes particularly to mind. In the early stages of our work we cooperated with the treasury and the RFC in a plan to unfreeze the deposits in closed banks. The bank holiday had closed a large majority of the nineteen thousand banks in the country, and among the first acts of the incoming administration was to get the sound banks open again. The plan was for the RFC to lend fifty percent of the total assets in all of these banks and thus bail out one-half of the deposits without going into the difficult and unsatisfactory job of evaluating the assets. We all realized the RFC would suffer some loss, but the loss would be negligible in comparison with the good to be accomplished in saving the banks and releasing this huge block of purchasing power. After all, we were in a real depression, and heroic measures were required. Jesse, always cool and calculating, was not to be hurried. He insisted on negotiating with each bank for an appraisal of its assets by his representative. As a consequence the release was delayed for months, but a superb job was done and the objective attained.

Over the years this independence irritated FDR no end and finally resulted in the famous 1945 letter telling Jesse that Wallace would take over. I always did feel that Jesse had little in common with FDR, that he was never really in favor of the president's policies. Roosevelt would have eliminated him much sooner save for Jesse's association with Jack Garner and Texas politicos generally. FDR, however, always believed in working along the lines of least resistance, biding his time, and later getting his own results. The president had Jesse properly appraised and rated. He knew that Jesse had some but not great strength in Texas politics. As a matter of fact, the real leaders in Texas had no great regard for Jesse personally, no respect at all for his political strength, despite his immense holdings as well as his two newspapers. Roosevelt also knew that he was a symbol of big business, and he did not wish to sever the cord that would leave the New Deal with no tangible evidence of association with business. It should not be forgotten that in the days before World War II, any man from business and industry who took office in the Roosevelt administration was as a rule charged with treason by his former associates.[7]

Then there was Dan Roper, secretary of commerce, who attended the sessions of the Executive Council with regularity. I can still hear Dan, when his opinion was asked about some new policy or idea, responding with the same hackneyed reply: "Mr. President, I have just appointed a committee to study and report on the matter. I am sure they will go into it thoroughly and bring us a very intelligent report."

Dan had formed a commerce advisory committee consisting of some of the outstanding businessmen of the country and would expound to them on the many problems confronting the administration and request advice as to their solution. In all seriousness Secretary Roper would then tell his committee, few of whom had any sympathy for Roosevelt, that "their recommendations would receive most serious consideration."

On one occasion prior to a regular meeting of the Executive Council, Dan called upon me with a proposal from one of his foremost business executives. The secretary said that it was a splendid proposal made by an outstanding industrialist and was the answer to all of the executive committee problems. The suggestion was that the president appoint a businessman to head up all emergency agencies, some sixty or seventy in number. This executive would have the same powers as are assigned in a corporate structure to a company president. Such a man, he said, should be a person of character, business experience, good judgment, tact, force, and should be an expert in finance. I reported Dan's recommendation in strict confidence to the president. After I had outlined in precise detail the type of man for whom Hugh Johnson, Peek, Lewis Douglas, Ickes, Marriner Eccles, and the others all were to work, the Boss, as so often was his custom, said, "Frank whom would you suggest? Whom would you suggest for this position?"[8]

I replied, "The Lord! Although I don't know how He would do on financial matters."

The president laughed most heartily and said, "I'm going to make that proposal at the meeting."

I begged him not to, but his mischievous spirit compelled him to tell the council, much to my embarrassment and also Dan Roper's. I don't think Dan ever forgave me for this remark of mine to the president, made quite innocently and in fun.

By the fall of 1933, in the course of reviewing and analyzing the operations of the various governmental departments and examining the weekly reports filed with the Executive Council, it soon became apparent that there was a vast amount of confusion in the field activities of the numerous agencies. This confusion increased from day to day. Complaints of conflicts, overlapping, and confusion were coming to our attention. It became evident that steps would have to be taken to coordinate the field activities. Thus was the National Emergency Council created by Executive Order 6433-A on November 17, 1933, to make "more efficient and productive the work of the numerous field agencies of the government" established under the federal relief acts. In each state an outstanding man was appointed as state director. It became his duty to keep himself informed as to the operations of government in his field and to report each week to Washington. The field problems were handled by representatives in much the same fashion.[9]

It was our intention to organize the National Emergency Council, get it started functioning in orderly fashion, then combine it later with the Executive Council. Thus it later came to pass that the two councils were merged and the title of National Emergency Council was retained. The first meeting of the National Emergency Council was held on December 19, 1933. I held the title of executive director.

Just the day previous, December 18, by Executive Order 6513, the president transferred all of the functions of the special Industrial Recovery Board. This same order also made all members of the recovery board members of the National Emergency Council and bestowed on the emergency council the powers previously given the Industrial Recovery Board.

Looking back over the years, I will not say that I believe Frank Kent to be absolutely correct in his comparison of me with the preacher. But I will concur in his view that there was much confusion in the speedily organized emergency agencies, that their separate functions were not too clearly defined, and the various means to attain our goal were confusing and sometimes really clouded. In most instances the agencies were headed by men of varying and very decided views. Some of them had qualities of genius. All of them were pretty strong characters. It required a man of some parts to get individuals of the types of Ickes, Johnson, Harry L. Hopkins, General Robert E. Wood, Louis Howe, Eccles, John Fahey, Douglas, and many others pulling smoothly, evenly, and tractably in any given direction.[10] With the human equation involved it is not easy to get perfect or even good results. It was not the simplest of tasks.

The "few weeks" so optimistically referred to by the president and Mac ran on and on into the months, into nine months, with Walker still at the helm and trying desperately to keep the ship on an even keel. Finally, in June 1934, eleven months after my flying trip to help out, the illness of my uncle, M. E. Comerford, compelled me to return to business.[11]

When I left Washington that first time I felt that in some measure I had gotten things started, that I had gotten some order out of the chaos attendant upon the creation of so many diversified branches of a new venture in government. I can truthfully say that I had reason to be extremely proud of the result I had obtained. Admittedly, the result was not a completely unified organization, but in my own defense I think I can point out with justification that under the circumstances unity was not easy of accomplishment. When one contemplates the new beginnings of so many experiments in government headed by strong personalities, ambitious men with new ideas, many of whom felt that in their own department alone lay the answers to the serious problems confronting the nation, one must admit that it would have required a coordinator of unusual force, ability, and great capacity to keep them all happy and still attain the real objective.

8

A GALLERY OF NEW DEALERS

A frank confession is good for the soul. If I were asked to render honest judgment as to the general esteem in which I was held by some of the personalities whose names I have taken in these pages—Johnson, Hopkins, Ickes, Wallace, and the rest—I think I would have answered that their individual collective opinion of Frank Walker could best be summarized in Al Smith's famous colloquialism about matters that didn't concern him overmuch, "gave it the wave of the left hand."[1] Hugh Johnson, in his book *The Blue Eagle: From Egg to Earth,* protested as he beat his breast that he was most anxious to have the New Deal's Executive Council, of which I was head, guide and govern the activities of all agencies and particularly his own. Knowing Hugh's innate honesty and forthrightness—he was both honest and forthright—I think he made that statement in all sincerity. Yet insofar as giving any evidence of cooperation I gleaned but little.

In fact, Hugh Johnson and his NRA gave me quite a few headaches. Hugh, as is well known, was really a high-powered fellow, a lone wolf, and as temperamental as Ickes and Hopkins combined. A real dictator, he cracked the whip over the heads of businessmen and industry leaders like an old Butte ore teamster over his team of six. He cursed and swore and expostulated from morning until night. I always had the feeling he was about to have a stroke of apoplexy. To borrow one of Hugh's own expressions, he at all meetings of the council struck me as "having ants in his pants." I always thought he rather looked down his nose at the Executive Council. Save on some matter involving a code or NRA function that he wished to obtain clearance on, Hugh always left me with the impression that discussion of activities of other agencies was a waste of his time.

Hugh had great assurance. He thought he had all the answers and was not concerned as to whether his policies interfered with those of Wallace or Peek in agriculture, Hopkins in the emergency relief program, or with Ickes, who was interested in oil. NRA was Hugh's baby, and by and with it he was going to save the country from economic chaos. All other problems to him were of lesser moment. Many times I heard "Old Ironpants" refer to some other department or agency as child's play. As for his colleagues on the Executive Council, he didn't care a damn if he stepped on their toes but would yell to high heaven if any one of them even looked in the direction of his field of endeavor.

There are three incidents that stand out in my memory concerning Hugh. Each one brought out clearly and distinctly the different qualities that were a part of him. For me it was really an interesting study in human nature to engage in a discussion, not to mention a controversy, with him on any matter that was near and dear to his heart.

My first really colorful session with Hugh occurred in his office. I had dropped in on him seemingly for a casual visit. Really I was bearding the lion in his den. Though I didn't tell him so at the outset, I came with instructions to take the oil code from Old Ironpants and place it with his archenemy, Harold Ickes. The Boss, smilingly and with seeming innocence, had turned this pleasant task over to me with the suggestion that it would please him greatly if he could have this little matter accomplished so that he could announce it at his press conference the following morning.

After engaging in a few pleasantries with Hugh about the weather in Washington and the general improvement brought to business conditions by the NRA, I cautiously ventured the suggestion that Hugh was taking on too much work. That he had too many irons in the fire, and though he was admittedly a superman, he should be relieved of some of his less-important tasks so that he could devote more time to his general code plan.

Blunt as only Hugh could be, he said, "Walker," and I quote, "Walker, what have you really got in mind? You didn't come over here to pay me a social visit at this hour of the evening." It was then close to seven o'clock. He said, "Walker, I've got a seven-thirty engagement at the Occidental Restaurant with Governor Pinchot.[2] What's on your mind?"

My response was, "Hugh, I'd like to turn the oil code over to Ickes."

There was fire in his eye, and in that rough, coarse voice of his he blared out, "Walker, you'll do it over my dead body! That damn designing Ickes has wanted to get hold of oil for some time and damned if he'll get it! You and I are good friends, Frank, and you have a tough job with all those prima donnas you're trying to handle for FDR. But I tell you here and now, you can go back to Roosevelt with my resignation, effective forthwith, and this is my final decision!"

Hugh and I argued for six hours. To be more exact, for ninety percent of that period I just listened. But I had a real fondness for the old general; he was tough and hard, yet a sweet, soft sort of a fellow.

As I left him at 1:00 A.M. he graciously surrendered and said, "Walker, if the Boss wants it that way I'll go along. He has more problems than I and he's a great fellow."

Hugh and I then left his office and he joined Governor Pinchot, who had been waiting for him five and one-half hours. Next morning the papers carried the story about the fury of Pinchot, kept waiting at the Occidental by Hugh Johnson. But the press knew or said nothing about the agony I suffered whilst Pinchot waited.

Despite his weakness Hugh was—I have used this word before for him and I use it again, advisedly—a sweet kind of person, a man of real capacity with a fine sense of loyalty. While we had many differences during the years we worked together, socially and personally we got on well.

He was forceful, dynamic, a man of action, a real dictator. But we were as far apart in action and also, I think, in our conception of philosophy and economics as two men could be. Hugh was honest and forthright and you always knew where he stood. I shall always feel, though, and I say it with a kindly spirit, that he was wrong far more often than he was right. To give a touch of Decatur, "Right or wrong, he was always for Johnson's philosophy."[3]

The next incident about Hugh and me in violent opposition arose more or less out of the Schechter "sick chicken" case. This occurred in 1934, when the case was still in the lower courts. In May 1935 in its decision on this case, the Supreme Court knocked the NRA into a cocked hat.[4]

Even in the preliminary stages of this legal fracas, Johnson was smart enough to realize that the case might be decided against him. In addition, the Darrow Committee was preparing to swing into action and there was no doubt as to the tenor of its forthcoming report.[5] So to circumvent the criticisms and to, almost literally, silence the opposition, Johnson prepared himself and the NRA staff for a newer and bigger, a more expansive and a more expensive, NRA, with a newer and bigger blue eagle to place in all the windows.

Through the grapevine I had learned of this big, grand scheme. I learned that his publicity men had worked for weeks, using all their exploitation methods, their imagination, their creative powers, to make this the biggest show of all time. Barnum had nothing on this new plan. The presses had gone to work—the advertising, the circulars, the pamphlets were all set.

I made my plans as head of the Executive Council to "put in a real block," as Jim Crowley of the "four horsemen" used to say, and arranged to meet the Boss on his return from a cruising holiday.[6]

But Hugh had anticipated such a move on my part. I believe that Hugh's son, Captain Johnson, working with his father in the NRA, gleaned from some conversations with me that I was not in sympathy with the general's extravagant program.

Returning from his trip—he had been out on the *Houston*, as I recall— the president landed in Florida.[7] Smarty Hugh, hoping to beat me to it, rushed to Florida by car, and narrowly escaped being hit by a train in the process, with an order for his NRA in his pocket ready for the president's signature. Somewhere on the trip north—I have the impression somehow that it was around Charlottesville—Hugh got the Boss's ear and sold his bill of goods. Five minutes after the presidential train arrived in Washington the presses started printing all the new rules and regulations for the revised NRA program. As far as I know, though, the printers received no overtime for that bit of work. I think I had the first appointment once the president was back in his office. In reply to my question, FDR admitted he had signed Hugh's order. Thereupon I told him of the many valid and serious objections to the proposed plan. The president authorized me to call young Hugh (Captain Johnson) so as to hold all proceedings until the following day. The president called Hugh in; the order he had signed was revoked, and the "new NRA" did not come into being.

Hugh knew that I was responsible for this frustration, but he and I, although we saw each other many times, never discussed it.

Although it happened a few years later on, I remember another sad and pathetic, yes almost tragic, incident, which found me involved with the Boss and Hugh. Even though the time was 1937, when my connection with both the Executive Council and National Emergency Council was already part of the past, I will relate the story here since it is so characteristic of Hugh.

Johnson became a columnist for a time after he left Washington. He joined those who became most critical of the president and his policies. I always felt that the general was controlled more by his emotions than by his brain, though he was a brilliant man. He was most impetuous, possessed a good intellect. He wrote with clarity but lacked the advantage of a sound or deliberate mentality. He was susceptible to emotion and to the flattery of friends. During the summer of the Supreme Court fight—that would be 1937—he wrote a most unfair article in his column about the much-discussed Joseph Robinson Supreme Court appointment. I'm quite sure he did not think the matter through and accepted the version of some of his fair-weather friends, who convinced him that Roosevelt had promised Senator Robinson the appointment with no intention of keeping the promise. Johnson said in so many words that when Robinson heard or realized that Roosevelt did not intend to appoint him to the court, the shock struck him with such force that it brought about his death.[8]

Shortly after this article appeared—it was in July 1937—I think remorse struck at Hugh, and he asked for and received an appointment with the president. He had been consistently bedeviling the president in his column, and this, intensified by his accusation that FDR was responsible for Robinson's death, created a tense atmosphere as the two met.

I had an appointment with the Boss immediately after. When Hugh left it was as dramatic a moment as one could contemplate. When Hugh passed me coming out, I noticed that he was in tears.

As I entered the Boss's presence he seemed to be white and tense. "Frank," he said, "I just told Johnson he was a blankety-blank liar and that I would never forgive him for the lie he wrote about my part in old Joe Robinson's passing." The Boss continued, "Hugh cried and said, 'What can I do to a man in a situation of this kind? What can I do, man to man, in a situation of this kind?'" By "situation" Johnson meant, of course, that he could take no action against a helpless man. Roosevelt was chained to his desk and Roosevelt knew and deliberately took advantage of Hugh's frustrated helplessness.

"Frank," Roosevelt said to me, "Frank, I told him—I said it coolly and calmly and deliberately—I never felt so bitter in my life. He was wrong and he had no alternative but to accept it."

I have heard much from those who knew firsthand of the Robinson matter. I read many articles by those who wrote of it with convincing authenticity. I think Hugh was as wrong as he could be, but I think also that he came to know that he had written too impetuously and that he had done the Boss an injustice. All in all, this must have been the greatest ordeal Hugh Johnson ever suffered.

Yet, strong and courageous and forthright as he was, he accepted it in fine and soldierly fashion. The incident served to convince me that, though a man of some weaknesses, he was really a grand character. In my judgment Hugh Johnson was a real honest-to-god man as we knew them in the West. A man of great emotion, he had many weaknesses, but he had intellect and force, character and integrity. According to my concept of life and of men, the good and worthwhile things he did in life will outbalance by far his trivial human failings. I shall always look upon him as a grand and gracious character, a generous character too. Admittedly he had his failings, but they were in keeping with his great-souled nature, nothing small or mean.

Turning to Harry Hopkins, the Civil Works Administration was a real godsend. Hopkins was the originator and driving force behind this emergency measure, and for its success he is entitled to full credit. And again I wish to reiterate my considered opinion that the wise way in which CWA was brought into being and handled may have been responsible for avoiding a revolution in this country.[9]

But as Bob Sherwood has noted, I did not always see eye-to-eye with Hopkins in his plans.[10] I felt that the later Works Progress Administration, which in effect was CWA's successor, was too broad, too expansive, and wide open to the creation of many nonessential, impractical, and ill-considered projects.

As for Harry's own character, and this of course is only my personal opinion, I don't think he was nearly as dependable or forthright as was his adversary, Harold Ickes. In many ways he was an opportunist, a cold, ruthless sort of person. And in addition rather a paradox. He was a social worker and yet himself had no little social ambition. He'd brush shoulder-to-shoulder with the common man and outwardly gave way easily to emotion. But to me he always appeared sort of an actor on stage. He could mix with a miner or a farmer, a John L. Lewis or an Averell Harriman.[11] Yet he seemed to be happiest with the Long Island set.

In saying this I do not speak disparagingly of him. Roosevelt could have had, and I say this thoughtfully, no better aide than Hopkins. He was smart, able, had a splendid intellect and a great capacity for living. Moreover, he was blessed with a sense of humor.

Harry had an almost intuitive genius for sensing FDR's hopes and ambitions; he arranged all his plans to conform with the Boss's objectives.[12] I never knew any man who had a quicker perception of what Roosevelt had in mind than he did. Almost literally he was Roosevelt's ears and eyes and legs when Roosevelt needed him, and he did a grand job for him.

Although it may sound strange, Harry Hopkins and I got on much better socially than Ickes and myself. Yet I always felt that Harold and I were much closer and really had more in common. Moreover, as regards their objectives, at all times I was much more a supporter of the Public Works Administration. In this field there was a great need for heavy industries, and the work to be done was essential, worthwhile, and a boon to our economy. Many of the PWA projects will stand for generations as a monument to the foresight of Roosevelt and Ickes and of the New Deal. It is not my intention, obviously, to dwell too much on the achievements of any particular agency, but it will take only a minute to mention several of the more celebrated PWA projects, such as the Triborough Bridge in New York, the Chicago Sanitary District, the Golden Gate Bridge in San Francisco. Too long to list here and deserving of at least a special paragraph would be the dams and the flood control and power projects.

Harold personally sometimes left me with the thought that he was a holier-than-thou sort of fellow. Yet as I came to know him better, I became quite sure that it was not an act on his part. I liked Harold and I had the feeling that he came to like me. I'm quite sure that he had the notion that I was not sufficiently assertive or aggressive. His appraisal may have been correct. He rather felt that I was an amiable, easygoing chap—he was always after me to pin Harry's ears back—but he, too, always wanted his own way. Smilingly I would listen to his vociferous declamations and then perhaps rule against him. Honesty compels me to admit, though, that Ickes usually then went in through the back door and got his own way with the Boss.

I have always felt that Harold Ickes was one of the most colorful characters I met. I am equally certain that I never met another person who had such a combination of qualities. He could be so irritating and yet almost lovable at one and the same time. He could register all the known emotions in as short a period of time as any person I ever knew. He loved to pontificate, yet I know he had much humility. At one minute he was arrogant beyond human belief, and a humble suppliant the next; caustic and vitriolic, yet he could be kind and considerate. He could hate with an intense, burning hatred; nevertheless, he could be kind and forgiving as well. One thing no one doubted: he was fundamentally honest. Though he was called Honest Harold partly in jest, never for a single moment did anyone deny the accuracy of the label.

It is equally certain that Harold was no shrinking violet. He had a notion, yes a deep-seated conviction, that he was right in all things. He also had great ambitions and felt with certitude that he was of the anointed. He never ventured opinions; his statements were always edicts and pronunciamentos. It almost goes without saying that with the written word Ickes was no less forceful than in verbal onslaught. He styled himself well in the title of his memoir, *The Autobiography of a Curmudgeon*.

There is one incident concerning Harold that I will always keep in mind. At this particular time Harold began to feel that he was getting more than his quota of flying brickbats, which seemed to be hurled only at his obstinate head. And patience, it seems superfluous to remark, was not one of his many outstanding virtues. So whatever the final straw may have been on this particular occasion, to use a modern slang term, Harold had it. No doubt at all, there was a conspiracy afoot to do him injury. So in his own characteristic style he indited a twelve-page letter to FDR concerning certain abuse being heaped upon him.

After much thought it seemed that he had come to the conclusion that certain (and far from unknown) individuals in and about the government were planning his complete annihilation and total extinction. Mrs. Roosevelt, Harry Hopkins, and General Johnson were a few of those he indicted.

At the close of his bristling apologia, if such a word is not too incongru-
ous, he asked Roosevelt to conduct a full and complete investigation into his
career as a government official. He suggested that it be done by a one-man
board of inquiry, which after examination of the evidence and due deliberation
would make a detailed report of his, Ickes's, conduct to the president with
appropriate recommendations as to the acceptance or rejection of his resignation. Quoting from memory, I believe Harold closed his document thus: "I
shall be confronted by witnesses; I shall be heard and insist that you appoint
an arbitrator to hear these false and defamatory charges. My choice is Frank
Walker for arbitrator."

His selection of me pleased me in a fashion, but I had no real zeal for the
task. The Boss called me in and showed me the document. While on this
point, may I say incidentally I doubt if this document was ever revealed to any
eyes save Roosevelt's and mine. The president kept it in his desk, and I don't
think he ever showed it to another soul. Without doubt it was a masterpiece
in the vitriolic.

I suggested to the Boss that I talk to Harold about it, for I really did not
take the matter very seriously. I went over to his office, got him in a good
mood, and we both laughed it off. Ickes was forthright but he too had a good
sense of humor. What had seemed such a serious controversy became a trivial,
soon-forgotten incident in the at times tempestuous activities of FDR,
Harold, and myself.

One thing, however, Harold refused to laugh off, and that was his very
real contempt for Harry Hopkins. Harry in turn detested Ickes. This recipro-
cal disaffection began in the Executive Council days and later in 1935 really
flared up during the works projects period. I know that each in turn, individually and jointly, kept me busy pouring oil and salving injured feelings when I
could well have devoted my time and efforts to better things.

Roosevelt really enjoyed these battles but rarely took part in them. He
laughingly and with design passed them on to me. The feud finally became so
intense that FDR decided to take his prize prima donnas on a cruise with him,
leaving me behind in charge of the works program and at peace. This particular
cruise, incidentally, was on the *Houston* toward the end of September 1935. Bob
Sherwood has a very amusing account of it in his *Roosevelt and Hopkins*.[13]

Henry Wallace together with Peek and Tugwell were the real triumvirate
in the Department of Agriculture. They formed still another group, with
which I was to establish liaison with the Boss. And also to use my best
endeavors to see to it that their programs and objectives would form a coher-
ent part of the New Deal program.

Wallace was, I am sure, as well informed on farming as any man associated with the administration. He was the son of a former cabinet member,

another Henry Wallace, who served in the same agricultural post under President Harding and survived his chief only a year, dying in 1924. He and his father before him—I'm talking about the New Deal Wallace now—were real students of farming and for years had been active in the public and political life of the American farmer. Not only did they operate and control a farm journal of considerable repute, but they both had done much in research. It had been said that they were Burbanks in corn and wheat. Henry on his own had evolved a new type of hybrid corn, which had made him independent financially and of increased stature in his own field.[14]

When I first met Henry, I very soon came to look on him in the same manner as did one of the commentators of his early days, who styled him a Protestant saint. I never to this day could make any sort of satisfactory or real analysis of Henry. To me he just did not seem to be part of this world. In any matter of policy that involved a difference of opinion, rightly or wrongly I seemed inevitably to find myself in opposition to Henry. In his quarrel with Peek, his pretended if not real disagreement with Tugwell, in his arguments with Ickes over the Bureau of Forestry, it seemed fated that Henry would be on one side and I on the other.[15] To say that I was disturbed when he came forth with his pig program is putting it mildly. I was shocked.[16]

To get ahead of ourselves for a bit, when Henry Wallace sought the vice presidential nomination against Harry S. Truman in 1944, I was definitely in Truman's corner. And I just wish to say at this point that I genuinely liked Henry Wallace, having served with him directly and indirectly for eleven years. It embarrassed me no little to oppose, openly as well as behind the scenes, his nomination.

After the 1944 convention was over, I thought it the nice and gracious thing to do to make a call upon Henry in his office. I did this and told him I hoped he would take no personal offense against me for either my attitude or my actions at the convention. I explained to him that I had no apology to make for anything I had done but just wanted him to know that the battle from my viewpoint was entirely impersonal. I thought my attitude correct, yet hoped the result would not interfere with our friendship. Henry was cordial and gracious and closed the conversation with these words: "Frank, I hope that twenty years from now you may tell me the real reason for your opposition to me." He did not say it in hostile fashion but left me with the definite impression that I was part of a deep-dyed plot against him.[17]

The intervening years since 1944 have, I think, clearly demonstrated how different it would have been, both for this country and the world, had Henry been nominated. Looking back upon it, how close we were to the edge of the cliff! Whether or not one had supported or opposed Harry Truman, it seems to me that we would do well to pause a minute and reflect, then soberly

Frank Walker with Henry Wallace, *left,* in 1941. Photograph courtesy University of Notre Dame Archives.

thank God that it was Harry Truman and not Henry Wallace who was nominated in 1944.

But as far as my overall opinion goes, the complete returns are not yet in on Henry Wallace. The few recognized geniuses I have met have been accorded my respectful awe. And if Henry was a genius, he was just beyond me. I will be the first to admit that I think he was an honest, sincere man of unusual capacity in many fields. One thing is definitely certain. In my rich and varied experience of sixty-odd years, he really was unique.[18]

Lewis W. Douglas was of Scotch descent, and this fact was obvious to any and all who had dealings with him. I think that Senator Byrd would be well classified as a spendthrift by the standards maintained by Lew.[19]

I always held Lew in high esteem, though I did feel he was set to the point of being adamant. His opinions were always strongly fixed. Economy was a real obsession with him and he had very little if any compromise in his makeup.

He was the only man I ever heard, either at Executive Council or cabinet meetings, place himself in open, violent, and very disrespectful opposition to the president's personally expressed views.

This particular discussion came up at a meeting of the Executive Council on a question of expenditures. The debate became heated. Lew turned livid and his voice rose in high, strident tones. Roosevelt, while at first seemingly cool and deliberate himself, turned white with rage. It was an ill-chosen time and place for Lew so forcibly to argue his point. It struck me that he could have served his cause and incidentally himself better in a private conference with FDR. I know that all present were embarrassed.

I do not think that FDR ever forgave Lew. Shortly afterwards—this was the summer or fall of 1933—FDR had Lew up at Hyde Park, and that meeting ended with Lew's resignation. I was at Hyde Park myself and saw the president right after his stormy encounter with his late director of the budget. And I remember Roosevelt told me then, "I surely had a wordy conflict with Douglas and I was never so damned mad in my life. I was white with rage, I think, and I called him an SOB to his face."

I doubt if Roosevelt ever forgave Douglas. I am repeating that statement despite the fact that Hopkins brought Douglas back during the war to serve in shipping. This was with Roosevelt's approval. And I know too that Roosevelt in discussions with me gave serious consideration to the appointment of Lew as Cordell Hull's successor in the post of secretary of state.[20]

Roosevelt assigned many tasks to me during my stay in Washington and also during the intervening period when I was not serving in an official capacity.[21] Some of these assignments were pleasant, interesting, and occasionally intriguing, others I found difficult and unpleasant, more than a few quite embarrassing. Roosevelt as much as any man I ever knew avoided the unpleasant things that confront men as they go through life. Most of us naturally are inclined to avoid meeting the unpleasant head-on. Because of his position and power, many unpleasant or distasteful decisions were inevitably set before Roosevelt. It was always amazing to me how adroitly he maneuvered and sidestepped rather than make a decision involving personalities.

This characteristic—I might call it a weakness on his part—was well exemplified in the latter part of 1933, when he issued a statement that members of the Democratic National Committee should forthwith resign their posts if they wished to continue practicing law in Washington. Soon after this announcement I dined with him alone one evening at the White House. With no warning he suddenly said, "Frank, I think it is a mistake to have a member of the cabinet serve as chairman of the national committee. I'd like very much to have you convey my thoughts to Jim Farley. Jim is a very efficient national chairman, but he just can't do both jobs and do them well. Tell him I think he should make his position as chairman a full-time job with a decent salary and resign as postmaster general."

I ventured the suggestion that this was a very personal matter and I thought he should handle it himself.

He was very insistent, however, that I take over. "We're all on the same team," the president said. "We have a program to carry out. We must now lay our plans for the next election because we cannot complete our program in four years. You open up this subject with Jim, get his reactions, and then I can go into it more fully with him."

I was of course hesitant to broach so delicate a matter to Jim, but since the president felt the matter was vitally important, I consented to carry the message.

Soon afterward I had Jim for dinner at my apartment. I advised him of my discussion with the president. Jim's reaction was not enthusiastic. He said he wanted to give the matter a little thought, and we went on to other topics. I reported to FDR and then forgot it. Apparently FDR said nothing to Farley nor Farley to the president.

Several months later FDR revived the discussion. Again I took the matter up with Jim, who on this occasion told me he wanted to submit his formal postmaster general's report of his two years in office. He would then resign and devote his entire time to the national committee. Once again I reported to FDR, and this was the last I heard of the topic until Jim did resign in 1940.

Roosevelt changed his attitude in later years, when he insisted despite my protests that I, having succeeded Farley as postmaster general, should also accept the chairmanship of the national committee.

I always felt that Jim held this particular request against the Boss. He may have held it against me too, though he gave no evidence of it. Jim's outward attitude, at least toward me, did not change until after the 1940 convention.

Speaking of Jim's attitudes, I recall that in the many gatherings I attended where the Boss and Farley were present I cannot remember one occasion where Jim pursued an argument. At times he would evince some slight manifestation of disagreement, but inevitably he wound up with the same statement: "You're the boss. Whatever you say goes with me. But I just wanted to express the viewpoint of someone who may have been talking."

To be perfectly blunt about it, Jim never seemed at ease with FDR. He always sat on the edge of his chair during these sessions and very seldom, if ever, relaxed. I rather think Roosevelt sensed this, and I honestly believe he enjoyed Jim's discomfiture. Many times I taxed FDR with this and teasingly accused him of left-handing Jim and keeping him back on his heels. He never affirmed this. He did not deny it either. He just smiled.

Once more, getting ahead of my story. I have noted that, outwardly at least, Jim's attitude toward me changed after the 1940 convention. I had remonstrated with him when he sought the presidential nomination of Cordell Hull. I always felt Hull did not have the slightest chance of being nominated. I am quite sure Jim did not like my frank statement concerning his possibilities. I felt that Jim's strategy at that time was to bring about the nomination of Hull and so obtain the vice presidential spot for himself. Jim always said he was opposed to a third term on principle.

I never questioned Jim Farley's honesty. Yet I sometimes wondered if his own ambition did not have at least a subconscious influence upon him in reaching this conclusion. I remember that he and Jack Garner were conferring very frequently in those days. I am sure that Jim felt if Jack missed out in his try for the top he would eventually line up behind a Hull-Farley ticket. To borrow an expression used often by my son, Tom, when he was a child, Jim "will be mad to me" for expressing this view. It is my well-considered opinion that I have appraised the situation properly. It is indeed very difficult, speaking of 1940, to reconcile Jim Farley's often-recorded advocacy of strict party organization with his conduct in that campaign.

I liked Felix Frankfurter.[22] I liked his quick mind. He was a man of great ability, yet his ideas and mine were quite different. This too applied to Mr. Justice Holmes and many of his protégés from the late 1920s on.[23] They were all quick on the trigger, smart, mentally alert; they had little respect for tradition and their philosophy was very modern. According to my conception of law and ethics, they had neither respect nor reverence for the philosophy of St. Augustine, St. Thomas Aquinas, or the philosophers who meant so much to me. I think that the so-called Harvard crowd—the slang term for them was "Frankfurter's hot dogs"—did more damage to the New Deal and to Roosevelt than any other faction that came to Washington.

I shall always feel that they suffered my presence because of my association with Roosevelt, not because of any approval of my mentality. I might properly say they were never less than a bit condescending with me.

Insofar as Frankfurter was concerned, I think he was a very able lawyer. But he was most voluble, gregarious, and did not seem to me to have the dignity that should go with a man who was sitting on the Supreme Court. Roosevelt had no little respect for his ability, however, and often took his advice, sometimes when I thought he should not.

I had many meetings with Roosevelt at which Bill Douglas was present. Douglas, associate justice of the court, always puzzled me. To my understanding he was always a very strange person. He was a man of great mental activity and capacity, there's no question about that, and was highly intelligent. I think he had a strikingly bad sense of taste and had not the slightest conception of culture in the niceties. Certainly the vile story he told at one of Russ Young's memorable dinners, for which Young publicly rebuked him, is sufficient indication of that.[24]

I also had many opportunities to see Tom Corcoran at work with Roosevelt, though I saw less of Corcoran than Roosevelt did.[25] Roosevelt used to see Corcoran quite often in the evening. Tommy and I were never close, and I never did feel at home in this group. I think he had respect for Corcoran's ability to accomplish the things he wanted accomplished. The president knew that Corcoran and I had little in common, either in thought or action.

Corcoran was a man of considerable ability. He was a bit on the fresh side. I was a great admirer of Jim Perkins, who had become president of the National City Bank.[26] He had been the first president of the Farmers Trust before that. Perkins came to see me many times when we were drafting legislation in connection with the banking and securities bills. I was quite open-minded about the scope and character of this legislation, and I think Raymond Moley was more or less so. Corcoran, however, felt quite differently. One night I remember Moley, Corcoran, and I had been working on the securities bill, and we met at my apartment. I suggested some ideas that Jim Perkins had advanced. I thought they had some merit. Moley was inclined to agree with me. But right here Corcoran displayed a facet of his character that showed unmistakably that he was not my type of person. "Listen!" he said. "We have them behind the eight ball (only he used a more offensive physiological term). We've put them right in their place. Let's keep them there."

Without in any way considering myself naive, I had thought we were trying to write some constructive legislation. I did not feel that the other crowd were enemies at all. To me it appeared much better to hear their side of the discussion, to try to effect a meeting of the minds, convince them by our arguments, and finally try to draft a fair bill that would be helpful not only to the country as a whole but also to those who had even opposed it. How well I remember how Tom, "Tommy the Cork," as FDR used to call him, exulted that we had them on the run and that the best thing to do was to prod them as they went.

That was my estimate of Corcoran at that time, and I am afraid it has not changed much. To me, Tom did not seem to have the correct sense of ethics; he always seemed to be wanting to win a battle. The principle involved, it appeared to me, did not concern him nearly as much as the desire to win a victory. He always seemed to look down his nose at most of the men on the other side. It might be regarded as an understatement to note that he possessed a superiority complex; he thought that he and his group were so far superior mentally to the crowd on the other side that to him there simply was no comparison between the two groups.

No, I had little faith in Tom. He went along with Roosevelt, and the president held him in high esteem for a very considerable period. Corcoran was quite active in the Supreme Court fight. Later the almost inevitable fate of all court favorites overtook him.

Dean Acheson became prominent in the first months of the New Deal. I always had great respect for Acheson. When I first went to Washington, Dean was undersecretary of the treasury. And when he went out it was on a question of principle. When Roosevelt went off gold, as the popular saying had it, Acheson, who had opposed this move as a matter of conscience, promptly resigned. For a long time after that Roosevelt felt very bitterly towards him. Personally, though, I felt very sympathetic to Dean; I felt he was a fine character, with great sincerity as well as great ability. I think really I had more respect for Acheson's ability and his philosophy of life than for any other of the Harvard group.[27]

Here it might be pertinent to devote a few words to the great inspiration of the Harvard group, Oliver Wendell Holmes Jr. That Mr. Justice Holmes possessed legal learning together with an incisive and epigrammatic wit, I will be the first to admit. Nevertheless, I was never a great admirer of Holmes. I think he was a man of ability and intellect. But he had so little faith in human nature and his philosophy of life was so far apart from mine that he just never could win me over.[28] I think that he and Frankfurter and others of that ilk did more to damage the minds of the young Harvard graduates in the twenties and thirties than any other single force or, for that matter, combination of forces that I can call to mind.

And in this respect I would class Jim Rowe as Exhibit A, though I doubt if Jim, now another prosperous lawyer and in partnership with Tom Corcoran, would appreciate this distinction.[29] As far as Jim is concerned, I have always had a feeling in my mind that I was somewhat responsible for his position in life and more specifically for his mental attitudes towards life. His father and I were very close, and I regarded him as one of the outstanding citizens of Montana. A way back, when Jim was finishing his "lit" courses at Harvard—I think he was aiming at an A.B., and he had about made up his mind he was going into journalism—one time when his father was in New York, he asked me if I would not have a talk with Jim and recommend what he should do. I agreed to see Jim and give him the best of my ideas. When he came down from Harvard once in his senior year, I took him to dinner and told him that instead of going into journalism the best thing for him to do was to take law. Somewhat to my surprise he followed my advice, and that put him under the guidance and tutelage of Felix Frankfurter. I am not sure that that did not lead Jim and his mental processes into channels that I had never anticipated and certainly would not have recommended. For Jim became a more than typical product of the Harvard group, about which I have already expressed my opinion.

Hope has not left me that Jim and a lot of those young fellows—at least I regard them as such and I certainly would not call their thinking mature— will still change their viewpoint and attain a commonsense outlook and knowledge of the correct philosophy. I may be a bit too optimistic. As far as I am concerned, my conscience has always bothered me a bit about Jim Rowe. I brought him to Washington and gave him his first job. He started with me; then, through Frankfurter or Corcoran, the then-retired Mr. Justice Holmes took him on as his secretary.

Jim and Holmes became very close. I remember one story that I thought was very cute. This story came from Jim. Holmes used to call him Sharkey. They were accustomed to take a daily drive through the park and over toward the Potomac River. On many occasions they had seen a certain particular bird—it was a stork, if I am not mistaken. One day, it seems, their ornithological acquaintance was apparently among the missing. So Holmes said, "Where's the bird today? We don't see him."

Jim said, "*I* can see him—there—across the river, across the Potomac."

To anyone familiar with Washington it is hardly necessary to state that the Virginia side was so far distant that nobody with even better than normal sight, and Jim was wearing glasses then, could see so large a bird.

Anyway, Holmes peered dutifully across the Potomac, turned to Jim, and said briskly "Yes, that's right. I see him, too, Sharkey. You dirty liar!"

Over the years I conversed many times with Frankfurter, Acheson, Corcoran, Rowe, Ben Cohen, and other such products of Cambridge-by-the-Charles.[30] I wondered, sometimes, if they would continue to carry on with the philosophy that they accepted so unquestioningly in the early days of the Roosevelt era. I was inclined to doubt it. It is my idea that more or less all of them toned down. But for better or worse, and on that point I have already entered my verdict, they were a part of the New Deal.

9

WAR

Editor's Note: Frank Walker did not leave any autobiographical account of World War II, during which he served as postmaster general and for a year as chairman of the Democratic National Committee. But he left something better—a diary. Sometimes he would not write for weeks or even months on end. But his entries, when he made them, are often memorable accounts of his connection, close as it was, with the president of the United States.

❋ ❋ ❋ ❋

Saturday, December 6, 1941. Hallie and I went to New York at 11:00 A.M. to attend the Treasury Hour program Saturday evening as guests of the secretary of the treasury, Henry Morgenthau. Toscanini conducted the NBC Symphony Orchestra. They played "The Star-Spangled Banner," and I have never heard it played more impressively.

Sunday, December 7, 1941. Tom's twenty-first birthday. I attended the annual Notre Dame holy communion gathering at St. Patrick's Cathedral and breakfast afterwards at the Hotel Roosevelt. Among those present at the breakfast were Bishop O'Hara, Secretary of State Michael F. Walsh, and Myron Taylor, the president's ambassador to the Vatican. Taylor gave his first public address since his appointment to the Vatican. He delivered a most inspiring talk—was most generous to the church and to His Holiness—a splendid bit of Catholic philosophy.

During breakfast I received word at the table that I had several calls from Father Drought from Washington.[1] I felt it was one of the usual calls about the Japanese conferences and did not respond, sending word out that I would take the call after the breakfast. When I returned home about noon was unable to reach Father Drought and, with Hallie and Maude, went to hear Laura Hallie sing in a beautiful little operetta up at Marymount at Tarrytown.[2] I was called from the performance by a telephone message from Bill Cronin in Washington. Bill advised that the president had called a special meeting of the cabinet for 8:30 this evening, because the Japanese had attacked Pearl Harbor and the Philippine Islands. I received this word about 4:45 P.M. Rushed immediately by car to La Guardia Airport. During the trip listened to the radio reports of the attack. All stations were broadcasting the story. In company with Vice President Wallace and Secretary Madam Perkins took 6:30 P.M. plane to Washington.[3] Went directly to White House upon arrival in Washington.

Entire cabinet met with the president in the Oval Room of the White House—also Harry Hopkins and Steve Early were present.[4] Later this group was joined by Senators Barkley, McNary, Connally, Johnson, and Austin, and Speaker Rayburn, House Leader Jere Cooper, House Minority Leader Smith, Congressman Bloom, Congressman Eaton of New Jersey, and Congressman Martin.

The president opened the cabinet session with the remark that this was the most historically important moment since 1861. The president imparted to us all the information he had received with reference to the Hawaiian attack. The data were practically the same as what was to be given out by the secretary of the navy, Knox, about ten days later upon his return from Hawaii. The attack came at about 7:35 A.M. Hawaiian time. Japanese Ambassadors Nomura and Kurusu waited upon Secretary Hull, at the very moment the attack was in progress, with a message indicating that the Japanese could not accept the terms of the U.S. government but with no indication of war. At the time they presented their message to Secretary Hull their planes had been bombing Hawaii for several hours.[5]

The cabinet meeting adjourned at about 10:30 P.M., and Attorney General Biddle, Vice President Wallace, and I consulted with the president about censorship. At our suggestion he authorized us to have J. Edgar Hoover take charge of censorship until an appointment of a director could be made. Left immediately for the attorney general's office where the vice president, the attorney general, Fred Ironside, and I met with Mr. Tamm and Mr. Clegg and discussed moves for censorship. I returned to the Wardman Park Hotel shortly after midnight.

Monday, December 8, 1941. At noon the president addressed a joint assembly of both houses of Congress in the House chamber—present were also the Supreme Court and the cabinet. I think this was the second time in history the Supreme Court had appeared for such an occasion. It was a solemn, dignified, and enthusiastic meeting. The president asked for a declaration that "a state of war has existed between the U.S. and the Japanese empire" as a result of Japan's "unprovoked and dastardly attack" and within minutes after he finished his address the Senate passed a resolution declaring war on Japan unanimously. Almost as quickly the House passed the same resolution with one dissenting vote from the congresswoman Jeannette Rankin.

The president joined us at the speaker's room before he appeared before the joint house, and with several other cabinet officers we discussed with him the general situation. Later in the day I conferred with the attorney general and J. Edgar Hoover, in which we outlined a plan for censorship. Met with bureau heads of Post Office Department to discuss various wartime policies to be adopted.

Tuesday, December 9, 1941. The president addressed the nation on Thursday night. I spoke with him on the telephone after he had completed his address. He seemed much relieved that he had told the story and suggested to me that he thought history would show our record in attempting to avoid the conflict was perfect. I am in hearty accord with this thought, and feel that no nation in all history has a cleaner, finer record for attempting to avert the terrible war that is now in progress.

At the cabinet meeting on December 12, Attorney General Biddle and I conferred with the president and he agreed to appoint Byron Price director of censorship. I also conferred with him on civilian defense matters. At the president's suggestion I called Mr. Price and asked him to come down to Washington the next day, Saturday, December 13. Saturday afternoon at 3:00 P.M. Early, Lowell Mellett, Price, and I discussed censorship, and Mr. Price agreed to accept the appointment as director.

At the cabinet meeting on December 19 discussion was had for first time of setting up an Allied war council. The president sought legal advice as to his scope as commander in chief and questioned whether or not agreement could be made with Britain and China not to agree on a separate peace. Also the question of whether or not we could agree not to cease hostilities save by mutual agreement. The president indicated at this meeting that Frank Knox's action in going to Hawaii was one of the finest things ever done by a cabinet officer since 1789. Said it had a wonderful effect in buying up the country.

I met with the president on another occasion the week of the seventh and discussed the radio controversy between communications and the broadcasters—the censorship question—and the general war situation. At that time he brought me up to date on advice he had received from the Pacific. The night I spoke with him on the phone he had just received the message that planes were seen off Hawaii. One day during the week of December 15 I discussed with the president, General Watson, and others the question of civilian defense, and I made some recommendations.[6] At that meeting we also discussed air mail rates for soldiers—the franking privilege or free mail for soldiers out of the country and the zone rates on parcel post to our various bases off the continent. At the cabinet meeting this week I received permission to take care of these questions.

Friday, January 16, 1942. Yesterday at 5:30 P.M. I visited the president to go over the books, papers, and data of Isaac Roosevelt, which were brought down to Washington by Mr. Alpern. We did not get to the actual examination of the books, but to give an example of the president's ability to relax during these critical times (yesterday the president announced that Donald Nelson would be the chairman of the War Production Board and in full charge of the administration of the Office of Production Management, and tomorrow he will appoint William Knudsen a lieutenant general in charge of actual production), I set down this most confidential and interesting story he told me.[7]

The president had taken a day off from his arduous tasks and had but two engagements for the day. As proof of how easily he relaxes, he told me when I arrived that he had just completed a one-and-one-half-hour nap. He said, "I am going to tell you a very personal story that I think is very interesting."

My grandfather had two sons—James, my father, and John. At the age of fourteen my father left home and went up on the hill to live with his grandfather, my great-grandfather. My father had been quite unhappy at home, largely because I think his brother John, who was a rather nice and pretty boy, received all the affection. At the time my father reached the age of twenty his grandfather died and left him half of his estate, together with the home on the hill, which was called Mount Hope, and all of its contents. The other half was left by my great-grandfather to my grandfather. This of course was not pleasing either to my grandfather or my father's brother John.

Five years later my father married and went to Europe. While there, the house on the hill was destroyed by fire and upon being advised of this my father returned home. Due to the stone construction of the house, most of the things on the first floor were saved. All these, which belonged to my father, were taken by him to his father's home. The two family Bibles, many paintings, and some very interesting books and ledgers showed the history of the family transactions of Jacobus and Isaac Roosevelt.

Watches, fobs and many other heirlooms were included. Later, my father's first wife died and my father moved to the place that is now my home—Hyde Park. He advised his brother John many times that he wanted to take with him all of the personal property that had been removed from the home of their grandfather, which belonged to him. However, John, never pleased because my father's grandfather had ignored him in the will and willed the property to Father, would never consent to the removal. My father did succeed in getting some of the paintings, and, eventually, succeeded in getting hold of the oldest of the family Bibles and some few trinkets.

Many times my father told me this story but always insisted he didn't want to have a family quarrel during his lifetime because he hated family quarrels, but he told me I should always remember that these family heirlooms were mine and he told me many times I should insist upon having them returned. When my father broached the question several times with my Uncle John, he would not consent to the transfer up to the time of the death of my father.

My Uncle John later died, leaving two daughters, Ellie Roosevelt and Mrs. Mary Clark, who are still neighbors of mine. As a boy I remember seeing many of these articles in and about my uncle's home, and after his death I opened up a conversation several times directed toward indicating to them that I would like to have these belongings. Apparently the feeling was transmitted to the second generation, for my Cousin Ellie would always purse her lips and indicate by her manner that she felt I was like my father, "quite grasping," and anxious to keep all the family heirlooms and treasures.

Upon the death of my Uncle John, he left an estate of more than $200,000. Since then this has dwindled to an amount, I think, of about $50,000, and my two cousins have had some difficulty in getting on. On one occasion Cousin Ellie came to the house and told me that in searching through some of the drawers she had found a large ring that belonged to my great-grandfather. It was a large blue ring—I recognized it immediately. If it had not been for the fact it was chipped it would have been of very considerable value, but by reason of the chip it lost its intrinsic value and retained only the value of an heirloom. However, I did purchase it for $150, which was much more than it was worth.

Another time she came with a fob I recognized as having been that of my grandfather, and I purchased that from her for $300. My sole thought in doing this was to give them some aid in this form because I knew my cousins were proud and needed some assistance.

On another occasion she came with a receipt from Benedict Arnold to my great-grandfather. This receipt was for some things great-grandfather purchased from Arnold, who was a merchant. She asked if I would like to buy it. I sent it to the Library of Congress for appraisal, and they appraised it at $7.50. I gave her $150 for it, with which she was delighted. On another occasion she brought in two small Dutch Bibles, which I also had appraised by the Library of Congress at $12.50. I gave her $500 for these. I suppose I shall have to go on doing this for some time. Despite the fact that I have helped them very often, they have taken some of these letters and books and ledgers, which I told them very often I would like to have, and sold them to collectors for practically nothing. The collectors in turn, knowing I would like to have them, have attempted to exact large sums from me.

Do you think I should institute suit against them, or just do as my father did and say, "I hate family quarrels," and pass this on to another generation?

We answered the question together, both saying we thought it was just as well not to have any family quarrels. He tossed his head back and laughed, saying, "I suppose I shall have to go on helping Ellie, and she will keep on making things miserable for me, all because of the nice boy, Johnnie."

The president also said: "One of the Poughkeepsie papers some time ago got out a history of Dutchess County and referred to the records of New York State's meeting for the adoption of the constitution. It gave credit to my Cousin Ellie for obtaining the information from the original records of the constitutional convention, which were in her possession. These really belong to me, but I cannot get them."

As I was leaving, Secretary Knox and Admiral Moreell came in, very apologetically, saying they knew he was making no engagements but they had to impose upon him.[8] When I left he was saying, "Frank, come back tomorrow, I have cabinet and a war board meeting tomorrow but come back after that. I want to finish this story."

Saturday, January 17, 1942. I met with the president about two o'clock today. He told me:

In about 1927 my mother's income seemed to be stripped a bit too far, and to relieve her I suggested that she deed to me the two brownstone houses, in one of which she lived and the other in which I lived, on Sixty-fifth Street, and that I would pay the taxes, which would give her $4,000 additional to spend. These cost her about $90,000. I lived there a good many years on and off. For some time I have felt there was no market for these. What do you think of the good luck that has just come to me? A representative of some foundation in New York spoke to Eleanor recently and told her they were interested in purchasing these from me to deed to some organization in Hunter College engaged in some cause for religious freedom. Eleanor told me of it and I told her to tell them that if they took it immediately I would accept $50,000, but that was to be rock bottom and no negotiating. I got word today, and I think they will accept it. What a windfall, for it gives me an opportunity to charge off a considerable amount of income tax because the value at the time they were given to me as a gift was about $90,000 and I am now selling them for $50,000. Another thing, I feared I would have them on my hands for many years to come. Isn't that a break?

The president told me also about buying some old prints, some Currier and Ives, from Bradley in his curio shop, which was down in a basement in New York years ago. He used to drop in there occasionally and acquire prints. When he asked about prints, Bradley advised him that he had just acquired some of the cleanest Currier and Ives he had ever seen and that because they had no value for him he would give them to him at a little profit.

> I told him I had no interest in that type—the set of five of them cost me twenty dollars [Bradley said] and I will give them to you for twenty-two dollars—a two-dollar profit in a half hour isn't bad. They were beautiful prints. I didn't know what to do with them though I had bought them. They were "Surprise," "Delight" (the ones that now appear in my study).
>
> Can you imagine what happened a few days later? I picked up the paper and saw that Currier and Ives were being sold from $180 to $210 to $250 apiece. Now they are worth much more.

When the president related what he had said—"I wouldn't be interested in them"—I said, "Oh, that was your Dutch cropping out—trying to make a good deal."

"No, I didn't want them, but the more I looked—so fine and clear."

[FDR] "Do you know that I figured that over the last several years I have averaged about fifty dollars a year winnings at poker?"

[Walker] "By the way, you play a good game of poker when you are winning, but you have not got as much Dutch in you as I have and you call too often when you are losing."

He said: "When I am losing I become very cautious."

[FDR] "When I came into the White House, I weighed 186 stripped. In 1936, I got up to 191. Today I weigh 185. I don't diet, I just cut down on my food. I am only sixty on the thirtieth and they are trying to make a diamond jubilee out of it. I don't even feel sixty. I am going to clean up the stuff on my desk this weekend and take things easy next week, but, by the way, we do have the cabinet dinner, don't we? When you take your trip keep your eyes and ears open and tell me what you hear."

Saturday, January 24, 1942. Saw the president yesterday after cabinet. He said:

> I turned to Churchill when he was here and said, "Winston, I am going to be more insistent on one proposal that has got to be set forth in the peace agreement when it is reached. I am going to insist now that I have your support in

it. Can I rely upon that?" Churchill said, "Well," very seriously, and quite alarmed that I should be discussing a matter of that kind at this time, he suggested he would surely give it every consideration and if it was at all possible he would be in accord with me, "But may I ask what it is?" [The president responded:] "I am sick and tired of boiled shirts, stiff collars, and white ties. After the war you and I will set the fashion in men's wear—no more dress suits, cutaways, tails, etc. We will wear soft shirts and soft collars and no white ties." Winston said he was in entire accord.

Just before December 7 I was talking with the president one day, when he said, "I am afraid you are going to be here for a long time." He said: "If Flynn takes a post"—an embassy or a legation, he said, "you will have to take over the national committee."

I said: "We will cross that bridge when we come to it."

He said: "There is one thing certain. If this war isn't over we will all be renting or renewing office again. You and I and a lot of the rest of us might be on an island down around the South Sea Islands."

Last night at the cabinet dinner the president said: "How are you getting on in your negotiations for the Roosevelt books?" I said: "I cut him down a little." He said: "Don't forget I am Dutch." The president made a beautiful talk at the dinner. At former cabinet dinners he was always opposed to toasts to those members who had passed on. He said last night, "I shall refrain from doing that tonight because I think they are with us." He said: "My sole toast shall be to the USA."

Monday, January 26, 1942. I was talking with the president Saturday and Sunday and again this evening. He said: "Wavell sent this message to MacArthur saying what he thought should be done. 'If you think it necessary I will come to you personally, however, I will outline my program of action. Will you please let me know what suggestions you have with reference to it. I will be very happy to get your advice and thought and I will be happy to follow it.' MacArthur wired back: 'Under no circumstances should you come. Your job is different than mine. Am in entire accord with your program. My job is here and yours is there and is entirely different. It is too great a hazard for you to come and you shouldn't do it.'"[9]

The question came up about Quezon.[10] It was felt it was necessary for Philippine morale to have Quezon carry on. Requests made from many sources to have Quezon brought from the Islands to Australia. MacArthur advised that the hazard was much too great. He said: "I too would like to have Quezon set up government someplace else but because of the submarines around the Islands, leaving here would be subject to too great telling attacks."

The president said: "I didn't know that an Irishman was a good trader. You must have some Scotch in you because you have worked out a better deal for those papers than even a Dutchman like me could do. Cousin Ellie is finally penitent. She left word for me that she has some more papers and that I can have all she has. I don't think she will sell any more. Isn't that grand?"

I told him Hallie and I were opening the Red Cross room in the post office today and he said, "What did she serve?" I told him, "Punch," and he wanted to know if there was a stick in it. When I told him, "No," he said, "Isn't that terrible to serve punch without a stick in it?"

I had quite a talk with him about Hopkins. He said once he had a strong physique and could take a Scotch at noon, one in the evening, and one before going to bed. He said: "I can never drink at noon. A drink or two before dinner is plenty for me. I think association with Winston will kill Harry, if it hasn't already done it."

[FDR] "I wish that on your trip you would keep your eyes and ears open and tell me frankly what you think about the country's reaction."

While I was with the president Friday, Justice Roberts called him and asked when he should give him his report on the Pearl Harbor attack.[11] He said, "Shall I come over this afternoon?" and the president said, "Wish you would come tomorrow instead."

"Frank," he said, "we will have many changes around here. I am going to need so much help and so much assistance. It's not these days I am so worried about, it's the days to come."

His secretariat and the crowd around the White House wanted to buy the books for him, but he said, "I told them I wouldn't allow them to spend their money on this, that I wanted to give my own personal check."

When he started to talk about his family he interrupted, saying, "When we get a little more leisure we will sit down and talk about these things. I have a lot of things to tell you about several generations of the Roosevelts."

Tuesday, April 7, 1942. Meeting at the White House—first meeting after the trip to the coast. Something very confidential was told that was described as a really startling revelation.

Monday, April 20, 1942. [Walker went to General Watson's house in Virginia over the weekend of April 11 and rode down with the president, who told some interesting stories.] As a youngster, his father had an uncle who was very wealthy but miserly. Although a man of considerable fortune, he lived in a shack down in Greenwich Village, and each Christmas during the holidays his family used to dress him and his cousin, a Bailey, who afterward became archbishop of Baltimore, a predecessor of Gibbons, and send them down to visit the old fellow, hoping that part of his great fortune would go to them.[12] But all this was to no avail because he left everything to Roosevelt Hospital, which is now a liability to the entire family because they are all making contributions trying to keep it together.

When [Walker] was leaving the president on their return on Sunday, April 12, he [FDR] said he was then going in to look at his charts. He said the charts were all up-to-date now and show where every outfit is centered over the entire world.[13]

He said he would like to see Owen Young nominated for governor because he is the only one he thought could win in New York. Said he thought he would bring Lehman down here shortly.[14] Said he offered a job to Kennedy but it wasn't a top-notch job and Joe wants nothing but a top job. He is very temperamental. He talked about Hugh Johnson, who died just a day or two afterwards. Said he never could have been a real West Point graduate because to be one of these a fellow had to be a scholar and a gentleman, and he said Hugh could never qualify as a gentleman.[15]

He told the story about Teddy R. being abroad at the time of the death of old King Edward and how Taft appointed him to be the representative of the U.S. government and how he was made a pallbearer. He said the old king and the queen had really never even been friendly, having not lived together for years, and he related how Teddy had reported that the queen had brought him in to view the corpse and observed to him, "Doesn't he look natural?" and he, never having seen him before, replied, "He certainly does."[16]

Teddy, not being a king or an emperor or a potentate, was assigned to carriage number sixteen, but then it developed that the potentates from some of the smaller and less important countries got into a row about precedence and he gave up his place to them and he went alone.

He said that Taft and Teddy were at the funeral of Whitelaw Reid and at the time Teddy was mad at Taft.[17] He said that just as Taft got to the casket after the ceremonies, a group of Marines started to pick up the casket, and there was a moment of confusion when Taft apparently didn't know whether to stop or go forward, at which point Teddy said in a stage whisper that could be heard all over the church, "I didn't know there was ever any question of precedence among the dead."

The president said he was always sorry that Taft and Teddy didn't settle their differences before they died.

He said he voted for Roosevelt against Parker.[18]

We discussed the negotiations with Japan before the war and I observed that we had exercised every possible means of settling our differences. He said that he thought we went much further in trying to avoid war with Japan than was our duty. I said if it wasn't for our conduct of these negotiations Germany never would have assailed Russia at the time they did, which gave us many needed months. He said if it hadn't been for the war party in Japan we might have been able to settle without war. He said this has killed Cordell Hull. Said he, Cordell Hull, did a grand job trying to avert it.

He said the time he met Churchill on the seas last summer that Churchill was very anxious to break relations with Japan then and he said he talked him out of it.[19]

He said Frank Murphy wanted to go to the Philippines but that he felt it would risk too many lives of a crew taking him over in a submarine and getting back.[20] Said he thought he would send him to Australia because Murphy and Quezon are good friends and he could do a lot of good in setting up the Philippine Government in Australia.

On April 13, 1942, said next six or eight months will be terrible.

Tuesday, July 28, 1942. Last Saturday, July 25, Mrs. W. and I went with X [President Roosevelt] to participate in the final trials of the good ship *Shangri-La* over the weekend.[21] The first trial was held the previous weekend. Over the weekend we were talking about the day before inauguration in 1933. He said:

> In conformity with the custom over the years, followed in every instance except in the case of Andrew Jackson's predecessor, Mrs. R. and I called at the White House to visit the president and Mrs. Hoover, and Jimmie went with us.[22] You know how large the Red Room is? Well, Mrs. H. was away over at one corner, I was at another corner, the president was a very considerable distance from me, and Eleanor was in still another corner. It was just like playing puss in the corner. The situation was very tense and embarrassing and it was very difficult to make conversation. Finally when I decided it was time to leave I suggested, as I rose, that in view of the fact he was so busy during these troubled times, let us agree that he would not have to follow the amenity of calling upon me. This was also a custom in vogue by all presidents . . . Can you imagine the answer that I got? Mr. H. said, "When you become president you will come to learn that the president of the United States calls upon nobody." Of course I was furious, Jimmie was mad enough to take a swing at him, and Eleanor turned white. As soon as we got in our car Eleanor said, "Let us think up somebody we can call upon in Washington very soon." If you will remember, three days later Mrs. R. and I called on Justice Holmes—it was his ninetieth birthday.

I asked the president if it wasn't a very long trip from the White House to the Capitol on the morning of inauguration. He said:

> It was terribly long, and frightful. We drove out of the northeast gate and a big crowd assembled there started to cheer. I very foolishly, should have known better, doffed my hat and waved, but he, with his dill-pickled

expression, made no response whatsoever. As we turned the corner below the White House, I said very courteously, "They were cheering you, Mr. President," but he merely grunted. The crowd kept cheering as we went on down Pennsylvania Avenue and I decided to wave in response. As we passed your building [the post office building, which was just being erected] I very inanely said, "Isn't that fine steel?" As we passed another building a moment later I said, "What building is that?" and he said very gruffly, "That's the labor building," and I said, "That's fine steel too."

You know Mr. and Mrs. H. were one of four couples [during the Wilson administration] who had the custom of entertaining each other at supper on Sunday nights. Franklin K. Lane was one of the others.[23] H. was anxious to indicate that he was a Democrat and wanted to get a few votes in the coming Democratic convention. Lane said that was a good idea and agreed to help him get a few delegates from California. He said, "You can have them vote for you on the first ballot, and then sign a letter withdrawing before the second ballot. That will give you the Democratic Party." This was agreeable to Hoover. However, sometime afterwards I was at dinner at the Lodges and we got discussing Mr. Hoover. I told her he was a Democrat and she said, "Oh, no, the old man [her husband, Senator Henry Cabot Lodge] took him into camp at dinner the other night and said he will run for president on the Republican ticket."

A very good friend of mine named Curtin, a contractor in Australia, told me that Hoover was doing some work in Australia with him and that a couple of months before the job was to be completed Hoover told my friend the contractor that he was going to return to America. He said, "You know I can't stay away from there too long because I expect to run for president sometime." He also told me that according to British authority one who votes in a general election in England becomes a citizen. If one votes in one of the smaller or supervisory elections it qualifies him to vote in the general election. It is established beyond the question of a doubt that Hoover had voted in supervisory elections and there is evidence that he had voted in a general election, which would make him a citizen, but it was never proved that he had voted in a general election.

I remember one Sunday evening I was sitting around the house in an old bathrobe and a soft shirt and Mrs. R. had on a wrapper. There was a ring at the doorbell and I answered and a friend of ours and his wife were at the door. I said, "Come in, delighted to see you," and just as we were seated the doorbell rang again and another couple came, and finally four or five couples arrived. It finally dawned on us that they were the same crowd we thought we had invited for the following Sunday. We only had a few things in the icebox but we scraped everything together and I gave them enough cocktails so that they didn't care whether they had anything to eat or not.

The maddest I ever got was the night of the Philadelphia acceptance speech.[24] I always get mad when the hinge on my brace loosens, and as Jimmie and I were coming in that night the brace loosened. I had my speech in my hand and the sheets went in all different directions. Jimmie had great difficulty, but with some aid he finally got the speech back together, with all the pages dirty, and we went through the crowd, and just at that point the mayor of the city came over and sat on my lap and said, "Mr. President, it isn't true we are charging $3.50 for a steak in Philadelphia." Joe Robinson got up and made a nice speech. I thought he was going to introduce me but instead he introduced Garner. Garner, who had never read a speech in his life, started to read a manuscript, and the papers would rustle against the mike and were making noise. Somebody told Halsey and he went up and started to whisper to Garner, "Pull down the sheets, pull down the sheets." The whispering could be heard on the radio and finally Garner asked, "Pull down what sheets?" When I got up that night I was madder than the devil.

I said, "Yes, that was the night you made the economic royalist speech?" He said, "Yes, that was the night."

He said he was a member of the firm (Carter, Nevin, and Milburn) when Mrs. William Leeds married the uncle of the present king of Greece and he was sent by the firm to draft the prenuptial agreement. He afterwards entertained the king here. They were afterwards separated and he drafted the will, which left so much to Billie Leeds, Jr., who married Princess Xenia, living out on Long Island.

He spoke very nicely of Jim Farley. Said he thought he would be a good candidate for governor, that he could win and ought to run. Said, "Never in my life felt unkindly toward Jim."

I went up to see Queen Wilhelmina and, you know, I was scared to death, and was telling Eleanor. She said, "What do you mean? That isn't true," and I told her she is one queen who is smart as the devil, she's a brilliant woman and has not been one that has no jurisdiction—she always ruled with an iron hand. While there the queen and I sat talking, and Crown Princess Martha and Juliana were also there and they were talking.[25] Afterwards Martha told me that Juliana had told her that her mother had said that "President Roosevelt is coming and I'm scared to death because he knows so much—he is so smart about the world's affairs."

Thursday, October 14, 1942. Australians [said the president] have shown no spirit and have fallen down terribly. Two or three times the force of Japs pushed them back eighteen miles; on the other hand, when the Americans attacked the Japs they went right through and the Australians don't understand why the Americans are able to do this and they cannot.

Just before Churchill went to visit Stalin, R. sent word to Stalin that he learned from what he thought to be a reliable authority that the Japs would not attack Siberia. Stalin asked Churchill what he thought, and he said he didn't know; consequently R. stuck his chin all the way out because, unquestionably, Stalin concentrated all his force on the Eastern [German] Front.

R. said that he didn't have any unkindly feeling toward Jim F. and that he thought he ought to be the candidate himself.

Saturday, November 12, 1942. In the middle of the ocean, with fourteen days to go, charts showed that fifteen submarines appeared in front of them. Convoy turned south to get away and the fifteen submarines turned south, but they avoided the submarines entirely. At about a hundred miles from the destination twenty submarines congregated and were sighted. The tides off Casablanca were against them, however, and only one of the transports was hit. It is true that they got the invasion boats off over one hundred miles from shore and succeeded in landing every man safely.

Monday, December 5, 1942. Conversation regarding candidate for 1944.

[Walker] "Well, there's one fellow you are playing up who hasn't got a chance in the world—that's H. W. [Henry Wallace]."

[FDR] "I think you are right."

[Walker] "You are the only one who would have a chance."

[FDR] "Get thee behind me, Satan."

Friday, December. 17, 1943. President returned from Cairo and Iran—cabinet meeting. Said Stalin kidded C. through most of the meeting. Said:

Stalin and I agreed on a division of Germany into five separate units. Up to the north around Hamburg the ports will be free to all nations; the Saar Basin and Ruhr will be under some protectorate.

At all their meetings they were apparently having difficulty in getting Stalin to agree to the freedom of Iran. I finally convinced him after I agreed that we would have an international port, which would give him a warm-water port. This he said sounded all right to him and he agreed.

I was surprised when he agreed about Manchuria. I thought there would be some opposition but there wasn't. He also agreed that we would have a port, Dairen, international in character, free to all nations, as we have at Hamburg, at a point in the north for an exit to Siberia.

Said he made the suggestion that we would have to have an international police force, and he said we would have to have international police stations so the force could immediately suppress any hostilities.

Said that somebody in our group must have slipped because he [Stalin] said, "What about Dakar?"

[FDR] said, "I always had this in the back of my head."

Stalin said, "Would you run Dakar?" and I said, "We would run it but as an agent for the United Nations." Somebody in our crowd must have slipped.

> I was inclined to think the view of Stalin would not be in favor of having China one of the Big Four. Of course Churchill was never in favor of having China—"Don't you think that is right, Cordell?" Hull said not only not in favor—much against it. Although he had been working on this subject for two years he hasn't agreed to give up Hong Kong and had said the day after they gave up Hong Kong, Chiang would take it over as a national state. Stalin said he didn't care whether China was one of the Big Four.
>
> I had more difficulty with Britain than either of the other two at the conference. Churchill said they would never give up Dakar and I have an expression I had used for similar statements of his on other occasions, "Oh, yeah?" which I used at that point.

Said it is very regrettable so many people seem to have the notion the war is over. Says we are going to have many more serious casualties—the war is far from over. So far as starting the second front early is concerned, we had considerable difficulty with Churchill but he finally conceded to our viewpoint.

> I found Chiang a very fine little person—quite serious and silent, but at times his face would light up with a beautiful smile.
>
> We didn't discuss Palestine.
>
> Came back on the biggest warship in the world, the *Iowa*. When I saw my little boat, which was to pick me up to bring me to Washington, I thought it had shrunk.[26] Had a grand trip. It was great fun.
>
> Churchill was very much in favor of a powerful French nation. Stalin said that the only thing that would ever save the French would be to get rid of the old leaders and elect new men under forty years who had nothing to do with politics. They are a decadent nation, decadent people—who had lost their spirit and it would take a long time before they became a great nation again. Stalin said he was in entire accord with us that we should take care of Germany—and we should see to it she is not able under any circumstances to start another war in twenty years: "I am anxious to do everything within my power to bring about their full and complete defeat at as early a date as possible. We must defeat them absolutely. So far as Japan is concerned, I hope you do to the Japs what I want to do to Germany."

Wednesday, December 22, 1943. Lunch with P. Said I ought to keep in the back of my mind that if they nominate Bricker or even Dewey we should try to get Willkie on our side.[27] Said he would make a deal with him. Asked him pointblank, "Who do you want for your VP candidate?"

"We have three candidates—Sam R., Jimmie Byrnes, and Wallace.[28] We could give Wallace some international assignment—Sam would be all right but I don't know whether he would be helpful politically." Said we have to talk politics once a week from now on.

I asked what he thought about Norman Baxter as publicity man for the committee—said he didn't know him. Said he wanted a tough SOB who could write short stories indicting Dewey, Bricker, Landon, Hoover, one after another, with skill and ease.[29]

I told him there were many bad situations around the country and he then said we have to meet every week. Agreed to have the reception for the national committee without the slightest hesitation, and agreed to see members of Senate and Congress.

I asked him what he was going to do about the R.R. strike and he indicated that he was inclined to take them over. I told him as forcibly as I could that I thought this would be the worst thing he could do—that the transportation system would break down, that he couldn't get men out of the army who could run the railroad system, that it would cause starvation and chaos, even for a day. He asked about a National Service Act—I told him I thought this would be better but that it meant political ruin. He said, "That's all right, it might do some good some other ways." I think I sold him the idea of not taking over the R.R.s. It would be a miracle if he could run them.

Churchill wasn't very well when he came over, and he said to him, "You're looking kind of pasty."

C. said, "I've got dysentery."

R. said, "Well, you don't mean to tell me you didn't bring your bottle of water with you from the boat?"

C. said, "You don't think water ever passed my lips, do you? I never drink water, Mr. P."

Said, "We ought to have a very late convention." I observed about the middle of July. He said, "No, the middle of July is much too early."

He is for Palestine. Said the head of the Arabian government told him that the only time he had been insulted was when an Englishman representing American J's came to him and offered twenty million pounds for a refuge for the J's.

Thursday, December 23, 1944. Bill Bullitt told me that he stayed in Paris [in 1940] at the insistence of the French government and at their expense, because they thought that if he stayed on he could help save Paris from being destroyed.[30] He said while he was there the president called him one night and said he should leave at once or he might become a prisoner of war and possibly lose his life. Bullitt asked him why he hadn't told him sooner because, he said, "I would look terrible leaving now." Bullitt said he put it straight up to the president about the army or navy. R. had promised him an appointment to either the secretary of war or navy, and he (Bullitt) said they wouldn't do anything to him in view of this if he would make the announcement of the appointment.

Bullitt said the president said, "All right, I will make the announcement of your appointment to the navy."

Bullitt says he was amazed, therefore, when within the next few days the appointments of Stimson and Knox came out.[31] "And when I came back about the twenty-fifth of June, I said, 'What the hell did you do to me?'"

The president said, "Why, didn't you know I sent you a telegram?"

I said, "You did no such thing."

"I did, didn't you get it?"

Bullitt said, "I will go over and check at the State Department," but then a twinkle came in the president's eye and he admitted he didn't send it.

The president recently gave Bullitt hell for disseminating the story about Welles. The damage that was done could never be undone. Of course Bullitt said he had to do it. The Boss had to get rid of this fellow.[32]

Churchill, by the way, was very much opposed to opening the second front across the Channel. Stalin simply said, "Do you want to fight or don't you?" On one occasion Churchill made about a ten-minute impassioned speech about blood and sweat, etc., but not arriving any place particularly, and when he finished Stalin said promptly, "And now have we got anything else to discuss?"

1944, undated. On the evening of July 19, Ed Flynn was sitting in Room 705 at the Blackstone Hotel describing the activities of one of the so-called political leaders.[33] He had just finished remarking that this leader reminded him of the old Irish woman named Sarah who had her head out the window all day long, leaning on her elbows and firing away to the woman across the alley, "Didya hear about so-and-so and so-and-so and so-and-so?" (this all with gestures), when the phone rang and the so-called leader advised Mr. Walker that he had just heard the rumor that the New York delegation had shifted to Wallace and that he had been trying to locate Mr. Flynn and that they better try to find him right away and advise him. Mr. Walker explained that he would try to locate Mr. Flynn and bring him up to date. He turned to Mr. Flynn and informed him of this new development, whereupon Mr. Flynn observed, "That's just what I mean."

Saturday, October 14, 1944. Yesterday he [Cordell Hull] called me from his bed and asked me to call upon him, which I did about 8:15 P.M. He had been ill for the past two weeks and had been confined to his bed. When I went in he was lying in bed, and after our greetings he said:

> I am going to tell you something in the strictest confidence. You are the only person outside of my wife who knows this. When I ran for the Senate the last time, a well-known specialist advised me I should not become a candidate because I had a spot on my lung and a touch of diabetes and I could not stand the campaign. My own doctor advised otherwise, and I made the campaign and I have been in very good condition for a number of years. As you know, during the negotiations which we were having with the Japanese a recurrence came in the lung condition, which according to the doctors had covered with tissue over the years. During part of these discussions I suffered greatly and at times had to use a morphine solution to soothe my throat. However, the condition cleared up very considerably as the days went on, until during the months of May and June this year I had so many things to care for and so many conferences to attend that it all created intense distress. The attack returned and the doctors now advise me that the diabetes has reached the advance stage and "this thing" on my lung is much worse.

He then broke into tears and said:

> Frank, this is the first time I have ever done this but I can't help it. I wanted so much to head up this great conference and to attain my objective of peace in the world, and here I find myself just unable to do it.[34] I am sure I will not be able to work again, and I am not sure I will ever be able to leave this bed.
>
> I wish you would tell this to the president. I am at the earliest possible moment going to draft a statement on foreign policy to cover the entire situation. I am very anxious to have Long, Acheson, and Berle proclaim my views.[35] It is so essential that our administration carry on and bring this to a successful conclusion.
>
> I very much fear that the newspapers will get a hold of this, which would just be terrible, because you and the president and my own wife are the only people to whom I have confided this information.

Friday, December 22, 1944. At the cabinet it was decided to stop racing in the United States. Reason was it proved very bad for the war effort and for the morale of soldiers. In Florida for example they have a track right next to a rehabilitation camp and the effect is bad. The government doesn't get anything out of all the money that is being gambled away, and automobiles and gasoline are being used and a lot of 4-Fs are used taking care of horses.[36]

Stimson said he wasn't unduly alarmed at this stage of the German break-through.[37] Said if the breaks go our way we will stem it, and if the Germans get in too far it will set us back more than a year. We are still holding two bases—the only bases of importance—and if we can stem this the war may end much quicker. Said this offensive is very much like the last three or four attacks the Germans made in 1918. Said he had been with the British and just left in time or he would have been captured.

We haven't got enough nurses to take care of people over there. The casualties are terrific. Said we must go into the higher categories of the draft. And told me that Mrs. Ameno's husband is up in front lines now.[38]

Said this was not unexpected and we are preparing for a counteroffensive but thinks we might have to put it off. Says we must be calm and careful in viewing situation.

Decided to go ahead with renewing contracts for shipbuilding instead of curtailing. New contracts will be let for Liberties, which they had stopped, and they will keep on program for Victory boats.[39]

Said we haven't enough nurses over there now and we have to do something about that.

They are shortening the training time at officers' camps from seventeen to fifteen weeks. Said Eisenhower said Hodges's job was magnificent in handling situation.[40] Terribly handicapped by rain and fog and every indication will continue serious handicap. Hoping Montgomery will do something with his troops. Said he is overcautious and will make no move until he is sure he will win.

Saturday, January 6, 1945. Secretary Stimson said yesterday that we have on the front 1,600,000 combat troops—800,000 supply and 250,000 reserves in France. In tonnage we lost only the equivalent of one day's delivery by shipping in this general attack. In combat now we have forty-seven American divisions, plus three reserve divisions—eight French divisions and fourteen British divisions. Patton says the 11th is right up with the Third Army now and that with any kind of a break at all we are going to win the whole war right here. However, Stimson doesn't agree with that at all. Stimson says that if we can cut off the German salient the amount of equipment, etc. that will be lost should be enough to wreck their army. We have seventy-two divisions and the Germans have the equivalent of seventy-two, but their divisions are not as large as ours. However, they can if necessary bring additional divisions from the east. We have purposely made a withdrawal from the south of the Seventh Army, a withdrawal that is orderly and planned, and if successful we will have the advantage of a two-pincers movement north and south to cut off the salient. If we succeed it will be disastrous to the Germans. Thus we have a great chance here but the secretary is making no predictions.

Frank Walker with his wife, Hallie, and daughter, Laura, at home in 1943. Photograph courtesy the Walker family.

We have lost in and around Leyte about sixty-four ships. A good many of these were destroyed by the new suicide groups. The Jap suicide groups consist of young men who are not their best-line fighters. They install them with great ceremony—dress them in silk, confer all war honors upon them, and then turn over a new plane to them. They are supposed to take the plane with explosives and dive right on one of our warships or transports. Very considerable damage was done in this fashion to the *Iowa*. It really became quite a menace, but we are handling the problem pretty well, now that we know what they are trying to do, and they haven't been doing as much damage recently as formerly because we understand and have larger guns on our aircraft and boats. We have a picture at the navy showing one of our battleships and three of these suicide groups missing the ship by as little as two hundred yards in front and on one side. One of these young Japs who had been duly installed was found by our men, and he told them that he had taken along a parachute when he found out that they were actually giving him an old plane at the time of the takeoff and he bailed out. Said he had been sold on the idea of doing this and was willing to do it but that they couldn't fool him with that trick. That if he was willing to do this, they should at least have been willing to give him a new plane.

April 15, 1945. Presidential train returning from Hyde Park. McNutt made a speech against giving the Philippines their independence this year. Josephus Daniels wrote the Boss and told him he had never tried to advise him on such matters because he was much wiser than he, but that he thought it would be terrible not to give them their independence.[41] The president wrote to him in return that he hoped to give them their independence on July 4 of this year, but then thought it would be better to give it to them on the Philippines Independence Day, which is August 6, and that he hoped to be there for it but was afraid that he couldn't.

Byrnes telephoned and insisted that he be assigned to one of the private cars going to Hyde Park and I am told that Farley asked permission to go to Hyde Park and was denied permission by Mrs. Roosevelt, but I haven't confirmed that.

I had luncheon with the Boss on March 16 and I am told that at the time he intended to ask me to withdraw from the cabinet and become his secretary. After I left him on that day and went into the Cabinet Room, Grace Tully asked him if he had made the request, and he said "I lost my nerve. I was afraid Frank might not want to leave the cabinet and that he might feel he would be stepping down, but I can let it go until later. I will ask him when I return from the trip.[42]

When we were talking with Mrs. Roosevelt on the car yesterday, returning from Hyde Park, she told Mrs. Walker and me that "Franklin had always looked upon me as one of his closest personal friends and felt that he always could count upon me." She also quoted the president as saying, "The Walkers always did their part in a very nice way."

Hallie and I, on our way from Hyde Park, dropped in to see the new president, and in the first room of the car we met Mrs. Truman, who was seated watching her daughter and Mrs. Hannegan play gin rummy.[43] I told her we had come to pay our respects to the president, and she said, "He would be very happy to see you." She started to take us in, but I asked her if she wouldn't announce us first. She did and returned, saying the president would be very glad to see us. As we were going in he rushed into his drawing room to put on his coat, as he had been in his shirtsleeves. When we came to the rear of his car Harold Ickes was there. Harold left very shortly.

The president and I had a talk, and Mrs. Walker and Mrs. Truman conversed with each other. The president said, "Frank, I appreciate your letter very much. I know nothing of foreign affairs and I must acquaint myself with them at once. I must make two speeches—one to Congress on Monday and

Frank Walker with his son aboard the *Cassidy* in New York Harbor in 1944. Photograph courtesy University of Notre Dame Archives.

another on Tuesday. These matters will keep me busy for the next two days. After Tuesday, I would like to have a two-hour talk with you. There are many things I would like to take up with you."

Bill Hassett told me the last official thing the president [FDR] did was to approve my recommendation that he purchase the United Nations stamp at the [United Nations] Conference from the postmaster of San Francisco.[44] Grace Tully told me that the president sent two letters to Jimmy Byrnes—the official letter and another, which he dictated to her.[45] The second letter read something like the following: "Dear Jim: I was shocked when I got your letter

Frank Walker with actress Jane Wyman in 1943. Photograph courtesy University of Notre Dame Archives.

of resignation. I had hoped you would stay on until the affair came near completion. . . FDR."

April 20, 1945. When FDR made the announcement of Clayton-Rockefeller and Stettinius, he left for Warm Springs, and Mrs. Roosevelt called him up down there and told him all about the repercussions and raised the devil with him, particularly about appointing Clayton. Anna Boettiger told me later when we were discussing these appointments that "Father hung up the phone on Mother."[46]

Today at the White House when the members of the cabinet and their wives came at my suggestion to bid good-bye to Mrs. Roosevelt, she said to me within earshot of most of the cabinet, "Frank, Franklin always had a great affection for you. He always felt that he could depend upon you to do anything that he wanted you to do."

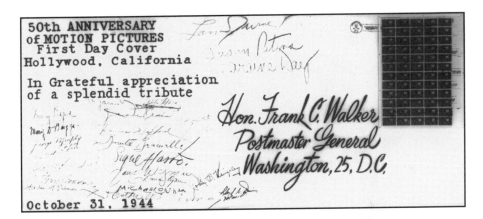

Some of these names are familiar. Photograph courtesy University of Notre Dame Archives.

Mr. and Mrs. Frank C. Walker in 1945. Photograph courtesy Santa Fe Railway and University of Notre Dame Archives.

10

CHOOSING A VICE PRESIDENT

resident Roosevelt on August 31, 1940, designated me as postmaster
general to succeed James A. Farley, who had submitted his resignation.
Farley had likewise resigned as chairman of the Democratic National Committee. As Farley's successor, the national committee selected Ed Flynn of the
Bronx, longtime confidant and political adviser to the president and his secretary of state when Franklin D. Roosevelt was governor of New York. In January 1943, Flynn resigned as chairman of the Democratic National Committee.
On January 17 of that year the national committee designated me as his successor. I accepted the post very reluctantly and only at the urgent insistence of
the president.

I made one point very clear before I became chairman of the Democratic
National Committee. It was that my tenure of office would be brief, lasting
only until a suitable successor could be found. In the summer of 1943 I
reminded President Roosevelt of this. For the next few months lists of prospective candidates were drawn up and their qualifications carefully examined.

It is interesting to note that the then junior senator from Missouri was
among those considered. The same factors that were later to be in his favor as
a nominee for the vice presidency also counted for him in 1943. He was from a
Midwest pivotal state, he had the respect and affection of his colleagues in the
Democratic Party, and he was a consistent supporter of President Roosevelt's
social and economic aims. Moreover, Truman was becoming more and more

Frank Walker turning over the chairmanship of the Democratic National Committee to Robert E. Hannegan in 1944. Photograph courtesy University of Notre Dame Archives.

favorably known to the public in his role as chairman of the Senate committee investigating the conduct of the war, better known as the Truman Committee. But in this capacity Senator Truman's contributions to the war effort and to the morale of the country were so effective that it was considered inadvisable to divert his energies to other channels.

So Truman was saved for a greater role, and on such seemingly insignificant incidents do the destinies of men and nations turn. For if Senator Truman had been offered the post of chairman of the Democratic National Committee, it is my opinion that he would have accepted. In all probability, then, he would not have been selected as President Roosevelt's running mate in 1944 and there would have been another occupant of the White House. It is equally probable, incidentally, that Dr. Gallup and Mr. Kaltenborn, among others, would not have suffered such acute embarrassment on November 3, 1948.[1]

Be that as it may, Robert E. Hannegan of St. Louis, then commissioner of internal revenue, was finally selected to succeed me. On January 21, 1944, he became chairman of the Democratic National Committee.

It was soon after this that Ed Flynn made one of his frequent trips to Washington to see the president. He was due at the White House one evening, but he had previously arranged to call me as soon as he left the president. I was in my office about ten that evening with Bill Cronin, then my executive assistant in the post office, when Flynn telephoned. He asked us to come directly to his suite at the Mayflower. We found him in a terribly agitated condition. He told us he was certain that Roosevelt would not even consider running for a fourth term. His health would not stand it. In any event FDR would not run. His mind was made up.

But as we know now, and neither for the first nor the last time in his life, Roosevelt changed his mind. There was very little discussion about anybody for the presidency in 1944, as I remember it, except Roosevelt. In 1940 there was a lot of discussion as to other candidates by Roosevelt himself, but in 1944 there was very little discussion about anybody running for president except Roosevelt.

Roosevelt didn't look well in my judgment, but I didn't think, nor did anybody who knew him intimately think, that his health was seriously impaired. For a long time he had been making very few public appearances and had used his braces very seldom; they had gotten to a point where they were very burdensome to him. He discussed on one occasion, I remember, getting a new set of braces and then decided not to do it. And I remember there was some discussion before he decided to be a candidate as to how he would make public appearances and then I remember he agreed he would not use braces and that he would make his speeches while seated rather than standing. The braces were very heavy and I don't think he had the same strength in his legs he had before. It was very difficult for him to move the braces.[2]

He made all his speeches in 1944, as I remember it, seated. I was with him the major portion of that trip. I was with him in Philadelphia, I was with him in Chicago, I was with him in Boston. I was with him in New York when he made his foreign policy speech. On every occasion, as I remember it, he was seated.

I sat in an automobile; I sat beside him in Philadelphia. I have never seen such enthusiasm—and they say he wasn't well!—as he had on that Philadelphia trip. He was very much pleased with the reception he got as we went through Philadelphia and very much pleased with the reception they gave him at the baseball field where he made his talk. I remember as we drove around the baseball field and were going out he made the comment: "Frank," he said, "isn't it strange? Women always jump up and down when they're excited. Men never do but women always do. Why is that?"

I also went to Boston with him one night. I joined the party in Connecticut. I remember Senator Walsh joined us before we got into Boston and I

Edwin W. Pauley with Frank Walker in 1943. Photograph courtesy University of Notre Dame Archives.

went and spoke to him about making an appearance with the president in Boston.[3] I think I asked the senator to introduce him. But Walsh was very hesitant and would not agree to do it. At that time I think there was a discussion also about Joe Kennedy making an appearance in Boston, and he sent word because of the recent death of his son that he wasn't making public appearances.[4] Dever, too, who was running for governor that year, evaded appearing with the president in Boston.[5] Roosevelt won, of course, and Dever lost, running way behind the ticket, and a lot of people thought he lost because of his failure to appear with the president.

Based upon conversations I had with various persons throughout the country, there was very little discussion of anybody for the presidency in 1944; there was some discussion in 1943 but only because nobody seemed to know whether Roosevelt would run again in 1944. But it was more or less taken for granted, I think, even in 1943, that he would be a candidate. By spring 1944 it seemed a sure thing that the president would run if the Democratic Party nominated him. And of that, of course, there was not the slightest doubt.

The next step was to select the most suitable running mate as the nominee for vice president. Henry Wallace was not nearly as active in 1944 as he was earlier in the war. But by 1944 quite a few of us were in doubt as to whether Roosevelt really wanted Henry. He didn't express himself. He did send a letter to Wallace in which he said that if he were a delegate and going to vote, he would vote for Wallace. But I think that was done more as a courtesy because, after all, they had been associated as president and vice president for four years, and for eight years before that Wallace was serving as secretary of agriculture. He was serving as vice president and Roosevelt felt the only thing for him to do was to vote for him, as he had said. Apart from that, I don't think he did want him—I never will feel that he really wanted Wallace as a running mate in 1944.

I don't think that Alben Barkley's famous rebellion from the floor of the Senate when the president made his celebrated veto of the tax bill weighed with Roosevelt in reaching the decision that Barkley would not be the right vice presidential candidate. It was Barkley's age more than anything else that brought Roosevelt to the conclusion that Barkley should not be the candidate.[6]

I think if Roosevelt could have had his own way and if he felt he could get the support of the convention, he would have selected Bill Douglas as vice president. He indicated that more than once.

Of all those considered, Jimmy Byrnes seemed the best qualified. So at the president's request I called for Byrnes one afternoon when we were leaving our respective offices. As we rode through Rock Creek Park, I sounded him out as to whether he would be receptive to a place on the Democratic ticket as the president's running mate. His answer was unequivocal. Barkis indeed was willing.[7]

We come now to the celebrated dinner at the White House on the night of July 11, 1944. Both George Allen and Jonathan Daniels have listed the names of the guests in their accounts of this same subject.[8] The president sat at the head of the table. Also present were Bob Hannegan, Ed Pauley, Mayor Ed Kelly of Chicago, Ed Flynn, and myself.[9] Anna Roosevelt's husband, John Boettiger, joined us later.

We had dinner with the president that night and afterwards met in the Oval Room, his study. We had quite a discussion that night about various candidates. I remember Rayburn was discussed, and Bill Douglas, Barkley, and Henry Wallace and Harry Truman.[10]

Something I had never seen indicated before came up in the discussion—that was the discussion by Ed Kelly. Ed Kelly was very strong in the support of Bill Douglas. Some writer, whose name I have forgotten, had written a magazine article, I think, about Douglas. At the time he was writing it he had gotten in touch with Kelly in Chicago and had discussed Douglas with Kelly. Kelly became quite enthusiastic about Douglas and so expressed himself at the meeting.

There was a discussion also about Jimmy Byrnes, as to whether or not his Catholicism would react against him, by that I mean his leaving the Catholic Church.[11] I think the consensus of opinion was that it would not, although I have heard others say it would be inimical to his interests.

There was some discussion by the president and others as to Jim Byrnes's labor record and his attitude on the Negro question. It seemed to be the consensus of opinion that the Negro question did not help his candidacy any and that his labor record was such that he surely would not get the enthusiastic support of the labor group.[12] I do not think there was any indication that anybody felt labor would be necessarily opposed to him, but I think they all felt they would not be enthusiastic about his candidacy.

There was quite a bit of discussion about Truman. Now, I have heard it said that Hannegan advanced the candidacy of Truman. I do not think that is true. In all my discussions with Hannegan, not once did he advocate the candidacy of Truman merely because of their friendship.[13] I think he weighed Truman in the balance, just as everybody else did, and I could not say that Bob was an impassioned advocate. He felt that Truman would be a good candidate. And I remembered something that I think most people had forgotten, that next to the president Truman was the most outstanding man in Washington due to the fine job he had done on his committee. I remember that when I had been in California, I had not run into Senator Truman myself. But I did see some members of the Truman Committee and heard many favorable comments about the very fine work he had been doing with his committee.

Ed Pauley spoke favorably of Rayburn; everybody there spoke favorably of Rayburn and Barkley. But I do not think these names were seriously considered at the meeting.

Ed Kelly, as I said before, spoke very favorably of Douglas, and the president did, as well. I think there was some indication, however, by whom I have forgotten, that Douglas might have some difficulty in getting any support in the convention as he had never been very active in the party.

The names of the most logical candidates for the vice presidential nomination were brought up, discussed pro and con, and then discarded. Every name except one—that of Harry S. Truman.

Finally the president looked around and said (I am quoting roughly from memory), "Boys, I guess it's Truman."

The president then turned to me and asked me to tell Byrnes that he was out, that he was not the chosen candidate for the second place on the ticket. I raised a natural objection to being picked for this unpleasant job. FDR, however, brushed my protest aside with the very correct observation that at one time or another we had all handled assignments like this—it was part of the game.

When the meeting broke up and we were all leaving the White House, I mentioned to Bob Hannegan that it would be as well to have some written confirmation by the president that Truman was his choice. I think I whispered, "Go back and get it in writing." Hannegan returned upstairs, ostensibly for a forgotten coat. When he came down and as we were getting into our cars he whispered to me, "I've got it." He told me the story in more detail the next day, that on the back of an envelope or on some scrap of paper the president had written a short message for Truman.

That same "next day"—Wednesday, July 12—there was an interval during which neither Hannegan nor I could be found in our offices. We were not together, though. Each of us was abroad on a different errand connected with the conference of the previous evening.

This was the message that, according to Mrs. Hannegan, the president wrote in longhand.[14]

July 19

Dear Bob:

You have written me about Harry Truman and Bill Douglas. I should, of course, be very glad to run with either of them and believe that either one of them would bring real strength to the ticket.

Always sincerely,
FR
Hon. Robert Hannegan

At this point it might be in order to go into detail a bit about this memorandum, which has taken on such a hue of mystery during the passing years.

First, the signature. It reads "FR," which to my knowledge was a signature the president was not accustomed to use. However, it was Roosevelt's custom

The handwritten note to Robert E. Hannegan by President Roosevelt designating Senator Harry S. Truman as his first choice for vice president in the campaign of 1944. Courtesy Harry S. Truman Library.

in signing an informal note to run the three initials, "FDR," together. So written hurriedly in pencil the scribbled "FDR" could be interpreted "FR."

It may be as well also to explain how the name of Mr. Justice (Bill) Douglas appeared in the memorandum. While the president appeared to favor him, the mention of his name aroused little enthusiasm among the others present at the July 11 conference in the White House. With the single exception of Mayor Kelly of Chicago, who was his strong supporter. As was also Harold Ickes, secretary of the interior. I have said, incidentally, that the president appeared to back Douglas. But I have always felt that Douglas's name was included in the memorandum more as a gesture of appeasement to Kelly and Ickes than as a reflection of Roosevelt's own preference.

The note itself was postdated "July 19" although really written eight days before. Moreover, the opening sentence was deliberately phrased as if it were in answer to a (purely fictitious) inquiry from Hannegan.

But to return now to that Wednesday morning of July 12. While Hannegan was busy at the White House, I was performing the unenviable task of informing Jimmy Byrnes that he had been (to put it colloquially) "passed over" for the nomination.[15] Byrnes was hurt, angry, and frankly incredulous. Originally Byrnes had been considered the most logical name for second place on the ticket. But his prospects had been lessened by certain factors such as his abandonment of the Catholic faith and the hostility of the colored and labor votes. An experienced politician such as the president could not fail to take all these into account. I might say here, however, that some of those very close to the president did not see eye to eye with him as to how much any or all of the above would influence the voters.

In any event Byrnes adhered stubbornly, and not too illogically, to the position that if the president did not want him as a running mate, then let the president tell him so to his face. This, however, Roosevelt would not do. And even though the unpleasant job was, so to speak, wished off on me, I think the president was entirely justified in his action. First of all, as in the case of Jim Farley four years before, it was not for the president to tell anyone he could not run or that the president did not want him to run for any office. And to have it known, and without impugning anyone's good faith it would most certainly have been known, that Roosevelt did not want Byrnes or anyone else to run with him would have had violent political repercussions. And finally there was the characteristic reluctance of Franklin Roosevelt to be harsh with or to seemingly cast off those who had been in his intimate circle.

Incidentally, in all I have read about the convention of 1944 there has been no mention of the fact that it was I who was delegated to administer the coup de grace to Jimmy Byrnes. We were never especially intimate after that, and I can in a sense understand his feelings. For even though I was only carrying out orders, he could not fail to regard me as a key conspirator in a plot that eventually was to slam the gates of the White House in his face.

Although I am getting ahead of my story, I might add here that, also balked in his ambition, Henry Wallace was very distant with me from that time on. So with no premeditated malice on my part I can now claim the somewhat unique distinction of having alienated two men in public life, each of whom may have felt that I, at least in part, was responsible for his not being in the White House.

But to return once more to that Wednesday. Byrnes remained implacable. Once I left him he evidently went into immediate action. Presumably he contacted Leo Crowley, foreign economic administrator and intimate both with Byrnes and with the president. Also, and whether it was his intention to kill two birds with one stone is not for me to say, he proceeded to telephone Harry Truman in Missouri to request him to place his, Byrnes's, name in nomination for the vice presidency. To this request Truman gladly assented. It was characteristic of his personal code, which places such a high premium on loyalty, that throughout the early days of the convention Harry Truman was steadfast in his declaration that he was a Byrnes man. And he abandoned this position only when confronted with the overwhelmingly and irrefutable proof that he himself and not Byrnes was the all but unanimous choice of the Democratic Party.[16]

Back in Washington, meanwhile, Crowley was in touch with me and, I imagine, the president. I explained to Crowley in unmistakable terms the import of the message the president had instructed me to deliver to Byrnes. It is safe to assume that if Crowley were in personal touch with FDR the president had confirmed my words. Roosevelt, however, persisted in his refusal to break the news to Byrnes personally. But as I have noted above, it is my opinion that he was thoroughly justified in this.

On Thursday, July 13, the tension continued to increase. My appointment diary for that day shows that Crowley was in constant touch with me. He phoned first, then came to see me personally. Then later after our conference he phoned me again. I have already remarked that Crowley was very intimate both with the president and with Jimmy Byrnes. By this time he certainly must have known what the score was. Anyway, he kept reassuring us that "he could fix it with Byrnes."

It was becoming more and more apparent, however, that Byrnes would not withdraw without a personal request to that effect from the president. But this we all knew would never be forthcoming.

Less than forty-eight hours remained before we must all get under way for the convention at Chicago. The president, who for this once would not appear at the convention, had already left Washington under conditions of military secrecy.[17]

Events now proceeded to accelerate. On Friday, July 14, Crowley arranged for Jimmy Byrnes and myself to lunch with him in his suite at the Mayflower. It was not a particularly happy meal. Only one subject was uppermost in the minds of us all. But Crowley, who had continually assured us that "he could fix it," kept shying away from that issue. It had not been an easy week for me, or for any of us, as far as that went. I lost patience, finally, and pinned Crowley right down. "You told the president," I said, "and you told me you'd fix it with Byrnes. Why don't you tell Byrnes right here to his face that you know the president told me to tell him he was out?" Crowley was trapped. But even this did not sway Byrnes's dogged determination to fight for the nomination unless

Frank Walker with the well-known stamp collector at the official opening of the thirty-eighth annual Christmas Seal sale of the Tuberculosis Association in 1944. Photograph courtesy University of Notre Dame Archives.

he received a direct veto from the president. As may well be imagined, we parted from the luncheon table, all of us, for various reasons, feeling frustrated and upset. Consequently, it could be nothing but embarrassing for my own party, i.e., George Allen, Ed Reynolds, Bill Cronin, and myself, to encounter Crowley and Byrnes on our Chicago-bound train.

The scene now shifts to Chicago, where Bob Hannegan and Ed Pauley were already at work superintending, both literally and metaphorically, the plans and progress of the convention.

As chairman of the national committee, Hannegan, of course, had his official headquarters. But he had a private hideout as well, an apartment loaned to him by a friend, Jimmy Coston. My own party arrived in Chicago on Sunday, July 16, and that evening I made my first appearance at Coston's apartment. Various topics were discussed, but the one item remained paramount: would Truman accept the nomination, especially in view of Byrnes's dogged determination to run?

Ed Flynn was late in coming to Chicago. As I remember, he did not arrive before Tuesday, and the convention was to open Wednesday morning.[18] The sentiment for Truman was growing, but the senator from Missouri replied to one and all that he was pledged to Byrnes and was going to place his name in nomination.

There is the fantastic episode of Truman making his way to Sidney Hillman's room by way of the fire escape only to hear from the labor leader that he, Truman, should be the next vice president.[19]

After Flynn's arrival there was another meeting in Coston's apartment, this time with the gloves off.[20] To Flynn it was all quite simple. "The Boss wanted Truman and Truman was the man." I, however, saw it differently, both from a personal and an overall angle. I myself could not be for Truman unless Byrnes was out. With this both Hannegan and Mayor Kelly agreed.

But at least I did what I could. I lunched with Hillman and Philip Murray and tried to sell them on Truman.[21] Both agreed that Truman was a good second choice but they were for Wallace first. Let it be said, incidentally, that they were men of their word. They went down fighting for Wallace and then switched to Truman.

By this time, however, Byrnes was learning the facts of life—not pleasantly. Previously Hannegan had told Byrnes that "he was in if he could deliver Hillman and Murray." Byrnes was confident he could do so. He was wrong. Then and only then did Byrnes retire from the scene. He left Chicago before the convention ended, and his name was not even placed in nomination.

The president's train had stopped long enough in the Chicago yards, always closely guarded as a military secret, for Hannegan to go aboard and confer with him. Then the president continued westward. It was from the naval base at San Diego on July 20 that he broadcast his acceptance speech, only nine days since that evening meeting at the White House.

In Chicago, meanwhile, there was some doubt that Roosevelt really did want Truman as his running mate. To clarify this once and for all, Hannegan from his suite at the Blackstone put a call through to the president. The president settled the matter beyond all doubt. He spoke to me last. "Frank," he said, "go all out for Truman."

That was the verdict and that was the result. Despite the almost hysterical activities of the Wallace adherents, who were convinced, from the famous "kiss of death letter," that the Iowan had White House backing.[22]

Truman had fulfilled his obligations to Byrnes. Now, as he allegedly put it, "I have been a soldier and I obey my commander in chief."

Although strictly not for publication, one calls to mind Bill Cronin's recollection of Truman, who, incidentally, did not talk to Roosevelt on the telephone, wandering bewilderedly around the suite at the Blackstone, hair down over his face, asking everybody, "Do you think I ought to run?"

As I remember it, three of us spoke to the president at the time, Hannegan and Ed Kelly and myself. And I was the last one to talk with him—I remember very clearly—because even though he told us he was for Truman, he might have changed his mind due to the unforeseen conditions that had arisen in the convention. Because Roosevelt could change his mind, and many times did. I don't say that as a criticism. I think he had a perfect right to do so if circumstances were such, if his own candidate could not be placed in nomination; he had a perfect right to work out a solution to the problem on a different plane.

That night or the following night Ed Kelly gave a dinner at the Blackstone Hotel. As I was leaving the dinner I saw Senator Barkley at a table and told him I'd like to see him later. The senator and I had been good friends, and I felt it was the right thing to do in view of the fact I had heard he had become a serious candidate for vice president. I felt the nice thing to do was to tell him that President Roosevelt had asked a group of us to support Truman for vice president. The senator, upon learning this, seemed to be in high dudgeon and very much put out about it. He indicated that he didn't know whether or not he would make the keynote speech the following morning. And being the bearer of the bad news, I seemed to incur, for the moment at least, the hostility of the senator. This I felt very much, because he and I had been friends over the years. Several times that night Les Biffle, secretary of the Senate, came to my room and indicated to me he was having great trouble with Senator Barkley in convincing him he should go ahead and make the keynote speech the following day. Finally, about three or four o'clock in the morning, as I remember it, Biffle came in and told me that Barkley had decided to go ahead with his speech but that he was still going to submit his name to the convention. Incidentally, I remember seeing the senator's son-in-law with Bill

Stanley the following day. They were both doing their utmost to advance the candidacy of the senator.

The rest was almost routine. We had many more votes promised for Truman than we used on the first ballot. Wallace led on the first ballot—it was really the groundswell from all the pent-up enthusiasm in his behalf—with 429.5 votes, but Truman was second with 319.5. The strategy was working and the plans were being carried out. I did not bother to wait for the second ballot. The result was a foregone conclusion.

The curtain was not to fall without a touch of comic relief. As I was leaving the convention hall, Harold Ickes rushed up to me and kept repeating, "It's going to be an impasse. We've got to do something, Frank. I'll see you after this ballot."

I nodded noncommittally and continued my journey back to the hotel. The second ballot showed 1,031 for Truman and 105 for Wallace.

I might say here that I found myself in a very embarrassing position early in the Chicago activities. I was a delegate at large for the state of Pennsylvania. Several days before the nominations a caucus of the Pennsylvania delegation was called, but I was told that no action binding the delegates would be taken there. I went to the meeting, held in one of the hotels, and soon found myself in the center of the room, completely hemmed in. The room was so crowded it was impossible to find an exit. When the caucus was in session, Phil Murray, who was seated in back of me, got to his feet and moved that it be the sense of the caucus that we support Henry Wallace for vice president.

I did not wish at that stage of the proceedings to indicate definitely that I was supporting Truman. I did not think it was wise to do so at that particular time. But I had no alternative.

I rose to a point of order, rather to a point of information, and asked the chairman, Dave Lawrence, mayor of Pittsburgh and a prominent Democratic politician in Pennsylvania, if the resolution would contemplate binding the delegates at the convention. If so, I said, I was not going to be bound and that I would like to leave the caucus if the instructions were supposed to be binding instructions.

The chair ruled that the motion would not be regarded as binding, only as indicative of how the delegates felt.

I remember when the resolution was put to a vote that I, as a delegate at large, was the first to vote and that I voted against the resolution. Senator Joseph Guffey, also a delegate at large, followed me and voted for the resolution. But Dave Lawrence, who was a delegate as well as chairman, cast his vote with me, so I was not entirely alone in the Pennsylvania delegation.

Most of the Pennsylvania delegates who were present seemed to vote for the resolution. During the actual balloting at the convention, however, quite a number of the Pennsylvania delegates seemed to support Truman instead of Wallace. After all, the caucus was not binding.

A friend of mine from Pottsville, a delegate by the name of Hugh Brady, referring to the resolution asked the chairman to announce the vote. I turned to him and told him to keep quiet. Just as I did so I noticed that he was seated right next to Murray and that Murray, glancing my way, did not give me a very pleasant look.

As I was saying, at no time was I in doubt that Truman would be nominated. But I had some very strenuous days during the convention.

I recall one incident when I incurred the wrath of Ed Pauley. Pauley had the delegates from California pledge themselves for Truman. But several of them wanted to be released from their pledge so they could vote for Wallace on the first ballot and, by so doing, comply with the wishes of Helen Gahagan Douglas, Governor Olson, and some others. Pauley refused to release them from their pledge. Then the attorney general of California came to my room. That was the night, I think, before the convention. Kenny, Bob Kenny, was his name. Bob asked me if we couldn't release a few votes for Wallace on the first ballot. So I went to the delegation, to some of the delegates, and released them without telling Pauley. Pauley was furious about it. But I thought it better to have a little harmony in the convention, and besides, I was thinking ahead to the election. It was highly desirable to have the friendship of that group rather than their hostility. And so I gave quite a few votes away that Ed had had safely pledged to Truman. That, of course, was for the first ballot only. And I did it with the knowledge that we would surely nominate Truman on the second ballot.

Then there was the Honorable Sam Jackson, United States senator from Indiana, who was slated for the role of permanent chairman. In my presence Hannegan told Jackson inelegantly but firmly to remember "he was Hannegan's chairman and, by God, not to forget it."

But Jackson did forget. Perhaps his temporary authority went to his head. Whatever the reason, when the possibility of a deadlock appeared for the vice presidential nomination, every favored son thought the lightning might strike. "And why shouldn't the lightning strike on the banks of the Wabash?"—or so Jackson may have reasoned. At any rate he decided he "wanted in" as a compromise candidate for the vice presidency. On the rostrum as permanent chairman, Jackson could not be too obvious about his own self-inspired boom. With what I hope was not too open amusement I watched Jackson trying to secure Senator Kenneth McKellar's attention—and his support. The senior senator from Tennessee carried his eighty years well, but he had grown quite deaf and he could not grasp the import of Jackson's feverish whispers. "What's that?" McKellar kept repeating, *"What's that?"* Jackson, much embarrassed, abandoned his newly hatched ambitions and returned to the more congenial role of "Hannegan's chairman."

And so it was that Harry S. Truman set foot on the path that within a year was to place him in the White House.

In closing, I call to mind that thus far two of my actions during those crowded days have escaped public notice. The first, as I have already mentioned, and it was known to the others at the White House conference, was that I was to "tell Byrnes that he was out." The second also concerned the doings of that eventful night. For from July 11 on, for a few days at least, with the exception of the president and possibly Mrs. Hannegan, I was the only living person who knew that Bob Hannegan had in his possession Roosevelt's note endorsing Harry S. Truman.

11

THE ROOSEVELT PORTRAIT

I 'm very much inclined to doubt if Franklin Roosevelt ever read a book—
really read a book, as I understand the term—during the time I knew him.
I think I am in a position to back up that statement, too. For if a man has the
habit of reading, that is what he turns to in his moments of relaxation. I have
been with Roosevelt when he was making trips by train and by boat. And if it
was relaxation he was after, the first thing he would turn to was his stamp collection. It was well known, of course, that philately was his acknowledged
hobby. With respect to books, Roosevelt made no pretense of being a book-
worm. When *Forever Amber* was the main topic of conversation, someone
asked FDR if he had read it. "Only the dirty parts," he replied, with a broad
grin.[1]

It was not Roosevelt's way to get his information from books. He managed that by discussion, by drawing people out, "picking a fellow's brains," as
the saying goes. And this gift, plus a marvelous memory, served him in good
stead on many occasions.

Take his jousts—and I think that word fits, too—with C. F. Kelley.[2]
Roosevelt had never forgotten the high prices the navy was forced to pay for
copper back during World War I, when he had been assistant secretary. Con
Kelley asked me to arrange for a conference with the president. The
appointment was arranged, in December 1933 I think it was, and I was with

them the whole time. Too much so for my own peace of mind, as I will explain in a moment.

Anyway, Roosevelt reopened the sixteen-year-old question of the price of copper back in 1917. Without a single note or a pause to check any reference, the president gave Kelley chapter, book, and verse on prices to the last decimal point, and tonnages and totals to the last ounce.

There was not much Con could say; he certainly was not prepared to challenge the figures Roosevelt hurled at him. But after we had left the White House he turned to me and said, "What a memory! Isn't it amazing what a marvelous memory that man has?"

I said I had been present at the entire meeting between the president and Con Kelley and too much so for my own peace of mind. An incident took place that caused me acute embarrassment at the time and that, although it was eighteen years ago, is still vivid in my recollection.

While we all were talking, the president's luncheon was brought in to him. It was served to him while he was holding forth with Kelley. I do not think anybody would have thought a thing about it if he had made some apology about his lack of time, the pressure of appointments, etc. But apology or explanation was certainly the farthest thought from Roosevelt's mind. Instead, "Have some luncheon, Frank," he said, waving me to a chair and pointedly ignoring Kelley. I certainly could not refuse. You can imagine my feeling, though, sitting there being served by the president while he went on talking to Con.

Now Roosevelt had been schooled in all the graces, and when he so desired there was no one more hospitable or a more charming host. It was evident, though, that he had never forgiven Kelley for his attitude during World War I, and he took this opportunity of being openly insulting to him. It's not for me to apologize for Roosevelt. After all, he knew what he was doing. He was a gentleman born. Perhaps the only explanation lies in that quotation from Michael Arlen, "A gentleman is one who is never rude unintentionally!"[3]

Whatever his attitude on this occasion may have been, I will say frankly that Roosevelt had firm control of his temper. I can go further and state that I never saw him lose it.

The time I saw him closest to going off the deep end was back in the thirties. I think it was soon after he had won his overwhelming victory in the 1936 campaign, and he, Mrs. Roosevelt, and I were together. As I recall it, Mrs. Roosevelt had recently returned from a trip through the South—I think she had gone as far as Texas—and she was still burning with indignation over the sights she had seen, the slums, the ignorance, the utter lack of hygienic and educational facilities, etc. And Mrs. Roosevelt wanted immediate action, something should be done right away quick. The president was trying to calm her down, to slow her up a bit. "But Eleanor," he kept saying, "these things take time. You can't change conditions overnight. Educating the people is the only way. Otherwise you get them mad and you're worse off than when you started."

Mrs. Roosevelt was too wrought up to be placated by any soft words, and she kept on insisting that as president and just reelected by an overwhelming majority besides, it was his duty to take immediate action right now.

Roosevelt, naturally, did not see it that way and just kept repeating, "Now Eleanor, be reasonable!" All to no avail, until finally his "Now Eleanor!" carried a distinct note of irritation and I was becoming embarrassed at being forced to witness a (First Family or not) spirited husband-and-wife quarrel.

It was not that the president did not sympathize with Mrs. Roosevelt's point of view. But first, last, and always, Roosevelt was a politician, and he realized that you cannot hurry educational or social changes. Whatever his personal feelings, he never would have championed a civil rights bill or antagonized the South the way Truman did in 1948.[4]

As a matter of fact, Roosevelt would seldom express an opinion on anything. He would listen, never arguing, and—though the speaker might not realize it—never completely agreeing.

"Grand!" was his favorite expression; it was as characteristic of him as the flashing white teeth and the hearty "Deelighted" was the trademark of his uncle and predecessor in the White House.[5] But "Grand!"—expressed as only Roosevelt could express it—did not necessarily mean, in fact it never did mean, that Roosevelt went along one hundred percent with the speaker. It could signify that the idea was good or that the speaker had made a forceful presentation or that the president admired the speaker's enthusiasm, or anything, except Roosevelt's adoption of whatever point was under discussion.

As I have said, Roosevelt would listen; he was judicial in his attitude; would gather in all the opinions and then, if a decision had to be made, it would be *his* decision that would be made.

It was quite in order for the others present to offer their views to the president, but he had no patience for arguments or discussions among those present as to the relative merits of the point at issue. There were two reasons for this, the first being the logical belief that, as his word was final, all preliminary discussion should have taken place before the question was referred to him. Secondly, and I am not sure Roosevelt would have denied it, the president had a well-nourished streak of vanity. *He* was the center of attraction, and he did not welcome any person or any discussion that might force him to share the spotlight. It was for this reason, I think, he never played bridge, or rather did not play if he could avoid it. Not a skilled player himself, he was reluctant to put himself in a position where a partner or an opponent could criticize his play. He preferred poker, where he could stand or fall on his own.

Frank Walker with the president at Hyde Park, and a new sheet for the philatelist. Photograph courtesy Notre Dame Archives.

One thing about Roosevelt that always puzzled me was his apparent lack of any emotional feeling. His undoubted charm and magnetism always struck me as a trifle on the cold side. He was of Dutch descent, of course, and they are not an emotional race.

No one could have been closer to Roosevelt, or more loyal, than Marvin McIntyre or Louie Howe or Missy LeHand.[6] As you know, they all three died during his tenure of office. Yet never at any time did I ever hear him express a sentence of regret or a feeling of personal loss at their passing.

Probably Pa Watson's death was felt most by the president. During his years as White House aide, Roosevelt had become very fond of the general.[7] He was typical "regular army," of the earth earthy, always prepared to draw on his collection of military jokes, which were more fundamental than subtle. Don't make any mistake about it, though, Pa Watson was nobody's fool. His casual bonhomie was an effective shield for a keen brain, and he was a very shrewd judge of human nature. In many respects he served Roosevelt well and was invaluable to him.

Watson was much more acute than Harry Hopkins. Hopkins was a cold-blooded, ambitious opportunist who did not run from any conflict or tussle

Frank Walker at a Front Porch Rally at Hyde Park in 1940 with President and Mrs. Roosevelt. Crown Princess Martha of Norway is to the right of Mrs. Roosevelt. Photograph courtesy University of Notre Dame Archives.

and could be as tough and as deceptive as any ward politician. Hopkins's great value to Roosevelt lay in this. Whatever the president wanted, Hopkins was for one hundred percent, and sometimes he seemed to anticipate Roosevelt's words or wishes. Serving the president, he was serving himself, and in the furtherance of the mutual objective he could be as designingly cold-blooded and double-cross with the best of them.

To me, Franklin Roosevelt had charm but no depth. He won you over immediately. He liked people but he never relaxed for an instant. He always had his guard up. Even as regards his much-publicized tie with his mother. To me, it did not seem to be affection, at least as I understand the word, as much as a sense of obligation.

There did not seem to be a great deal of exuberance in his public or even private social relations. Always what the French would call "correct."

Roosevelt was always attracted to women of charm and breeding, what the French would call soigné. Princess Martha of Norway was an example. He liked to be in their company. I understand that Woodrow Wilson had this same faculty.[8]

A while back I spoke of Roosevelt "keeping his guard up" even while he was friendly to you. But you had to keep your guard up, and it was not easy, believe me, when you were trying to avoid some project he was trying to pin on you. As I found out from experience, the only way to beat Roosevelt at that game was to present him with the name of an acceptable substitute at the very time you were trying to get out from under.

Take what happened in 1940, for instance. In the first place the president announced my appointment as postmaster general—it was up at Hyde Park—after he had definitely promised me he would do no such thing. I was not even sure in my own mind yet.

One thing I was sure about, however, was that I did not want to be chairman of the Democratic National Committee and run the 1940 campaign. When Farley took his celebrated walk in that year after the Chicago convention had nominated Roosevelt for the third term, Jim had resigned both as postmaster general and as chairman of the national committee.

The president wanted me to take over the chairmanship of the national committee as well as the post office. I could not see that. But I did know that I would be stuck with it unless I could offer the president another acceptable name. I knew Ed Flynn wanted to be chairman and that Roosevelt, in view of their long friendship and Flynn's political services, could not very well refuse him the post if I turned it down. So when the time came for me to discuss it with Roosevelt, I ducked and counterpunched by suggesting Ed Flynn's name. And that was how I evaded that assignment even though later on I did take the chairmanship for a year.

I should like to point out that it was not intuition but sad experience that taught me all this. It was in March 1935 that Congress passed the Work Relief Bill. It was obviously impossible to name either Hopkins or Ickes to the top job, and the president wanted me to move in either as buffer or referee, I'm not sure which. He talked to me about it and I didn't give him a final answer. He could not have been mistaken on that point. Yet the Associated Press had the story—it could only have come from the White House—and they got me on the phone while I was spending that April Sunday down in Atlantic City.

Even though the president nailed me on that one, he did not get all he wanted, though. For I got out from under on two points. I got Red Legget in from his other National Emergency Council work to make the announcements of allotments and approved projects to the press.[9] Secondly, I passed right back to Roosevelt himself the job of giving the final approval to the projects, whether they were PWA or WPA. I still have very vivid recollections of Louie Howe's original version of the Relief Bill, drawing the circles in the diagram to explain the plan. Louie wanted to make me the goat on the final approval of all projects.

I said a while back I never actually saw the president lose his temper. He did blow up on several celebrated occasions, but I have never been quite sure how much of his outbursts was temper and how much was stage effect. Probably the most famous incident was his scene with Joe Patterson of the *New York Daily News* after Pearl Harbor.[10] Patterson had come to the White House to make amends and to ask what he could do in the war effort. Yet Roosevelt chose this time to be smart-alecky and to alienate a vigorous and vindictive newspaper editor.

I have already said that Roosevelt would listen, at least for a while, to what his visitors might say. But however courteously he might be paying attention, real or feigned, the simple fact was that he really did not have much respect for the views of those who disagreed with him. He might not dispute their sincerity, but they just did not know and he did.

A lot of people seem to accept it as fact that Roosevelt never forgave anyone who opposed him. That is not strictly true. Take both Acheson and Lew Douglas. Both of them resigned and yet Roosevelt was glad to have them back in the war days.

One thing for sure. You could not wisecrack or kid the president out of any decision he had made. Even Ed Flynn, who had been his secretary of state at Albany and whose political acumen was highly regarded by Roosevelt, even Flynn never tried that. As I have said, the only way I ever succeeded was to drop the matter for the moment, then later try to catch the president in a more amenable frame of mind or come up with an acceptable alternative.

There was one time, though, when someone did use a slightly jeering tone at Roosevelt, but that was before he became the occupant of the White House. It happened in Albany, and the other party was Basil O'Connor, his former law partner. You recall the Jimmy Walker hearings before the governor and the political reactions that were bound to come, no matter what the governor's decision would be.[11] I happened to be there by pure accident. In fact, if I had known what the object of our visit to Albany was, I would have remained behind. But it was only a few weeks before election day in 1932, and when Jim Farley, Arthur Mullen, and some others asked me to come up to Albany to see the governor, I went along, believing some issue of the campaign was to be discussed.

Once we were with Roosevelt and I realized the purpose of the trip, I stayed in the background and did not utter a word. After all, it was not my business.

Arthur Mullen and all the rest were urging the governor to let Walker off with a reprimand. Even though the victory seemed certain, why take chances and antagonize Tammany?

Roosevelt listened and gave no hint of his decision. That was when Basil O'Connor—he'd had a few drinks, I believe—started to jeer at the governor and said, "So you'd rather be right than president would you?" He repeated this several times in a jeering tone.

Still no word from Roosevelt. It was just at this moment that word came from New York that Walker had resigned. Arthur Mullen states that his son called him from New York to announce the news. Incidentally, in his book describing this scene Mullen comments rather acidly on the belligerent tone of O'Connor toward Roosevelt.[12]

To this day no one can say with certainty what Roosevelt's decision would have been. Some believe he intended to let Walker off with a reprimand. Mrs. Roosevelt believes Walker would have been removed for "nonfeasance" rather than misfeasance. Ray Moley, Al Smith, and Jimmy Walker himself all were sure that Roosevelt would have ousted Walker.

But no one can say for sure what Roosevelt would have done. And you can be certain that he was too astute a politician ever to put himself on record. So his ultimate decision in the Jimmy Walker case will always be a matter for speculation.

This is not the place for me to attempt any final expression of my opinion of Roosevelt. For one thing, such a task will not be easy. I feel that no man in American history left a greater impress on the nation and people than he. Few men, if any, in political life, or for that matter in all history, accomplished more for the common man than he. I had great respect for the man and his ability and real affection for him. I was interested in his main objectives, and I think he knew that. In the main I had been since early youth for most of the things for which FDR stood. In this narrative I shall point out a few differences we had during my association with him; in every one of these I frankly and forcibly but, of course, respectfully, pointed out the various issues on which we did not agree. And among such issues were the Agricultural Adjustment Act program, the "plowing under," and the "pig question." The air mail contracts. The labor question, and John L. Lewis in particular. The work relief program where I advocated cutting the program in two and more emphasis on the heavy work (Public Works Administration) projects. The senatorial "purges" in 1938, against Walter George and Millard Tydings. The setting of class against class. And the left-wing tendency from 1936 on, where I opposed the Works Progress Administration and Hopkins drive, as well as the Harvard group. But my differences of opinion on principles were few. Never were they, as I soberly weighed them, of sufficient force or weight to compel me in conscience to break with him.[13]

At this point, though, I can say regretfully that to me Franklin Roosevelt was not the great man he could have been. To me he failed in becoming a truly great man.

Frank Walker and President Roosevelt at the dedication of the Franklin D. Roosevelt Library at Hyde Park, 1940. Photograph courtesy University of Notre Dame Archives.

12

LATER YEARS

hen FDR died, Walker was ready to get out of government. He had been working for Roosevelt since 1930, fifteen years, and the president was no easy taskmaster. Walker had to keep his wits about him as the Hyde Park squire asked him or nudged him to do this or that. The war made matters more difficult, even though the postmaster general ordinarily would not have been in the center of war management. In Roosevelt's cabinet he was a handyman to take on whatever missions the president had in mind. For a while he did double duty as chairman of the Democratic National Committee.

When he told the new president he was tired, Truman did not argue, though Walker promised to stay on until it was possible to nominate a successor.

A confusion momentarily arose, to have a quick solution. Truman needed an expert negotiator to help arrange German reparations to the Soviet Union and asked Walker to go abroad on this task, suggesting that he continue to hold his cabinet seat because that would make him a more impressive negotiator. Walker meanwhile discovered that Chairman Hannegan of the Democratic National Committee wanted to be postmaster general—and the Truman plan would keep Hannegan out of the cabinet. The way out was easy enough, for Walker did not want the reparations post and told the president so, and suggested he resign from the cabinet to open a place for Hannegan.

And so Walker gave up all connection with government—but only for a few months, because the president asked him to attend the first part of the first session of the United Nations General Assembly, meeting in London beginning in January, 1946. By this time the Walker family, which included Mrs. Walker and daughter Laura Hallie (son Tom was still in the navy), was back in their apartment in New York City, at Eighty-fifth Street and Fifth Avenue. Laura Hallie accompanied her father on the London trip, and the U.N. work proved more interesting than Walker expected, for there were important tasks to accomplish. In the course of them he saw much of Eleanor Roosevelt, a great lady by any measurement. She charmed him with her simple manners, even if she threatened sometimes to outwork, "overwork" might be the word, her fellow delegates. Mrs. Roosevelt never rested, and went straight for any goal she set.

The close association with Mrs. Roosevelt in London led to an interesting episode recorded by Walker in his London diary.

President Truman called me this morning and said: "Will you do me a favor? Elliott Roosevelt's writings and comments are causing me a lot of trouble. I am naturally wondering if he reflects Mrs. Roosevelt's views, because I get reports that she is not very well pleased with the policy we have established. You know I put her into the United Nations picture and I would not want to incur her antagonism. Would you mind having a talk with her?"[1]

I told the president I would be glad to. I had a luncheon appointment with my son Tom and Martin Sweeney, so I talked with Mrs. Thompson and went down to see Mrs. Roosevelt right after lunch.[2] Mrs. R. said: "The Republicans are making a lot more out of Elliott's comments than is justified. Elliott is not a liar. He did not lie, but he was directing his observations at Mr. Byrnes and not at Mr. Truman. The things Elliott said are true so far as Franklin's appraisal of Churchill is concerned, that is, Churchill as a conservative. Franklin was never in accord with him as far as his conservatism is concerned. Of course, he had a real affection for him, but he always thought that when peace came he would be able to get along better with Stalin than Churchill. So far as the president and his international policies are concerned, I think Jimmy Byrnes has done very well, but not the best possible job. Jimmy Byrnes was not loyal to Franklin and he has not been loyal to Truman or to the administration—not even to Mr. Baruch, who is his great benefactor. There is only one person Jimmy Byrnes is loyal to and that is Jimmy Byrnes. I was with Franklin when he talked to Byrnes going through Chicago.[3] I heard what he said to Byrnes, so it isn't secondhand with me that Franklin didn't want him for vice president. In general I think President Truman is doing fairly well. I do not think his problems are his fault. I think he is doing as well as could be expected. Of course I don't know whether he was well enough equipped to take over a job like this, but if Franklin had to handle the present situation I'm not sure he could do so. I don't think he can be elected in 1948."

I said I don't think any Democrat can, and she said, "I don't either. Don't tell him I said this, but if he asks me I will tell him. I think he has done very well thus far, however. I think he has been loyal to the policies of Franklin and not only do I not feel unfriendly but I feel very friendly. When I go down in January, I will see him myself."

In relating the above, Walker was reminded again of his close relationship with Mrs. Roosevelt's late husband.

This reminded Mr. Walker of the time Jesse Jones called him and said, "I've been trying for months to see the Boss.[4] Will you try to arrange an appointment for me?" When I spoke to Roosevelt he said, "You tell him this: I will see him when he comes out for my man for governor in Texas. And I don't want him to tell this to me. He must put it in writing." Jesse wrote an editorial but didn't take sides. Roosevelt wouldn't even read the editorial. He said, "He was to put it in writing and sign it 'Jesse Jones.'"

This reminded Mr. W. of the time Mrs. Sara Delano Roosevelt, the president's mother, told the president to put his coat over his shoulders. They were riding in an open car with R. driving at Hyde Park. Mr. W. said this puts me in a fine spot—who shall I obey, the president of the United States or the mother of the president? Roosevelt had been objecting vehemently that he wasn't cold, but Mrs. R. said, "Franklin you put that coat on or you'll catch your death of cold." Walker said I'm going to obey the mother of the president, and put the coat over his shoulders.

This reminded Mr. W. of the time Mrs. R. and FDR and he were having dinner alone and they got into an argument. Mrs. R. said, "Franklin, you are not always as informed as you think you are. Just because you have a smattering of something, you think you know all the facts." He said, "Madam, I am sufficiently informed on this matter and perhaps you are not so well informed yourself."

Upon return to New York City the Walkers at last settled down. Academic boards and foundations now took some of the former postmaster general's time. He served as national chairman of the Notre Dame Endowment and as president of the university's board of lay trustees. In 1948 Notre Dame awarded him its Laetare Medal, given annually to an outstanding Catholic layman. He was a director of the Alfred E. Smith Memorial Foundation and the Franklin Delano Roosevelt Memorial Foundation, and treasurer of the Franklin D. Roosevelt Library.

He was careful to stay out of the politics that had consumed his life for a decade and a half. If something needed to be done—such as the call from

President Truman—he of course accomplished it. Otherwise he considered that he had passed the torch to younger leaders of the party, who had more time ahead of them.

Nor was Walker any social butterfly. He attended the de rigueur dinners and parades and funerals but did not look for more affairs to conquer—such as his neighbor across the street, Jim Farley, who went to every affair in the city, partly in his role as European head of Coca-Cola, mostly because he enjoyed going out. Walker saw principally people whom he liked, such as his great friends Father John Cavanaugh of Notre Dame, Martin Sweeney, a hotel executive, and a fellow former cabinet member, Frances Perkins, a fine and friendly woman.

One reason for staying out of as much political activity as possible, and avoiding the social circuit, was that the theater business needed attention. At the outset, in the latter forties, it was flourishing, with a continuing boom in attendance. If not quite as heavy as during the war years, it was still very large. The movies remained the principal place of entertainment for the American people. Walker still had superintendence of Comerford Theaters, Inc. There were several hundred. Keeping them going, watching over their physical condition, getting the right bookings, managing personnel, was a time-consuming operation. Many things went right, to be sure; but then many things constantly were going wrong.

By the end of the decade, the beginning of the fifties, the theater business began, at first ever so slightly, then in almost the manner of an avalanche, to go down, and that took attention. Walker asked his son Tom to come back into the business and go up to Scranton in 1952 and help get things in order. Tom stayed until 1956, when matters were in even less order than when he arrived. By the end of the fifties Comerford was down to less than fifty theaters. And what had once been bustling financial enterprises were now virtually financial disasters. Comerford had had some theaters in New York State, but most of its houses were in cities and towns in the surrounding states, with a heavy concentration in Pennsylvania. As luck would have it, the theaters often were in the centers of the cities and towns, the very places where real estate values tumbled as businesses went out to the new suburban shopping centers. Not merely was Comerford left with theaters that, as buildings, had little or no value, but the land on which they stood had little value as well.

The problem was television. It had nothing to do with the Walkers' management. No one's management, even that of the redoubtable M. E. Comerford, could have gotten the business out of its spiraling losses. No matter that television throughout the fifties was a less-than-attractive medium, full of silly spectacles such as Arthur Godfrey playing his guitar. No matter that movies

The presentation of the Laetare Medal to Frank C. Walker, 1948. *From left:* Bishop John Francis O'Hara, Frank Walker, Francis Cardinal Spellman. Photograph courtesy *New York Herald Tribune* and University of Notre Dame Archives.

actually got better. It made no difference; people liked to look at the television screen, even if Godfrey played in a snowstorm.

Another part of the problem was the postwar baby boom, which produced shoals of children who needed to be watched at home. An entire generation became accustomed to staying home rather than going out. The movies went out. It nearly broke Walker's heart to see the collapse.

He took refuge and pleasure in the successes of his children. Tom, after leaving the navy, had gone back to W. R. Grace and Company in New York, where just before he had gone to war he had started in Grace's commercial insurance business. After leaving for Scranton at his father's behest to help with Comerford Theaters, Inc., he left W. R. Grace and this time went to Florida, where again he was in commercial insurance, starting his own firm, which eventually merged with Fred S. James and Co. Tom did famously in insurance. For a brief time, nine and one-half months in 1966, he was also in public office: during that period he was the appointed sheriff of Broward County, of which Fort Lauderdale is the county seat.

Laura Hallie also did well. She was educated at Marymount Academy in Tarrytown, New York, and at the Parsons School of Design. In 1944 she married Robert Ameno, captain in the tank corps, who not long afterward went overseas, where he was killed during the Battle of the Bulge, the surprise attack upon Allied forces in the Ardennes. After the war, she accompanied her father during his service in London as U.S. delegate to the United Nations General Assembly. Later she married James S. Jenkins of New York, an insurance broker with Davis Dorland Co., Inc. Between the London trip and marriage to Jim lived in Greenwich Connecticut, and from the marriage there were six sons and a daughter. Laura founded the Arts Council and was president of the auxiliary of St. Vincent's Hospital, Westchester. After her husband's retirement she and Jim moved to Annapolis, to a house that looks out on the water.

The senior Walker and his wife vacationed in Florida with Tom and his family. They especially admired Delray Beach. In the North, closer to the apartment in the city, they could go up to Coonamessett Inn on Cape Cod, where they had a summer place. Occasionally, but not as often as in older days, they went out to Butte. It was an understandable thing about the trips to Butte. Before World War II it was pretty much necessary to take the train, a long and circuitous trip. After the war the plane quickly became far more convenient—no changing in Chicago and again farther west. But as the trip became easier, the Walkers made it less frequently. They greatly admired the little city of their youth, and their memories reached out to it easily; but as time passed their friends moved on or were gathered in St. Patrick's Cemetery and, inexorably, Butte became a different place.

The years passed, and toward the end of the fifties the erstwhile postmaster general, chairman of the Democratic National Committee, and before that head of Comerford Theaters, noticed problems with his breathing: he began to exhibit the telltale signs of emphysema. For years friends had told him not to smoke so much, but he had paid little or no attention. Because of some particularly insistent objectors he had gone over to filtered Kents. But it was too late; the harm was done. He had been smoking since college days, when he had rolled his own and sat in the grass lazily watching Father Crumley turn the corner near the presbytery on his way to Sorin.

For a while he was in St. Vincent's Hospital in New York. Nothing really could be done. They brought him home—by this time a suite in the Carlyle Hotel—and set up a full-time oxygen tent, with round-the-clock nurses. He was conscious until near the end.

Frank Comerford Walker died on September 13, 1959. John Francis Cardinal O'Hara of Philadelphia, former president of Notre Dame, presided at the solemn requiem mass. The celebrant was the Reverend Edward P. Joyce, executive vice president of Notre Dame. Afterward, the three surviving family members—Mrs. Walker, Laura Hallie, and Tom—were waiting in the back of the limousine in front of the church. *The New York Times* reported that some dignitaries, including Eleanor Roosevelt, were there. The door opened and a very familiar face appeared, former president Truman, who had flown in from Kansas City.

Burial was in the family plot in Butte, in St. Patrick's Cemetery.

NOTES

Chapter 1: Growing Up in Butte

1. Heinze, the well-known Montana copper king, was a mining engineer, handsome, charming, unscrupulous; he was the center of his era in Butte, known as "the Heinze days." For Frederick Augustus "Fritz" Heinze, see Michael P. Malone and Richard B. Roeder, *Montana: A History of Two Centuries* (Seattle: University of Washington Press, 1976), 167–177; and especially Malone's *The Battle for Butte: Mining and Politics on the Northern Frontier* (Seattle: University of Washington Press, 1981), 49–53 passim.

2. See David M. Emmons, *The Butte Irish: Class and Ethnicity in an American Mining Town, 1876–1925* (Urbana: University of Illinois Press, 1989).

3. The author of the poem was Burton Brailey.

4. After the turn of the century the movement gathered against saloons, often places of degradation, and many localities voted for local Prohibition. The movement triumphed with the Eighteenth Amendment in 1920.

5. John Patrick Carroll was a staunch conservative with much support in Butte, where he coupled his desire for Prohibition with an active dislike of socialism and unions. When national chaplain of the Ancient Order of Hibernians in 1912, he issued a denunciation of socialism and labor radicalism, remarking that "socialism threatened every substantial institution of civilization and that the adoption of its delusive principles would wreck the nation." See Emmons, *The Butte Irish*, 276.

6. The Butte, Anaconda, and Pacific railroad hauled ore from Butte to the smelter in Anaconda.

7. Irish Americans virtually established prizefighting in the United States, and John L. Sullivan did much to make the sport popular; but Corbett took him on in New Orleans on September 7, 1892, and won by a knockout. Corbett lost in 1897 to Fitzsimmons, the lightest man to hold the heavyweight championship. Two years later James J. Jeffries knocked out Fitzsimmons.

8. Hooper ratings, introduced in 1935, soon superseded Crossley ratings as the preferred system for judging audience reaction to the radio programs of the 1940s and 1950s. The basis of both was the telephone survey, but Hooper used a coincidental method, noting what the listener said he or she was listening to at the time of the call, whereas Crossley used a recall method, noting what the listener mentioned having heard during a period of a few hours.

9. Walkerville was not named after Frank Walker's family but rather the Walker brothers of Salt Lake City, who ran a mining company there. In 1876 they sent Marcus Daly to scout Butte, and he recommended the purchase of the Alice Mine. Daly himself put $5,000 on the purchase and began his own great fortune.

10. Glenn S. "Pop" Warner played on the Cornell University team, and because he was a little older than his teammates became known as "Pop." He coached at Iowa State Agricultural College in 1894–1895, and afterward at Cornell, the Carlisle (Pennsylvania) Indian School, the University of Pittsburgh, Stanford University, and Temple University.

11. James E. Murray was elected to the Senate in 1934 to fill the vacancy caused by the death of the illustrious Thomas J. Walsh (for whom see footnote 1, Chapter 3).

12. The American Protective Association was a secret anti-Catholic society founded by Henry F. Gowers in Clinton, Iowa, in 1887. The Panic of 1893 and ensuing depression raised concerns over employment and jobs, bringing much prejudice against immigrants, and by 1896 the APA reached a membership of one million. That year it divided over the free silver issue, and thereafter its membership went down rapidly, but it survived until 1911.

13. Senator Thomas H. Carter, born in Ohio, moved to Helena in 1882 and was Montana's first elected member of the House of Representatives. He served in the Senate in 1897–1903 and 1905–1911. He introduced bills for improvements of Yellowstone Park and was largely responsible for the establishment of Glacier National Park.

14. John D. Ryan was a famous figure in his day. He became president of Anaconda Copper Mining Company at the time when use of copper, especially for electrical purposes, was widespread. At his death in 1923 Anaconda was the world's largest producer of copper and copper products. For C. F. Kelley, see footnote 2, Chapter 11.

Chapter 2: Education

1. Minims were grade-school students.

2. The steel man was Charles M. Schwab, one-time associate of Andrew Carnegie, president of Bethlehem Steel.

3. William Jennings Bryan possessed a voice that could reach three city blocks before amplification by "loudspeakers" came into use in 1919–1920.

4. This is John C. Cavanaugh, not John W. Cavanaugh, the president of Notre Dame during Walker's college years.

5. At the time of this writing, 1996, the endowment of the Notre Dame Endowment is $1.3 billion.

Chapter 3: The Law

1. Thomas J. Walsh became one of the most illustrious senators ever to represent Montana in Washington. In a sensational series of hearings in 1923–1924 he uncovered the bribery of President Warren G. Harding's secretary of the interior, Albert B. Fall, by the oilmen Edward L. Doheny and Harry F. Sinclair.

2. Robert L. "Believe It Or Not" Ripley was author of a well-known newspaper column in which he described and illustrated nearly unbelievable oddities.

3. The Moyer-Haywood-Pettibone case arose out of the killing of a former governor of Idaho, Frank Steunenberg, by a bomb planted by Harry Orchard. The latter turned state's evidence and connected to the crime three men who were members of the Western Federation of Miners in Colorado: Charles H. Moyer, William D. Haywood, and George A. Pettibone, all of whom were extradited and tried in Idaho. Haywood and Pettibone were acquitted; Moyer was released.

4. The Industrial Workers of the World flourished during World War I. A broadly based union as opposed to the craft unionism of the American Federation of Labor, it aroused much concern over whether it was under socialist-communist influence. See Melvyn Dubofsky, *We Shall Be All: A History of the Industrial Workers of the World*, 2d ed. (Urbana: University of Illinois Press, 1988).

5. William D. Leahy, fleet admiral in World War II, was chief of staff to Roosevelt and Truman. See William D. Leahy, *I Was There* (New York: Whittlesey House, 1950).

6. Roy E. Ayres was a member of the House of Representatives in 1933–1937 and was governor of Montana in 1937–1941.

7. In one of the ugliest cases of mob violence during World War I, vigilantes murdered an IWW organizer, Frank Little.

Chapter 4: The Comerford Theaters

1. The "gentleman's C average" has passed into history because of grade inflation—in modern colleges and universities anyone who can breathe gets more than a C average—but in its day it was well known. Some students sought a straight C average so they would graduate yet not stand out from their fellow students.

2. M. B. Comerford was a nephew of M. E. Comerford; in both names the "M" stood for Michael, hence the use of initials. Adolph Zukor was one of the earliest film entrepreneurs. Years earlier he had imported a four-reel film from France, *Queen Elizabeth,* starring Sarah Bernhardt, and its success made feature films popular. The first feature made in Hollywood, *The Squaw Man,* was produced by Cecil B. DeMille and Samuel Goldwyn.

3. James H. Higgins was governor of Rhode Island in 1907–1909.

4. At the Democratic National Convention in 1924 the anti-Prohibition "wet" forces of Governor Alfred E. Smith of New York and the Prohibition "dry" forces of William G. McAdoo of California, secretary of the treasury in the Wilson administration, fought each other to exhaustion, after which the convention turned to the West Virginia lawyer John W. Davis. Davis lost to President Calvin Coolidge in the subsequent election.

5. Alexander Pantages was the owner of a circuit that was well known at the time.

6. The theater was in Buffalo.

7. Edward F. Albee (no relation to the playwright of the same name) had gotten his start as a tent boy for P. T. Barnum, later assisted B. F. Keith, and eventually managed seventy theaters, with the Keith-Albee Exchange representing three hundred.

8. A trailer was, and remains, either a still or moving picture advertisement sandwiched between vaudeville or screen events.

9. "Meco" stood for M. E. Comerford.

10. In January 1921 the roof of Washington's Knickerbocker Theater collapsed, causing 108 deaths. The "World's Fair" here referred to was probably the Sesquicentennial Exposition held in Philadelphia in 1926.

11. Will H. Hays, postmaster general in the Harding administration, had become president of the Motion Picture Producers and Distributors, an organization dedicated to "cleaning up" pictures through self-censorship.

12. Warner Brothers Vitaphone was a sound-on-disc system. It was severely handicapped by the possibility that film and disc might fall out of synchronization and was abandoned in 1931. Fox Movietone was a sound-on-film process.

13. Jolson's *The Jazz Singer*, premiering in 1927, was the first acclaimed talking picture.

14. The bank moratorium of early March 1933 was one of the first moves of the incoming Democratic administration, made necessary by mass "runs," the demands of depositors for their money, that spread from bank to bank and state to state. The treasury department reopened sound banks.

Chapter 5: The Roosevelt Boom

1. Walker is of course referring to the famous maker of men's suits.

2. As assistant secretary of the navy, Roosevelt supervised the administration of Haiti and the Dominican Republic. In Butte he said, "I wrote Haiti's constitution myself and, if I do say it, I think it a pretty good constitution." In San Francisco he averred, "Why, I have been running Haiti or San Domingo for the past seven years."

3. For Moses, see Robert A. Caro, *The Power Broker: Robert Moses and the Fall of New York* (New York: Knopf, 1974). The best resource for Edward J. Flynn is his autobiography, *You're the Boss* (New York: Viking, 1947). The construction of the Roosevelt candidacy is examined in David Burner, *The Politics of Provincialism: The Democratic Party in*

Transition, 1918–1932 (New York: Knopf 1968); see also Bernard Bellush, *Franklin D. Roosevelt as Governor of New York* (New York: Columbia University Press, 1955).

4. For Raymond J. Moley, an early and soon-disenchanted member of the New Deal's "brains trust," see his *The First New Deal* (New York: Harcourt, Brace and World, 1966), edited by Elliot A. Rosen; see also Rosen's *Hoover, Roosevelt, and the Brains Trust: From Depression to New Deal* (New York: Columbia University Press,1977).

5. See Elisabeth I. Perry, *Belle Moskowitz: Feminine Politics and the Exercise of Power in the Age of Alfred E. Smith* (New York: Oxford University Press, 1987).

6. On Joseph M. Proskauer, see his *A Segment of My Times* (New York: Farrar, Straus: 1950).

7. See Albert B. Rollins, *Roosevelt and Howe* (New York: Knopf, 1962).

8. Arthur F. Mullen, *Western Democrat* (New York: Funk, 1940), 254.

9. For William H. Woodin, to become Roosevelt's first secretary of the treasury, see *Dictionary of American Biography*, vol. 10, pt. 2 (New York: Charles Scribner's Sons, 1928–), 494–495. Wilson's confidant, Edward M. House, played a small part in subsequent national events and died in 1938.

10. See Burton K. Wheeler, *Yankee from the West* (Garden City, N.Y.: Doubleday, 1962).

11. By this time a very rich man, Kennedy hoped for a preferment during a Roosevelt administration. After becoming chairman of the Securities and Exchange Commission and ambassador to Britain, he broke with the president over aid to Britain. See Michael R. Beschloss, *Kennedy and Roosevelt: The Uneasy Alliance* (New York: Norton, 1980).

12. Gerard had been ambassador to Germany before American entrance into World War I. See James W. Gerard, *My First Eighty-Three Years in America* (Garden City, N.Y.: Doubleday, 1951). Joseph P. Guffey was to become senator from Pennsylvania. Lawrence A. Steinhardt became ambassador to the Soviet Union and died in a plane crash in 1950.

13. For Johnson, see John K. Ohl, *Hugh S. Johnson and the New Deal* (De Kalb: Northern Illinois University Press, 1985).

Chapter 6: Nomination

1. Raskob was a financier connected with the DuPont interests and General Motors. He was chairman of the Democratic National Committee in 1928–1932.

2. Shouse, a one-time Kansas congressman, a supporter of Smith in 1928, served as chairman of the executive committee of the Democratic National Committee in 1929–1932.

3. Michelson was publicity director for the Democratic National Committee. See his *The Ghost Talks* (New York: Putnam, 1944).

4. Joseph T. Robinson was majority leader of the Senate at the time.

5. Newton D. Baker had been President Wilson's secretary of war, and before that mayor of Cleveland. Governor Albert C. Ritchie of Maryland for a while seemed a presidential hopeful. So did Representative John W. Garner of Texas, who was to be Roosevelt's running mate and vice president during FDR's first two terms.

6. Joseph B. Ely was governor in 1931–1935. He later turned against Roosevelt.

7. M. B. Comerford died after an automobile accident in December 1935. In February of the same year M. E. suffered a severe stroke that forced his withdrawal from active involvement in Comerford Theaters, Inc.

8. George E. Allen was a political man for all seasons, present during the 1944 dinner meeting in which Democratic party leaders chose Harry S. Truman to replace the then vice president, Henry A. Wallace. Even then he was befriending General Dwight D. Eisenhower, with whom he would become close. See his *Presidents Who Have Known Me,* 2d ed. (New York: Simon and Schuster, 1960).

9. Reed was one-time mayor of Kansas City, a member of the machine of Thomas J. Pendergast, who became a senator. Harry F. Byrd was a business-progressive as governor of Virginia, then an opponent of New Deal fiscal policy as senator.

10. Hague was the boss of Jersey City.

11. Bernard M. Baruch, by his own testimony, made a fortune on Wall Street and became a power in Democratic politics. He was chairman of the War Industries Board in 1918. See Jordan A. Schwarz, *The Speculator* (Chapel Hill: University of North Carolina Press, 1981); see also James Grant, *Bernard M. Baruch: The Adventures of a Wall Street Legend* (New York: Simon and Schuster, 1983).

12. Robert Jackson, a New England businessman acquainted with FDR since the Wilson years, was Democratic national committeeman from New Hampshire.

13. Senator Alben W. Barkley was vice president under Truman. See his autobiography, *That Reminds Me* (Garden City, N.Y.: Doubleday, 1954).

14. For many years Hull served in the House of Representatives for Tennessee and entered the Senate in 1931, resigning his seat to become secretary of state in 1933.

15. See T. Harry Williams, *Huey Long* (New York: Knopf, 1969).

16. Long was attempting to create southern hostility to Roosevelt. Adopted in 1832, the rule of Democratic conventions was that a two-thirds vote of the delegates was necessary for nomination of presidential and vice presidential candidates. The rule made it possible for the southern states to control nominations.

17. Josiah W. Bailey was an "old school" politician, a senator from 1931 until his death in 1946.

18. See James A Farley, *Behind the Ballots: The Personal History of a Politician* (New York: Harcourt, Brace, 1938), 116–119.

19. Representative Underwood deadlocked the Democratic convention of 1912 against Speaker Champ Clark of Missouri and made possible the nomination of Woodrow Wilson. A senator in 1924, he was a favorite son of Alabama.

20. Walker was writing in memory of the conventions of 1952, both of which were televised extensively. Television was used at the conventions of 1948, and both were held in Philadelphia, in part so that the television technicians would not have to move their equipment. But at that time only a very small number of households possessed television sets, and most of the stations were on the East Coast. All this had changed remarkably by 1952.

21. James M. Curley was mayor of Boston. For Mullen, see his *Western Democrat* (New York: Funk, 1940), 274–278. William Randolph Hearst Sr. was the well-known newspaper publisher.

22. Senator Harrison was a popular if conservative figure who would challenge Senator Barkley for the post of majority leader in 1937 and lose by a single vote. Barkley was Roosevelt's candidate.

23. Smith, of course, had been one of McAdoo's opponents in 1924.

24. Mayor Anton Cermak of Chicago would go down in history as the man who, early in 1933, received a fatal bullet wound from a would-be assassin of Roosevelt while sitting next to the president-elect in an open automobile in Miami.

25. With the Democrats' nomination of the conservative John W. Davis and the Republicans' nomination of President Coolidge, liberals had no place to go. Senator Robert M. La Follette Sr. of Wisconsin revived the Progressive Party of Theodore Roosevelt, on whose ticket TR had run in 1912.

26. Wheeler was one of the leaders of the successful fight against Roosevelt's proposal to "pack" the high court.

27. Charles Bryan was the brother of William Jennings Bryan, the three-time presidential candidate.

28. The National Industrial Recovery Act (1933) created the National Recovery Administration.

29. Judge Samuel I. Rosenman was a Roosevelt speechwriter who eventually received the anomalous title of special counsel. The book is Rosenman's *Working with Roosevelt* (New York: Harper, 1952).

30. For Pittman, see Fred L. Israel, *Nevada's Key Pittman* (Lincoln: University of Nebraska Press, 1963); Betty Glad, *Key Pittman: The Tragedy of a Senate Insider* (New York: Columbia University Press, 1986).

Chapter 7: The Executive Council

1. McIntyre was the president's appointments secretary.

2. The blue Oval Room was on the south side of the mansion's second floor.

3. The assistant secretary was, of course, Franklin Roosevelt.

4. This is a surprising appraisal, considering the praise heaped upon the Bureau of the Budget for bringing order out of chaos during the administration of President Harding. The first director of the bureau was a large figure in finance and politics, Charles G. Dawes, and he as well as Harding received much credit for the bureau's work. Lewis W. Douglas served under Roosevelt until they broke over the level of New Deal expenditure in 1934.

5. A sticker displaying a blue eagle with outstretched talons was the symbol of the National Recovery Administration, or NRA.

6. Hull's voluminous memoirs (2 vols., New York, 1948) are less than revealing. For Welles, see Irwin F. Gellman, *Secret Affairs: Franklin Roosevelt, Cordell Hull, and Sumner Welles* (Baltimore: Johns Hopkins University Press, 1995). For figures in agriculture, see John M. Blum, ed., *The Price of Vision: The Diary of Henry A. Wallace, 1942–1946* (Boston: Houghton Mifflin,1973); Bernard Sternsher, *Rexford Tugwell and the New Deal* (New Brunswick, N.J.: Rutgers University Press,1964); Gilbert C. Fite, *George N. Peek and the Fight for Farm Parity* (Norman: University of Oklahoma Press, 1954). Ickes's massive diary has been published through the year 1940: *The Secret Diary of Harold L. Ickes,* 3 vols. (New York: Simon and Schuster, 1953–1954). See also Graham White and John Maze, *Harold Ickes of the New Deal: His Private Life and Public Career* (Cambridge: Harvard University Press, 1985). The Works Progress Administration was the program directed by Harry L. Hopkins that initially created jobs for the unemployed. The Public Works Administration, easily confused with the WPA, under Ickes handled large-scale construction projects and generally long-term works.

7. Roosevelt privately referred to the head of the Reconstruction Finance Corporation as "Jesus H. Jones," and because conservative Democrats in Texas greatly embarrassed the president in 1944 by refusing to vote for him at the national convention, and because he suspected the hand of Jones in this business (one of Jones's nephews was among the ringleaders), he arranged to get Jones out. The way he did it was exquisitely painful to Jones, for during the war Roosevelt had allowed Vice President Wallace to clash openly with Jones and then pronounced a plague on both their houses. When Wallace lost a bid for renomination at the Chicago convention in 1944 (see footnote 15, Chapter 10), the president arranged for the vice president to take any cabinet post he wished except the state department. Smarting over the contention with Jones, Wallace chose commerce, then under Jones. The president offered Jones an embassy, but the Texan flatly refused such a decorous retirement.

8. For Douglas, see footnote 19, Chapter 8. Eccles was chairman of the Federal Reserve Board.

9. See Lester G. Seligman and Elmer E. Cornwell Jr., eds., *New Deal Mosaic: Roosevelt Confers with His National Emergency Council, 1933–1936* (Eugene: University of Oregon, 1965).

10. For Hopkins, see titles in footnote 1, Chapter 8. Wood was head of Sears, Roebuck and Company.

11. Here Walker is in error. During his months in Washington he had commuted to New York to continue his duties with Comerford Theaters. After the National Housing Act was signed in June of 1934, he intended to remain in New York. But the president asked him to continue with the National Emergency Council, which he did until December 1935, when M. B. Comerford died after an automobile accident. M. E. had suffered a stroke in February; although he never took a full part in the business thereafter, he recovered somewhat. He died in 1939.

Chapter 8: A Gallery of New Dealers

1. These men have had recent and careful appraisals: See John K. Ohl, *Hugh S. Johnson and the New Deal* (De Kalb: Northern Illinois University Press, 1985); Henry H. Adams, *Harry Hopkins* (New York: Putnam, 1977); George McJimsey, *Harry Hopkins* (Cambridge: Harvard University Press,1985); Graham White and John Maze, *Harold Ickes of the New Deal: His Private Life and Public Career* (Cambridge: Harvard University Press, 1985); T. H. Watkins, *Righteous Pilgrim: The Life and Times of Harold L. Ickes* (New York: Holt, 1990); Graham White and John Maze, *Henry A. Wallace: His Search for a New World Order* (Chapel Hill: University of North Caroline Press, 1995).

2. Gifford D. Pinchot was governor of Pennsylvania in 1923–1927 and 1931–1935. A follower of Theodore Roosevelt, he had played a prominent part in the break between TR and the latter's successor, President William H. Taft, by accusing Taft's secretary of the interior, Richard A. Ballinger, of withdrawing lands for power sites from government control. This was the so-called Ballinger-Pinchot affair.

3. The oft-repeated "Our country! In her intercourse with foreign nations may she always be in the right; but our country, right or wrong" is attributed to a toast given by Commodore Stephen Decatur in 1816.

4. The court voided the NRA's live poultry code because Congress had delegated too much legislative power to code authorities. It said the defendants, four brothers who slaughtered chickens in New York City, were not engaged in interstate commerce.

5. Early in 1934, complaints about the monopolistic features of NRA codes became so numerous that President Roosevelt appointed a committee headed by the well-known lawyer Clarence Darrow to investigate. An old-line progressive of socialist leanings, Darrow brought in a highly critical report.

6. It is perhaps unnecessary to point out the Notre Dame football reference to the four horsemen, and that a cruising holiday meant a Rooseveltian vacation aboard ship.

7. One of the president's favorite ships for recreational voyages was the heavy cruiser USS *Houston*, which would be lost in the Battle of the Java Sea.

8. The Senate majority leader died in his Washington apartment just when the Roosevelt-sponsored bill for reorganization of the federal judiciary—including possible enlargement of the Supreme Court to prevent the overthrow of New Deal legislation—came before the upper house. Critics said he worried himself to death over the forthcoming fight over the court, and Roosevelt haters whispered that as a

reward for helping put over the judiciary bill the president promised him a place on the court but had no intention of keeping the promise.

9. The CWA, an emergency relief program over the winter of 1933–1934, put four million men to work and pumped $1 billion into the lagging economy.

10. See Robert E. Sherwood, *Roosevelt and Hopkins*, rev. ed. (New York: Harper, 1950), 53–55.

11. President of the United Mine Workers, Lewis represented—from Walker's point of view—poverty when compared to the wealth of W. Averell Harriman, son of the railroad titan E. H. Harriman.

12. It was said in Washington that Hopkins would do anything the president wanted, and that if FDR asked him to jump off the Washington Monument, the only question in Hopkins's mind would be whether it should be with or without a parachute.

13. In the ship's paper, *The Blue Bonnet*, appeared the following news item:

> Buried at Sea
> The feud between Hopkins and Ickes was given a decent burial today. With flags at half mast . . . the President officiated at the solemn ceremony which we trust will take these two babies off the front page for all time.
> Hopkins, as usual, was dressed in his immaculate blues, browns and whites, his fine figure making a pretty sight with the moon-drifted sea in the foreground.
> Ickes wore his conventional faded grays, Mona Lisa smile and carried his stamp collection. . . .
> Hopkins expressed regret at the unkind things Ickes had said about him and Ickes on his part promised to make it stronger—only more so—as soon as he could get a stenographer who would take it down hot.
> The President gave them a hearty slap on the back—pushing them both into the sea. "Full steam ahead," the President ordered.

As Sherwood observed, this particular bit of shipboard badinage could only have been written by the president himself: see Sherwood, *Roosevelt and Hopkins*, 78–79.

14. *Wallaces' Farmer* circulated throughout the Middle West and told farmers how to plant and market crops. Henry Wallace made a name for himself among farmers by breeding corn, and his Pioneer Hi-Bred Corn Company made him wealthy. Luther Burbank (1849–1926) was a pioneering horticulturist.

15. Peek had been a proponent of the McNary-Haugen bills of the 1920s, which proposed no restriction on agricultural output but rather buying up and dumping annual farm surpluses to provide "parity" (or pre–World War I) prices for farmers. The New Deal inevitably went over to restricting production. Tugwell, a member of the "brains trust," was a trained economist and naturally disagreed with the New Deal programs

that were less the result of planning than of improvisation. Wallace and Ickes quarreled over whose department would contain the Bureau of Forestry.

16. To raise pork prices, an early New Deal program provided for killing little pigs, reducing the pig population.

17. For the 1944 nomination, see footnote 2, Chapter 10.

18. After World War II, Wallace recorded an enormous oral history, now in the Oral History Collection, Oral History Research Office, Butler Library, Columbia University, New York, N.Y. He died in 1965. His papers are at the University of Iowa in Iowa City.

19. See Robert P. Browder and Thomas G. Smith, *Independent: A Biography of Lewis W. Douglas* (New York: Knopf, 1985).

20. Douglas served as deputy war shipping administrator in 1942–1944. Hull's replacement in 1944 was Edward R. Stettinius Jr.

21. Walker is speaking of the years between his resignation as executive director of the National Emergency Council in 1935 and appointment as postmaster general in 1940.

22. Felix Frankfurter was professor at the Harvard Law School and a Roosevelt appointee to the Supreme Court.

23. For Holmes, see footnote 28.

24. William O. Douglas, *The Court Years, 1939–1975* (New York: Random House, 1980), displays its subject's better side.

25. Thomas G. Corcoran was a drafter of New Deal legislation and a Roosevelt intimate who later lost influence with the president.

26. James H. Perkins was chairman (not president) of the National City Bank.

27. Acheson's *Present at the Creation: My Years in the State Department* (New York: Norton, 1970) relates his animus toward Roosevelt, which he described as "admiration without affection." He was undersecretary of the treasury when he resigned in 1933.

28. See G. Edward White, *Justice Oliver Wendell Holmes: Law and the Inner Self* (New York: Oxford University Press, 1993).

29. James H. Rowe Jr. was administrative assistant to Roosevelt in 1939–1941.

30. Benjamin V. Cohen worked with Corcoran in drafting New Deal legislation.

Chapter 9: War

1. Father James Drought of the Maryknoll order was seeking to prevent war through private negotiations with Japanese diplomatic officials.

2. Maude Galen Walker was the wife of Frank Walker's brother Tom. Laura Hallie was playing the part of a Japanese princess.

3. This is Frances Perkins, secretary of labor.

4. Stephen T. Early was presidential press secretary. The Oval Room is on the second floor of the White House and is not to be confused with the president's office in the west wing. The latter office, incidentally, was not at that time known as the Oval Office.

5. Ambassador Kichisaburo Nomura and Special Ambassador Saburo Kurusu were instructed to present their message, a note, at 1:00 P.M. Washington time, which was minutes before the striking hour, close to daybreak Pearl Harbor time. Through the inability of a Japanese embassy official to type the note quickly—he was employing the two-finger method and making numerous mistakes—the ambassadors arrived after the attack had begun.

6. Major General Edwin M. "Pa" Watson was presidential appointments secretary at this time.

7. William S. Knudsen had been president of General Motors.

8. Vice Admiral Ben Moreell was in charge of the navy's construction battalions, known as Seabees.

9. General Sir Archibald Wavell commanded British defenses in India and the Far East; Lieutenant General Douglas MacArthur commanded American forces.

10. Manuel Quezon was president of the Philippine Commonwealth, the provisional government that would usher in independence on July 4, 1946.

11. Owen J. Roberts, associate justice of the Supreme Court, was chairman of a commission to investigate the Pearl Harbor disaster.

12. James Cardinal Gibbons was archbishop of Baltimore for forty-three years, until his death in 1921.

13. Here is a reference to the so-called map room, the secret operations room with maps and charts and Allied dispositions that was maintained in the White House.

14. Owen D. Young, chairman of the board of General Electric, arranged the Young Plan of 1929 for reparations. Herbert H. Lehman succeeded Roosevelt as governor of New York.

15. Johnson graduated from West Point in 1903.

16. Edward VII died in 1910.

17. Reid, who died in 1912, was publisher of the *New York Tribune*.

18. Judge Alton B. Parker was the Democratic nominee for president in 1904.

19. Here the president refers to the Argentia Conference, held at Placentia Bay in Newfoundland, of August 1941. See Theodore A. Wilson, *The First Summit*, rev. ed.(Lawrence: University Press of Kansas, 1991).

20. An associate justice of the Supreme Court, Murphy had been high commissioner of the Philippines.

21. The *Shangri-La* was one of the new carriers that would overwhelm the Japanese navy. At the time of Pearl Harbor the Japanese had ten carriers to five American carriers.

22. The president was in error; it was President John Adams—not John Quincy, who preceded Jackson—who refused to call on his successor, Thomas Jefferson. James Roosevelt was the president's eldest son.

23. Lane was secretary of the interior during the Wilson administration.

24. This was at the Democratic National Convention of 1936.

25. After the German invasion of the Low Countries in 1940, the queen of the Netherlands, Wilhelmina, came to the United States. Martha, crown princess of Norway, in exile in America because of the German occupation of her country, was a great favorite of the president. Princess Juliana would succeed her mother as queen of the Netherlands.

26. The president was referring to the yacht USS *Potomac*.

27. Senator John W. Bricker of Ohio and Governor Thomas E. Dewey of New York were likely Republican candidates. In 1943 the president sent the candidate of 1940, Wendell L. Willkie, on a round-the-world trip in hope of separating him from the GOP.

28. James F. Byrnes, senator from South Carolina, an associate justice of the Supreme Court at the beginning of the war, soon came into the White House, where Roosevelt appointed him "assistant president" in charge of domestic affairs while the president handled military and foreign affairs.

29. Alf M. Landon, former governor of Kansas, was Republican nominee for the presidency in 1936.

30. William C. Bullitt, ambassador to the Soviet Union and France in the 1930s, became estranged from the president during World War II—as his conversation with Walker reveals.

31. Henry L. Stimson, secretary of war during the Taft administration, secretary of state during the Hoover administration, was again secretary of war. He and Knox, both Republicans, appointed to the cabinet during the fall of France in the summer of 1940, represented a Rooseveltian attempt, prior to the presidential election in November, to arrange a coalition government.

32. Sumner Welles, undersecretary of state and a Roosevelt favorite, had been feuding with his superior, Secretary Hull, for years. Hull forced Welles's resignation in 1943 by accusing him of being homosexual.

33. Walker is referring to the Democratic National Convention that summer in Chicago.

34. Hull is speaking of the conference to establish the United Nations Organization that would be held in San Francisco in April–June 1945.

35. Breckinridge Long, Dean Acheson, and Adolf A. Berle were assistant secretaries of state.

36. Under the Selective Service Act, men in the category of 4-F were exempt from the draft for physical or medical reasons.

37. Stimson was speaking of the Battle of the Bulge, of December 1944, in which the German Army nearly achieved a breakthrough in its drive toward Paris.

38. Walker's daughter, Laura Hallie, that year had married Robert Ameno, a tank captain. He was killed in the fighting.

39. The mass-produced Liberty ships were the nautical workhorses of the war; the Victory ships, which were faster, were for postwar use.

40. General Courtney H. Hodges was commander of the U.S. First Army during the Normandy invasion and the Battle of the Bulge.

41. Paul V. McNutt, federal manpower commissioner, was a former high commissioner of the Philippines. Josephus Daniels, secretary of the navy during the Wilson administration, when FDR was assistant secretary, was in retirement but often wrote the president about matters of common interest.

42. Grace Tully was the president's private secretary. The president was speaking of a forthcoming trip to Warm Springs.

43. Robert E. Hannegan was chairman of the Democratic National Committee.

44. William D. Hassett, correspondence secretary for presidents Roosevelt and Truman, was at Warm Springs when FDR died. The president called Walker on the morning of April 11, the day before the president's death, concerning the new UN stamps, and in the course of the conversation spoke with the postmaster general's son, Tom, home on leave from the navy. Like the president, Tom suffered from infantile paralysis.

45. Byrnes had resigned as "assistant president," director of war mobilization, on April 6.

46. After the resignation of Secretary Hull in November 1944, William L. Clayton and Nelson Rockefeller became assistant secretaries of state, Stettinius the secretary. Anna Roosevelt Boettiger was the president's daughter.

Chapter 10: Choosing a Vice President

1. Truman told a later military aide, Harry H. Vaughan, that Walker asked him to take the post and he refused. See Charles T. Morrissey, Vaughan Oral History, 1963, Harry S. Truman Library, Independence, Missouri. The well-known poll taker George Gallup and the radio broadcaster H. V. Kaltenborn both predicted Truman's defeat in the election of 1948.

2. Walker's assertion that no one who saw the president frequently was alarmed over his health is interesting and may have rested on the fact that he saw the president so often. He may also have hesitated to say in a memoir he hoped would be published how ill Roosevelt was—although he was frank about other judgments. Walker's

papers contain no testimonies in letters, or private memoranda, about presidential illness. The men with whom he cooperated in the anti-Wallace movement were acting
from two beliefs: that Wallace had no political judgment, and that whoever obtained
the vice presidential nomination would become president. The leaders, of course, did
not know about Roosevelt's cardiovascular disease, which by 1944 was far advanced.
They did not know that on March 28 of that year the president underwent a physical
examination at Bethesda Naval Hospital, where he was seen by the staff cardiologist,
Lieutenant Commander Howard G. Bruenn, who found him in heart failure. Bruenn
put him on digitalis, which made his heart more efficient, and placed him on a diet,
for the president at 185 pounds was overweight, and all his weight was in his arms and
chest, his legs and hips having atrophied. Beyond that the physician could only recommend rest and relaxation, an impossibility for a president of the United States. See
Robert H. Ferrell, *Ill-Advised: Presidential Health and Public Trust* (Columbia: University of Missouri Press, 1992), 28–52. Walker's concern that the president's braces were
too heavy and about the lack of strength in FDR's legs was entirely misplaced: the
weight loss had made the braces loose.

3. David I. Walsh was senator from Massachusetts.

4. Joseph P. Kennedy Jr., serving in the army air forces in England, had undertaken a
dangerous assignment, and his plane blew up.

5. Paul A. Dever was governor of Massachusetts in 1949–1953.

6. Barkley in 1944 was majority leader and arranged the passage of a presidential tax
bill. To his consternation the president airily said he, FDR, would veto the bill. When
the veto message came down it added insult to injury by stating that the bill favored
the rich. The Kentucky senator advised his colleagues to override and announced he
would resign as majority leader. Roosevelt at once backed down. The senator's problem with the vice presidential nomination, however, as Walker described it, was age:
born in 1877, Barkley was five years older than the president.

7. In Charles Dickens's *David Copperfield,* the cart driver Barkis proposes marriage to
young David's nurse, Clara Peggotty, by asking David to include in his letter to Peggotty the suggestion "Barkis is willin'."

8. Jonathan Daniels, son of Josephus, and a White House assistant during the war,
published an authorized biography of President Truman, *The Man of Independence*
(Philadelphia: Lippincott, 1950), in which he described the White House dinner conference. Allen described it in the first edition of *Presidents Who Have Known Me* (New
York: Simon and Schuster,1950).

9. Edwin W. Pauley was treasurer of the Democratic Party.

10. Sam Rayburn of Texas was Speaker of the House.

11. Brought up in the Catholic Church, Byrnes had forsaken it for the Episcopal faith
of his wife.

12. Byrnes's South Carolina roots may have made him anathema to black voters, and as Roosevelt's wartime assistant he had antagonized labor in 1943 by asking laboring men and women to "hold the line" and refused to allow wages to go up—despite increases in the cost of living.

13. Hannegan had been a Democratic leader in St. Louis. In the 1940 Senate primary, when Truman was running for his political life against Governor Lloyd C. Stark and the prosecutor of the Pendergast machine in Kansas City, Maurice Milligan, Hannegan brought in 8,000 machine votes, giving Truman victory: he won the state with a plurality of less than 8,000. After Hannegan lost out in St. Louis the next year, when the Democrats fell to squabbling, Truman sponsored him for the local collectorship of internal revenue. Hannegan did so well with this appointment that the Roosevelt administration brought him to Washington as commissioner of internal revenue. Early in 1944, when Walker desired to give up the chairmanship of the Democratic National Committee, Hannegan was a natural candidate for the post. Incidentally, his sponsor for the chairmanship is uncertain, and could have been Byrnes. See Robert H. Ferrell, *Choosing Truman: The Democratic Convention of 1944* (Columbia: University of Missouri Press, 1994), 8–10.

14. Robert Hannegan died in 1949, and for some years his widow had in her possession the handwritten and later typed versions of the letter. She eventually gave them to the Truman Library.

15. Hannegan that morning went out to the Wardman Park Hotel in Washington, Northwest, and there sought to tell Vice President Wallace that he was out.

16. Technically, in the overwhelming vote of the Chicago convention's delegates for Truman on the second vice presidential ballot, Truman was the convention choice. In actual fact the supporters of Vice President Wallace were close to a majority and gave up only because it became apparent that the president wanted the senator from Missouri.

17. On Thursday evening the president left by train for Hyde Park from which he traveled westward to San Diego, where he took ship for Hawaii in order to confer with his military commanders. He returned by way of Alaska.

18. Walker's memory is wrong—Flynn arrived Monday afternoon.

19. Hillman was vice president of the Congress of Industrial Organizations (CIO) and headed its powerful political action committee. Walker may be wrong about Truman going to Hillman's suite via the fire escape. Hillman did occupy a suite accessible both through a hall door and by a fire escape, and photographers waited next to the fire escape and took pictures of politicians ascending to Hillman's rooms, but Truman learned the news from Hillman during a breakfast in the suite that could not have been disguised from reporters. There would have been no reason to use the fire escape. Moreover, the senator very probably would not have done such a thing: Harry S. Truman was a dignified man.

20. Here again a slip of memory. The argument with Flynn appears to have been in Hannegan's suite in the Blackstone.

21. Murray was president of the CIO. In what was a tangled series of negotiations impossible to hold in memory, the meal with Hillman and Murray was dinner on Monday evening.

22. Here Walker means the letter the president sent Senator Samuel D. Jackson of Indiana, permanent chairman of the convention, relating that if he, FDR, were a delegate (which he was not), he would vote for Wallace. It was too faint in enthusiasm to be effective, and of course the wily Roosevelt meant it that way.

Chapter 11: The Roosevelt Portrait

1. The 1944 novel by Kathleen Winsor was the subject of much conversation.

2. C. F. "Con" Kelley had been vice president and general counsel of the Anaconda Copper Mining Company and by the time Walker was writing had become chairman of the board.

3. Arlen was a novelist of the 1920s and 1930s.

4. The preceding year, 1947, Truman had arranged the release of an incendiary report concerning civil rights in the South and at the Democratic National Convention in 1948 accepted a strong civil rights plank that brought the exit of southern conservatives and the organization of a southern presidential slate: the States' Rights Democratic Party, or Dixiecrats. All this during an election when disaffected liberals had organized another splinter party headed by Henry Wallace, the Progressive Party, successor to the parties of the same name in 1912 and 1924.

5. Theodore Roosevelt was the fifth cousin of FDR.

6. Marguerite "Missy" LeHand was FDR's private secretary until her retirement and death during the war.

7. Watson died aboard ship on the return from the Yalta Conference in February 1945.

8. Wilson was the father of three daughters. His first wife died in 1914, and in the next year he courted and married a Washington widow, Edith Bolling Galt.

9. Patterson, owner of the *Daily News,* was the cousin of Eleanor Patterson of the *Washington Times-Herald.* Both were cousins of Robert R. McCormick, owner of the *Chicago Tribune.*

10. James J. Walker was mayor of New York, and his corrupt administration had brought matters to a head, forcing this case upon the governor at the moment when Roosevelt was running for the presidency. The governor did not want to alienate Tammany Hall.

11. Arthur F. Mullen, *Western Democrat* (New York: Funk, 1940), 286–287.

12. To assist farm income by creating scarcity, the agricultural program sought to "plow under" crops. Another measure was to slaughter young pigs rather than have them glut the market. The president cancelled private contracts to carry mail and gave the task to the army air corps: the result was several fatal crashes. After the failure of

the bill to reform the judiciary and if necessary enlarge the Supreme Court, the president sought to defeat Democratic senators who had failed to support court reform. Critics referred to his campaigning as an attempted "purge" similar to the purge trials in the Soviet Union.

Chapter 12: Later Years

1. Elliott had published *As He Saw It* (New York: Duell, Sloan and Pearce, 1946), with an introduction by his mother, which purported to reveal much wartime conversation with his father. Although Truman's name is not in the index, the book was highly critical of foreign policy after April 12, 1945. "Somewhere, at some point in the months since Franklin Roosevelt's death, his brave beginning has been prejudiced. It may be that 'prejudiced' is too mild a word. It may be that it should read: The peace is fast being lost" (247). The son of Truman's predecessor was visiting the Soviet Union in November-December 1946, and he said in Moscow that the Democrats' defeat in the congressional elections that year had occurred because of their failure to follow his father's policies. Among other courtesies, Elliott Roosevelt was granted an interview with Joseph Stalin.

2. Malvina Thompson was Eleanor Roosevelt's secretary.

3. Here Mrs. Roosevelt is probably speaking of the telephone conversation between Byrnes and her husband on Tuesday morning, July 18, 1944, the day before the Democratic National Convention opened in Chicago. Byrnes did not see Roosevelt when the latter's train passed through the city the preceding Saturday, July 15. In the telephone conversation aboard the presidential train en route to San Diego, the president did say to Byrnes that although Vice President Wallace had his liabilities as a running mate in 1944, "you did too, and there still remains the four things they [the party leaders] cited as objections." These things were Byrnes's forsaking the Catholic Church, the objections of blacks and labor to his candidacy, and Byrnes's age (he was three years older than Roosevelt). By that Tuesday morning, to be sure, Byrnes's candidacy had collapsed, the president having told the party leaders the night before to "go all out for Truman."

4. Evidently Walker was dictating this account.

INDEX

Robbins, Herman, 45
Roberts, John, 43–44
Roberts, Gwen J., 118
Robinson, Joseph T., 65, 97–98, 122
Rockefeller, Nelson, 132
Rockne, Knute, 9, 26
Rogers, Saul, 42
Rogers, Will, 45
Roosevelt, Eleanor, 100, 115, 120–122,
    130, 132, 151–152, 157, 160–161, 165
Roosevelt, Ellie, 114–115, 118
Roosevelt, Elliott, 160
Roosevelt, Franklin D., vii–viii, xiii–xx,
    35, 52, 159; preconvention, 53–63;
    nomination, 64–82; Executive
    Council, 83–93; New Dealers, 94–
    109; World War II, 110–132; vice
    president (1944), 134–140; portrait,
    150–158. *See* Franklin D. Roosevelt
    Library; Franklin Delano
    Roosevelt Memorial Foundation
Roosevelt, Isaac, 113
Roosevelt, Jacobus, 113
Roosevelt, James (father of FDR), 113–
    114, 118
Roosevelt, James (son of FDR), 122
Roosevelt, John (uncle of FDR), 113–114
Roosevelt, Sara D., 115, 154, 161
Roosevelt, Theodore, 57–58, 119
Roosevelt and Hopkins (book), by Robert
    E. Sherwood, 101
Roosevelt Hospital (New York), 118–119
Roosevelt Hotel (New York), 110
Root, Jesse B., 35
Roper, Daniel C., 90–91
Rosenman, Samuel I., 80, 125
Rowe, James H. Jr., xviii, 108–109
Rupple, Louis, 82
Russia. *See* Soviet Union
Ryan, John D., 15
Ryan, Joseph, 44
Ryan, William, 44

St. Anne's Hospital (Anaconda), 7

St. Ignatius Loyola Church (New York),
    vii
St. James Hospital (Butte), 5–6
St. Lawrence's Church (Walkerville), 9,
    16
St. Patrick's Cathedral (New York), 110
St. Patrick's Cemetery (Butte), 164–165;
    School, ix, 2, 5–9, 14
St. Vincent's Hospital (New York), 164;
    (Westchester), 164
Samuels brothers, 40
Saudi Arabia, 125
Scallon, William, 15
Schaefer, George, 50
Schechter Poultry Corp. v. United States, 96
Scheier, John B., 20
Scholastic (Notre Dame periodical), 22
Schwab, Edward H., 23
Senate, 72, 80, 112, 125, 127, 135, 138
Shangri–La, U.S.S. (carrier), 120
Sharer, Professor, 43
Shea, Harry, 45
Shea, May 45
Shea, Michael, 41–42
Sheehan, Winnie, 42
Sherwood, Robert E., 99, 101
Shouse, Jouett, 64, 70–71
Silver Bow Club (Butte), 35
Singing Fool (moving picture), 49
Sisters of Charity of Leavenworth,
    Kansas, xi, 2, 5–7
Slater, William, 11
Smeck, Roy, 48
Smith, Alfred E., xvi–xviii, 40, 54–57, 59–
    60, 64–70, 75, 94, 157, 163 *See* Alfred
    E. Smith Memorial Foundation
Smith, Ben, 70
Smith, Howard, 113
Socialist Party, 29, 34
Southern Hotel (Butte), 4
Soviet Union, 119, 159. *See* Stalin,
    Joseph V.
Spanish–American War, 6, 14
Spiegel, Harry, 43